Advances in Preventing and Treating Violence and Aggression

Series Editor

Peter Sturmey
Queens College and The Graduate Center
City University of New York
Flushing, NY, USA

The series publishes books focused and developed across three domains. The first is understanding and explaining violence and aggression. Books in this domain address such subject matter as genetics, physiology, neurobiology, cultural evolution, biobehavioral, learning, cognitive, psychoanalytic, sociological and other explanations of violence. The second domain focuses on prevention and treatment for individuals and couples. Examples of books in this domain include cognitive behavioral, behavioral, counseling, psychopharmacological, psychosocial, couples, and family therapy approaches. They also explore extant treatment packages for individually focused treatments (e.g., mindfulness, cognitive analytic therapies). Within this domain, books focus on meeting the information needs of clinicians and professionals who work in youth facilities, emergency rooms, special education, criminal justice, and therapy settings. Finally, books in the third domain address prevention and treatment for groups and society, including topical focus on early intervention programs, school violence prevention programs, policing strategies, juvenile facility reform as well as socio-legal and ethical issues. Books in this series serve as must-have resources for researchers, academics, and upper-level undergraduate and graduate students in clinical child and school psychology, public health, criminology/criminal justice, developmental psychology, psychotherapy/counseling, psychiatry, social work, educational policy and politics, health psychology, nursing, and behavioral therapy/rehabilitation.

More information about this series at http://www.springer.com/series/15332

James K. Luiselli
Editor

Applied Behavior Analysis Treatment of Violence and Aggression in Persons with Neurodevelopmental Disabilities

Springer

Editor
James K. Luiselli
Melmark New England
Andover, MA, USA

Series Editor
Peter Sturmey

Advances in Preventing and Treating Violence and Aggression
ISBN 978-3-030-68548-5   ISBN 978-3-030-68549-2   (eBook)
https://doi.org/10.1007/978-3-030-68549-2

© Springer Nature Switzerland AG 2021
This work is subject to copyright. All rights are reserved by the Publisher, whether the whole or part of the material is concerned, specifically the rights of translation, reprinting, reuse of illustrations, recitation, broadcasting, reproduction on microfilms or in any other physical way, and transmission or information storage and retrieval, electronic adaptation, computer software, or by similar or dissimilar methodology now known or hereafter developed.
The use of general descriptive names, registered names, trademarks, service marks, etc. in this publication does not imply, even in the absence of a specific statement, that such names are exempt from the relevant protective laws and regulations and therefore free for general use.
The publisher, the authors, and the editors are safe to assume that the advice and information in this book are believed to be true and accurate at the date of publication. Neither the publisher nor the authors or the editors give a warranty, expressed or implied, with respect to the material contained herein or for any errors or omissions that may have been made. The publisher remains neutral with regard to jurisdictional claims in published maps and institutional affiliations.

This Springer imprint is published by the registered company Springer Nature Switzerland AG
The registered company address is: Gewerbestrasse 11, 6330 Cham, Switzerland

Preface

Applied behavior analysis (ABA) is a scientific approach to understanding and changing human behavior, grounded in operant learning theory, and dedicated to technologically sound procedures that are empirically evaluated, replicable, and socially valid. From inception, and spanning five decades of treatment research, ABA has contributed greatly to improving the lives of persons who have neurodevelopmental disabilities including those who demonstrate violence and aggression. This volume should be in the Springer Series, Advances in Preventing and Treating of Violence and Aggression, addresses the most contemporary ABA practices for assessment, intervention, training, and supervision (https://www.springer.com/series/15332 / Advances in Preventing and Treating Violence and Aggression). Section chapters summarize the research foundation of many methods and procedures that clinicians, psychologists, behavior analysts, and related professionals can implement effectively with children, youth, and adults in multiple service settings. As well, the chapters highlight the multidisciplinary context of ABA treatment in the current day.

I am grateful to Dr. Peter Sturmey, Series Editor, for supporting a book devoted to ABA. Notably, the book was completed at the height of the 2020 COVID-19 pandemic and only possible due to the skilled production staff at Springer, dedicated chapter authors, and support of my colleagues at Melmark New England. And to my family, Tracy, Gabrielle, and Thomas, thanks for everything you teach and give me so generously.

Andover, MA, USA   James K. Luiselli

Contents

Part I Measurement and Assessment

Measurement and Data Recording of Aggression 3
Amanda N. Zangrillo, Seth G. Walker, Henry S. Roane,
William E. Sullivan, Dominik L. Keller, and Nicole M. DeRosa

Functional Behavior Assessment 27
Jill M. Harper, Juliya Krasnopolsky, Melissa C. Theodore,
Christen E. Russell, and Eris J. Dodds

Functional Analysis of Violence–Aggression 45
Ashley M. Fuhrman, Brian D. Greer, and Wayne W. Fisher

Behavioral Risk Assessment of Violence-Aggression 71
Joseph N. Ricciardi

Social Validity Assessment 85
James K. Luiselli

Part II Intervention, Training, and Supervision

Communication-Focused Treatment of Violence-Aggression 107
Valdeep Saini and William E. Sullivan

Behavioral Treatment of Sexual Offending 129
Duncan Pritchard, Heather Penney, Veda Richards, and Nicola Graham

Inpatient and Residential Treatment of Violence Aggression 153
Nicole L. Hausman, Michael P. Kranak, Molly K. Bednar,
and Louis P. Hagopian

Training and Performance Management of Care Providers........... 169
Raymond G. Miltenberger, Jennifer L. Cook, and Marissa Novotny

**Mindfulness Care Giving and Support for Anger
and Aggression Management**.................................... 189
Nirbhay N. Singh, Giulio E. Lancioni, and Yoon-Suk Hwang

Index... 203

Part I
Measurement and Assessment

Measurement and Data Recording of Aggression

Amanda N. Zangrillo, Seth G. Walker, Henry S. Roane, William E. Sullivan, Dominik L. Keller, and Nicole M. DeRosa

Abstract A foundation of ABA treatment is objective, reliable, and valid measurement of client responses preceding, during, and following intervention. This chapter reviews measurement and data recording methods for documenting the effects of behavioral treatment with persons who demonstrate aggression. The authors describe design and implementation of these methods within clinical and research settings including operational definitions, construction of measurement protocols, assessing reliability, and summarizing data outcomes.

Keywords Aggression · Measurement · Data analysis

Measurement and Data Recording of Violence-Aggression

Violence-aggression includes those acts that are intended to cause physical harm (National Collaborating Centre for Mental Health, 2015). The current chapter adopts an operant account of violence-aggression in which the intent of behavior is not an assumed variable of interest. Henceforth, we refer to violence-aggression by the term "aggression."

A. N. Zangrillo (✉) · S. G. Walker · D. L. Keller
Munroe-Meyer Institute, University of Nebraska Medical Center, Nebraska Medical Center, Omaha, NE, USA
e-mail: Amanda.zangrillo@unmc.edu

H. S. Roane · W. E. Sullivan · N. M. DeRosa
State University of New York Upstate Medical University, Syracuse, NY, USA

© Springer Nature Switzerland AG 2021
J. K. Luiselli (ed.), *Applied Behavior Analysis Treatment of Violence and Aggression in Persons with Neurodevelopmental Disabilities*, Advances in Preventing and Treating Violence and Aggression,
https://doi.org/10.1007/978-3-030-68549-2_1

Aggressive behaviors are commonly observed in young children, specifically in early childhood, when children are beginning to interact with peers outside of their family and navigate their social world (Fletcher, 2011). Aggressive behaviors are considered a part of typical development in children, although there are a number of differing definitions of what constitutes "normal" behavior across cultures (Hirschi, 1969). Developmentally, one expects these behaviors to reduce between the ages of 3- and 5-years-old due to the improvement of the child's language skills and emotional regulation (Underwood, 2003). Additional risk factors, such as age, sex, language abilities, adaptive functioning, cognitive abilities, genetic or biological determinants, prescribed medications, and educational history, may further impact the development of or persistence of aggression. Of particular note, individuals with autism spectrum disorder and other neurodevelopmental disabilities demonstrate a relatively high prevalence of aggressive behavior (Hill et al., 2014; Kanne & Mazurek, 2011; Schroeder et al., 2014). Among those who develop aggressive behaviors, there is a risk of lower quality of life, increased stress, reduction in access to services and supports, and caregiver burnout (Fitzpatrick, Srivorakiat, Wink, Pedapati, & Erickson, 2016). Thus, the development of efficacious treatment for individuals displaying aggression is critical to long-term success, growth, and development of individuals with neurodevelopmental disabilities.

Various disciplines have sought to explain the development, subtyping, and definition of aggression. Although not the focus of this chapter, it is quite important that readers understand the complex interplay between biological, psychobiological, and environmental variables impacting how various disciplines view aggressive behavior. A host of explanatory mechanisms for the occurrence of aggression have emerged over the last century. Theoretical perspectives for the causal determinants of aggression have included contributions from unresolved unconscious states, instinctual drives, and social learning theory (Roane & Kadey, 2011). Although these perspectives warrant discussion, the present chapter focuses on environmental influences, or an operant-behavior perspective, on the occurrence of aggression.

Regardless of the one's perspective on aggression, such behaviors are considered "aberrant" or of clinical significance warranting intervention when they: (1) increase in intensity or severity to cause physical or emotional harm; (2) impact participation in home, school, and community activities or placements; and (3) persist beyond the "normative" developmental window. To differentiate normative and clinically significant levels of aggression, clinicians may evaluate the behavior using interviews, checklists, questionnaires, and rating scales. These indirect measures of clinical significance can support a clinician's decision for intervention and the severity of the aggression observed or reported, relative to established norms; however, indirect measures do not yield individualized operational definitions that would inform accurate, reliable, and valid measurement. The use direct assessment methodologies, which is one key feature of applied behavior analysis, provides means for an objective measure of aggression.

For nearly 50 years, the field of applied behavior analysis has provided a framework for the assessment and treatment of socially relevant behavior. This technology has been applied across different settings, ages, and topographies of behavior with the purpose of both increasing prosocial behaviors (e.g., language skills) and decreasing problematic or destructive behaviors (e.g., violence-aggression). In general, the primary components of a behavior-analytic framework include: (1) identifying and defining the behavior targeted for change, (2) measuring the occurrence of the target responses during baseline and treatment, and (3) analyzing the immediate and long-term effects of treatment on the target response. The measurement of the target response is of particular importance in: (1) developing a valid baseline measure, (2) evaluating the effectiveness of treatment programming, and (3) discontinuing ineffective treatment programming (Cooper, Heron, & Heward, 2020).

In this chapter, we discuss key considerations in the development of accurate, reliable, and valid measurement systems specifically for the purpose of evaluating the efficacy of behavior-analytic interventions in the treatment of aggression. We review (1) development of operational definitions, (2) construction of measurement protocols, (3) means for assessing interobserver agreement, and (4) summarizing and displaying data outcomes. To assist in conceptualizing each area, the chapter begins with a case example to illustrate each step in the development of measurement and data collection systems.

Case Example

Quinn is a 15-year-old female diagnosed with moderate intellectual disability and autism spectrum disorder (ASD). Quinn was born prematurely at 35 weeks' gestation. She experienced neurotypical development of motoric milestones (i.e., rolling over, sitting up, crawling, walking); however, she experienced a significant regression in language, communication, and social behaviors at approximately 18 months of age. Quinn communicates using single words and gestures. Her caregivers noted "red flags" related to her aggression beginning at about 2 years of age and felt that this was the point where her aggression increased in intensity and severity. Caregivers reported that Quinn rapidly developed an intense interest in water play and extreme food selectivity. She typically only consumes brand-specific chicken fingers, cheese pizza, and crunchy carbohydrate-rich foods (e.g., crackers and chips). Quinn is of a large stature due to her high caloric intake and low caloric output (i.e., many of Quinn's preferred activities are sedentary). She is placed in a special-purpose private school program where her individual education program goals are focused heavily on decreasing aggressive behavior, increasing functional communication, and increasing compliance with and acquisition of daily living activities. She is supported by a 1:1 aide for her academic activities. Quinn's aggression impacts their ability to care for Quinn while keeping themselves and her infant sibling safe. Behavior also impacts the family's participation in community events and significantly impacts Quinn's participation in her academic programming. Specific referral concerns include frequent bouts of verbal threats and cursing, spitting at others, scratching, and biting others, which results in significant redness, swelling, and breaks in the skin.

Development of Operational Definitions

> *Once in possession of a set of terms we may proceed to a kind of description of behavior by giving a running account of a sample of behaviors as it unfolds itself in some frame of reference. This is a typical method in natural history...It may be classified as a narration...From data obtained in this way it is possible to classify different kinds of behavior to determine relative frequencies of occurrence. But although this is, properly speaking, a description of behavior, it is not a science in the accepted sense. We need to go beyond mere observation to a study of functional relationships. We need to establish laws by virtue of which we may predict behavior, and we may do this only by finding variables of which behavior is a function.*
> —B. F. Skinner (1938, p. 8)

Applied behavior analysis typically uses direct observation to identify the occurrence of behaviors of interest. Direct observation produces two distinct advantages for addressing behaviors such as aggression, namely allowing for data collection in virtually any applied setting, and providing a more thorough detection and recording of the range of responses that research participants and therapy clients exhibit (Page & Iwata, 1986).

An initial step in developing any data collection system includes operationally defining target responses. Well-developed operational definitions include four critical characteristics. First, they are objective, which means the definition only includes aspects of the behavior that can be observed and are not based on assumptions. Second, they are clear so that others understand what the behavior "looks like." Third, the operational definition must specify when an occurrence of the target response begins and when it ends. Finally, the definition must include examples and non-examples of the behavior that further clarify the definition.

Using the hypothetical example of Quinn, an operational definition of biting might be written as "Upward and downward motion of the mandibles which results in contact between Quinn's teeth and another's body or clothing." In this operational definition, the target behavior is described to include that Quinn must open and close her mouth (i.e., jaws) such that her teeth come into contact with any part of someone's body or clothing. It does not specify if a specific body part is targeted by Quinn's aggression. Moreover, the definition highlights that the behavior must include movement of the jaw and contact with her teeth, thereby disqualifying any behavior that does not involve those components.

The four core characteristics of operational definitions ensure that there is agreement among professionals about what behaviors are to be included in the measurement (Hawkins & Dobes, 1977). To inform development of operational definitions, clinicians may use indirect assessment strategies such as interviews and/or direct assessment strategies such as observation of the individual engaging in aggression. Table 1 provides a list of common topographies of aggression (e.g., hitting, biting, kicking, pinching, and scratching (Brosnan & Healy, 2011)) and sample operational definitions that may be used to describe these behaviors.

Table 1 Sample operational definitions

Response topography	Sample operational definition
Hitting/ punching	Contact of hand (open or closed) or arm (with or without another object) from a distance of 6 in. or greater against any part of the therapist's body Example: Client slaps the therapist on their face Nonexample: Client high-fives the therapist
Kicking/ stomping	Contact of foot, leg, or knee with any part of the therapist's body (includes stepping on therapist's foot) from a distance of 6 in. or greater Example: Client kicks the therapist on their shin Nonexample: Client trips over the therapist's foot
Pushing/pulling	Applying force to the therapist's body, attempting to move the therapist, or pulling any part of the therapist's body (including hair) Example: Client pushes the therapist by placing their hands on their shoulder and applying force, which moves the therapist away from the client Nonexample: Client takes the therapist's hand and attempts to pull them toward an activity as they appropriately ask for the therapist to join them in the activity
Grabbing	Applying force to the therapist's body, putting at least one hand around any part of a therapist's body such that the skin is either indented or reddened (this includes choking; may also include clothing) Example: Client grabs the therapist's shirt and refuses to release their grip on the therapist Nonexample: Client grabs the therapist's hand to walk with them when transitioning and does so without causing the therapist's hand to indent or become red

Throwing	Projecting any object at, or in the general direction of, the therapist (includes spitting)
	Example: Client throws a chair at the therapist
	    Client projects their spit toward the therapist's face
	Nonexample: Client throws a chair at the wall when the therapist is in the room. The chair is not thrown in the direction of the therapist
	    Client spits on the floor

Pinching	Closure of client's thumb and at least one other finger around therapist's skin such that the skin is either indented or reddened (may occur through therapist's clothing) Example: Client closes with force their thumb and pointer finger around the skin of the therapist's hand Nonexample: Client closes their thumb and pointer finger around the therapist's shirt as they state "this shirt is nice." No force is used in by the client when pinching the shirt
Scratching	Contact of client's fingernails against or along therapist's skin Example: Client drags their fingernails with force across the therapist's arm, which results in red marks on the therapist Nonexample: Client scrapes their fingernails across the therapist's hand when attempting to take an object from the therapist after it is offered to them

(continued)

Table 1 (continued)

Response topography	Sample operational definition
Head butting	Contact between client's head and any part of the therapist's body from a distance of 6 in. or greater Example: Client hits their head against the therapist's arm with force Nonexample: Client turns their head and bumps their head into the therapist's arm. This is not done with force
Biting	Closure of client's teeth around any part of the therapist's body Example: Client closes their teeth around the therapist's hand Nonexample: Client puts their mouth around the therapist's fingers when offered food, but does not bite down on the food until the therapist has removed their fingers from the client's mouth

Verbal aggression	Vocalizations made by the client toward the therapist that are intended to harm or threaten to harm the therapist, such as cursing, screaming, threats of violence-aggression
	Example: Client screams when they are turned toward the therapist
	  Client states "F*%#* off"
	  Client states "I'm going to punch you" when they are turned toward the therapist
	Nonexample: Client makes a high-pitch scream when playing with a toy, but is not turned toward the therapist

Aggression with a weapon	Client grabs an object and uses the object to hit or attempt to hit the therapist Example: Client picks up a book and hits the therapist forcefully with the book Nonexample: Client picks up a pencil and places it in the therapist's hand

Construction and Selection of Measurement Protocols

The operational definition is the foundational unit of behavior analysis. After a target response is operationalized, practitioners can construct and select the most appropriate measurement system(s). At this point the practitioner can identify the impact of environmental changes on the target response and thus, begin to understand functional relations that may be present in the environment. There are many properties of responses under consideration, and only a limited number of response properties can be captured by a given measurement procedure. Below we discuss three critical characteristics of measurement strategies: accuracy, validity, and reliability.

Accuracy describes the degree to which the measurement strategy reflects the true exhibition of the target response (Kahng, Ingvarsson, Quigg, Seckinger, & Teichman, 2011). The second characteristic of measurement is *validity*, the extent to which the measurement procedure records what it purports to measure (Kahng et al. 2011). The last characteristic, *reliability*, refers to consistency in outcomes obtained and consistency in outcomes between two independent observers. All measurement strategies vary across these three critical characteristics. In combination with careful consideration of the applied setting, resource availability, and the target response, practitioners can arrive at selection of a measurement strategy. Common indirect and direct measurement strategies employed in behavior-analytic research and practice are discussed below.

Indirect Measurement Strategies

Depending on the applied setting and resources available, indirect measures may appeal to researchers and practitioners due to ease of implementation and lower resource need relative to direct measures. However, ease of implementation comes at a potential cost in the areas of accuracy and validity, particularly if implemented in isolation. These procedures also may be implemented using a pencil and paper, meaning they require minimal technology and instrumentation in order to conduct measurement. Given that aggression in individuals with neurodevelopmental and related disorders is the behavior of interest for the present chapter, we will only review measures that best capture the relevant dimensions of that topography (e.g., event recording, rating scales, and permanent products).

A wide variety of established and validated interviews, checklists, questionnaires, and rating scales that are relevant to an assessment of aggression exist in the literature. Researchers and clinicians may use this measurement strategy that infers the repeatability, temporal extent, and intensity of a target response based on the reporter's perception of occurrence. Examples of checklists or rating scales include the Child Behavior Checklist (Achenbach & Rescorla, 2001), Behavior Problems Inventory (Rojahn, Matson, Lott, Esbensen, & Smalls, 2001), Aberrant Behavior Checklist (Aman & Singh, 1994), and Behavior Assessment System for Children (Reynolds & Kamphaus, 2004).

Permanent-product recording is another indirect measurement strategy that infers the repeatability and intensity of a target response based on the impact it has on the environment. To use permanent-product recording, the general strategy is to document the change in the environment after the target response has occurred, for example, damage to property in the form of broken furniture and glass.

Note that permanent-product data are not a direct measure of the target response and require a degree of inference, which sacrifices some accuracy and validity of these data. The tactics of measuring permanent products vary depending on the topography of interest. For example, when collecting the pictorial examples of a sustained bite mark provided in Fig. 1, permanent-product data would include tissue damage that resulted from the bite mark; however, additional information of the aggressive act, such as the number of bites (frequency) that occurred would not be represented.

We may also rely on other adaptations of established measures for recording damage produced by a response. For instance, self-injurious behavior may be measured via description of surface tissue damage via the Self-Injury Trauma (SIT) Scale (Iwata, Pace, Kissel, Nau, & Farber, 1990). Although the SIT Scale may be used to document the surface tissue damage targeted toward implementers of behavioral interventions that is not its original intention.

Fig. 1 Pictorial example of sustained bite marks

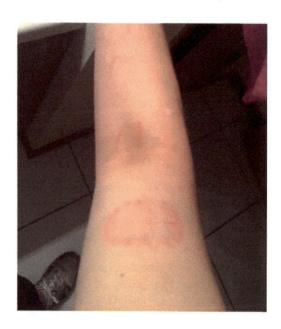

Direct Measurement Strategies

Continuous measurement. Continuous measures are common in behavior analysis and typically yield the most accurate data (Kahng et al., 2011). Continuous measures are most frequently employed in situations where a practitioner desires to measure all possible occurrences of a target response during a prescribed observation period. However, using continuous measures is resource intensive and may not be possible in all applied settings (LeBlanc, Raetz, Sellers, & Carr, 2016). Frequency, duration, latency, and intensity are the most commonly used continuous measurement procedures.

Frequency measures attempt to capture the repeatability dimension of a target response and require minimal instrumentation. To conduct a frequency measure, one simply counts the occurrence of the target response. For example, we might count the number of times that Quinn throws a toy at another student.

One could also divide the total count of the target response by the duration of the observation period to produce *response rate*. Response rate is an important frequency summary measure because it controls for uneven observation periods. That is, in scenarios where session durations are not constant, comparing frequency without considering observation time may skew the data; response rate equates across these different observation durations. For example, if we measured Quinn's scratching across observations periods of 5 and 8 min, the relative frequency of occurrence might be 5 and 3, which are fairly similar. When calculated as a rate, the relative occurrence is 1.0 responses per minute and 0.38 responses per minute, respectively.

Duration recording is used to capture the temporal extent, or the time that passes between the onset and offset of a target response. To use a duration measure, one must identify onset and offset criteria, then begin a timing device (e.g., stopwatch or timer) when onset criteria are met and stop the timing device when offset criteria are met. Duration is helpful when targeting responses with a long temporal extent. It may also be beneficial for responses with a brief temporal extent, which also have a rapid rate of occurrence. Duration can be summarized in a number of ways. The measure can be summarized with frequency of the target response to produce the *duration per occurrence* of target responses. The total duration of a target response can be divided by the observation period to derive a *percentage duration*. Lastly the duration per occurrence of the target response can be averaged to determine the *mean duration* of the response. Again using Quinn's verbal threats as an example, we might collect duration data on the number of seconds that she is engaged in threatening others (76 s). Calculating these data against a 5-min observation period would yield a percentage of occurrence of 25.3%.

Latency is similar to duration but captures the temporal locus of two events. Latency is typically used to identify when a target response occurred in relation to some other environmental event. For instance, if an instruction is given to Quinn, and then she engages in aggressive behavior toward the instructor, the time that elapses between instruction and aggression is the *response latency*. To conduct this measurement procedure, clear criteria are needed for when the observer is to start and stop their timing device. *Interresponse time* is a variation of the latency procedure where, instead of timing the latency from evocative stimulus (e.g., instruction) to target response (e.g., aggression), one records the latency between the cessation of one target response to the onset of the next. Latency measures are summarized as the average of the latencies recorded in the observation period or *mean latency*.

Intensity recording captures the magnitude of a target response. This measurement strategy may be more difficult to conduct in applied settings due to instrumentation requirements. Intensity is measured depending on the topography of the target response. For instance, if an individual engages in screaming behavior, intensity may be captured by a decibel meter. If the target response includes aggression toward others, intensity could be measured by a pressure plate or having care providers rate their perception of pain produced from aggression (Parenteau, Luiselli, & Keeley, 2013; Urban, Luiselli, Child, & Parenteau, 2011). It is often easier to measure intensity by the permanent products the target response leaves after its occurrence or by rating scale. Figure 2 provides an example of a rating scale that may be used to gather information regarding intensity or severity of aggression.

As mentioned above, the use of rating scales is a less desirable measure to determine the occurrence of aggression as observers must make a subjective evaluation of the intensity of the target response. Thus, rating scales should not be used alone in measuring serious aggression unless there is no other option. In resource-limited situations, it may be best to use permanent-product recording.

Discontinuous measurement. Discontinuous measures are most frequently employed in situations where a practitioner desires to record sample measures of a

Sample Rating Scale Depicting Varying Levels of Violence-Aggression Severity

Severity Range (check all that apply)

Level 1	=	*Aggression* resulting in (a) <u>no</u> marks on body and (b) <u>no</u> blows close to or contacting the eyes
Level 2	=	*Aggression* resulting in (a) reddening of skin, and/or (b) mild swelling
Level 3	=	*Aggression* resulting in (a) light scratches, (b) small or shallow breaks in skin, and/or (c) moderate to severe swelling
Level 4	=	*Aggression* involving blows close to or contacting the eyes or resulting in (a) scratches that leave scars, (b) breaks in skin that leave scars, and/or (c) trauma resulting in broken bones or lasting tissue damage or disfigurement

Fig. 2 Sample Rating Scale depicting varying levels of violence-aggression severity

target response during a prescribed observation period. Discontinuous measurement procedures require dividing an observation period into equal intervals and recording the occurrence of responses across those intervals. Discontinuous measures are most appropriate for target responses where the dimension of interest is repeatability and temporal extent. The discontinuous measurement procedures estimate the occurrence of the target response and, in turn, do not produce data that are as accurate as frequency and duration recording.

Notably, interval length is a feature of discontinuous measurement that impacts the degree of accuracy. Typically, shorter intervals (5–15 s) produce the most accurate record of the target response. As interval length is increased, accuracy is adversely affected (LeBlanc, Lund, Kooken, Lund, & Fisher, 2019). The primary benefit of discontinuous recording procedures is that they are typically easier to use than frequency or duration measures as they do not require precision in the recording of the exact occurrence of the target response. Three main types of discontinuous measurement are partial-interval recording, whole-interval recording, and momentary time sampling. When summarizing the following discontinuous measures, it is standard practice to report the occurrence of the target response in percentage of intervals or percentage of the observation period.

Partial-interval recording involves first dividing the observation period into equal observation intervals (e.g., 10 s). If an occurrence of the target response occurs at any point in an observation interval, the target response is reported as occurring for the entire interval. Partial-interval recording often overestimates the occurrence of a target response and can be beneficial when used with behavioral interventions where the main goal is to decrease the occurrence of the target response. For example, if we divided a 1-min observation window into 6, 10-s intervals, we might observe Quinn to engage in aggression at least once in 4 of the 6 intervals. Given this, partial-interval recording of her aggression would be 66.7%.

Whole-interval recording involves first dividing the observation period into equal intervals. The occurrence of the target response is only recorded if the target response persists for the entirety of an interval. Due to the requirement that the response persists for the whole interval, whole-interval recording tends to underestimate the occurrence of the target response. Because of this underestimation, it is not advised that whole-interval recording be used for responses which are targeted for reduction. To illustrate whole-interval recording, if we again divided a 1-min observation window into 6, 10-s intervals, we might observe Quinn to engage in aggression at least once in 4 of the 6 intervals but only throughout the entire interval twice. Given this, whole-interval recording of her aggression would be 33.3%.

The final common discontinuous measurement procedure is momentary time sampling. Like the above discontinuous procedures, the observation period is split into equal observation intervals. For most of the interval, the observer does not look for the occurrence of the target response, but rather looks up at the end of each interval for an observation check of approximately 1–3 s. If the target response occurs at any point during the observation check, the target response is recorded for the entire interval. Momentary time sampling has the potential to both overestimate and underestimate the occurrence of target responses. These errors are typically a function of the observation interval length and characteristics of the target response. Fiske and Delmolino (2012) provide a more in-depth discussion of the factors that impact error rate in momentary time sampling than what is possible in this chapter. Suppose that we were observing Quinn's aggressive behavior in her classroom. We might observe her for 3 s at the end of each 10-s interval but not during the remaining 7 s of each interval. As with the previous examples, if Quinn engaged in some aggression during 4 of 6 total intervals, but only three of those occurrences in the 3-s observation window, the momentary time sampling measure would reveal aggression to occur during 50% of the observation (i.e., underestimation relative to partial-interval and overestimation relative to whole interval).

The Table 2 provides a summary of the direct measurement procedures listed above:

Selecting Measurement Procedures

Understanding the various measurement procedures available to researchers and practitioners is a critical first step in obtaining reliable quantification of aggression. In combination with the development of the operational definition, selection of a measurement procedure(s) sets the stage for determining baseline levels of aggressive responding and is the foundation from which we evaluate the impact, or lack thereof, when applying an intervention. Thus, we next turn our attention to a descrip-

Table 2 Summary of continuous and discontinuous response measures

Event (no meaningful duration)	State (meaningful duration)	Initiation (starting behavior)	Completion (completing behavior)
Frequency Rate Partial-interval	Duration Whole interval Momentary time sampling Partial-interval	Latency Percent	Percent compliance Percent correct

Note: Adapted by B. K. Martens from "Procedures for Collecting Data" by P. A. Alberto, and A. C. Troutman, 2013, *Applied Behavior Analysis for Teachers*, p. 101. Copyright 2013 by Pearson Education Inc.

tion of decision-making models to assist practitioners in selecting the most appropriate measure for analyzing aggressive behavior.

Kahng et al. (2011) provide a decision-making model for selecting appropriate observational methods when frequency or duration is the behavioral dimension of interest. The practitioner is guided through a series of "yes" or "no" questions (e.g., "Is constant observation possible?") arriving at various recommendations for a selected measurement.

In a more recent example, LeBlanc et al. (2016) provided a clinical decision-making model for selection of measurement procedures in day-to-day practice. Similar to other decision-making models (e.g., Fiske & Delmolino, 2012; Geiger, Carr, & LeBlanc, 2010; Grow, Carr, & LeBlanc, 2009), LeBlanc et al., presented a series of questions to guide practitioners toward selection of the ideal measurement procedure(s) given the identified operational definition and context specific factors such as physical surroundings, personnel, and available technology. The model presents questions to the practitioner in a prescribed order to guide the selection of an appropriate data collection procedure.

These decision-making models provide a brief overview of how measurement selection may occur for *most* topographies of behavior. However, when considering high-risk destructive behavior like aggression, as is the main focus of this book, additional considerations beyond those suggested by LeBlanc et al. (2016) and Kahng et al. (2011) warrant attention. For example, there may be relevant environmental variables and dimensions of behavior one must consider before selecting the ideal measurement procedure(s) for targeted aggressive behavior. Potential environmental considerations that may impact the selection of a measurement system include:

- Does the environment support occurrence of aggression in either a free operant or restricted operant format?
- Are other vulnerable individuals present?
- What is the appropriate duration of observation?
- Can protective equipment (e.g., arm guards, hand guards, chest protectors, gloves) be utilized for individuals in the immediate environment?
- Are safer alternatives appropriate (e.g., precursor analyses, measuring attempted or blocked aggression)?

- Can the selected measures translate to different contexts and generalization settings easily (i.e., is data collection portable?)

Additionally, one must consider the relevant dimension(s) of the target response when selecting a measurement method. That is, more than one observable dimension of a target response may greatly impact the efficacy of an intervention and should be vetted early in the development of operational definitions and measurement systems. We suggest that practitioners consider how selection of a measurement system may best inform a socially and clinically significant reduction in aggressive behavior. Consider the following sample data for Quinn. If frequency is considered in isolation, practitioners may conclude that a significant reduction has occurred. However, when combined with another measure, such as an intensity rating, one might note that a low rate of aggression behavior that continues to send staff to the emergency room is clearly unacceptable.

Interobserver Agreement

Due to the reliance of behavior analysts on direct observation to record behavioral data, it is important to ensure reliability of the occurrence of target responses. Reliability in measurement can be thought of as the stability, dependability, and consistency of recording occurrences of the target response (Mitchell, 1979). It is important to note that the accuracy of behavioral data is related to the measurement strategy used in direct observations (e.g., frequency, duration, interval recording) and the reliability of the data is determined by the degree to which two independent observers agree on the occurrence of the target response. The strategy typically used to ensure that direct observations are reliable is called *interobserver agreement* (IOA).

To collect IOA data, a primary and secondary observer simultaneously and independently record the occurrence of responses targeted by a behavioral intervention. These independent observations could occur at the same point in time or asynchronously if the research or therapy session is video recorded. Then, records from each observer are used to calculate the extent to which they agree target responses occurred. Interobserver agreement scores are typically displayed in percentage agreement and can be calculated in several ways, which are discussed further below.

Total Agreement. Total agreement is a simple calculation that is often used with frequency and duration measures (Fig. 3). The calculation is performed by taking the two observation records and dividing the one with the smaller number of recorded occurrences by the larger number of occurrences. For instance, if the primary observer recorded the occurrence of aggression nine times during an observation period and the secondary observer recorded the occurrence of aggression 10 times in the same observation period, the total agreement calculation would be 9/10 = 0.9 and an IOA score of 90%. The same calculation could be used with a duration measure by converting the total duration of the target response to seconds

Total Agreement Equation

$$\frac{Smaller\ number}{Larger\ number} = Total\ Agreement$$

Fig. 3 Total agreement equation

Interval Agreement

Primary Observer	+	-	-	+	-	+	-	-	+	+
Secondary Observer	+	+	-	+	+	+	-	-	+	+

Note. The "+" indicates the occurrence of the target response and "-" indicates the nonoccurrence of the target response

Fig. 4 Interval agreement. *Note.* The "+" indicates the occurrence of the target response and "−" indicates the nonoccurrence of the target response

and performing the same calculation. Although a total agreement calculation may hold utility due to the ease of producing IOA scores, it has the limitation of being unable to indicate whether each observer recorded the same instance of behavior.

Interval Agreement. To address the above issue with total agreement, many researchers and practitioners perform an interval agreement IOA calculation. This first requires that the entire observation period be divided into smaller intervals. The occurrence of the target response is then recorded within those smaller intervals. Once the observers have collected data for the entirety of the observation period, agreements and disagreements are identified between the two records. Agreements are identified when both observers score the presence or absence of a target response in the same interval. For instance, in interval 1 of Fig. 4, the primary and secondary observers agree that the target response occurred. In interval 3 of Fig. 4, both the primary and secondary observers agree that the target response did not occur. A disagreement is identified any time the two observers do not have the score for the same interval. To calculate the interval agreement, one must first identify and count all agreements, then divide that number by total number of intervals. For instance, in Fig. 4, there are eight agreements and a total of 10 intervals which would produce the equation 8/10 = 0.8 and an interval IOA score of 80%.

There are three important variations of the interval agreement calculation. The first variation is the *occurrence agreement* or *occurrence only* (Miltenberger, 2016). The occurrence agreement may be beneficial for researchers or practitioners who

Measurement and Data Recording of Aggression

Occurrence Agreement

The "+" indicates the occurrence of the target response and "-" indicates the nonoccurrence of the target response

Primary Observer	+	-	-	-	-	+	-	-	-	-	+	+	-	+	-
Secondary Observer	+	-	-	-	-	-	-	-	-	-	+	+	-	+	-

Note. The "+" indicates the occurrence of the target response and "-" indicates the nonoccurrence of the target response.

Fig. 5 Occurrence agreement. *Note.* The "+" indicates the occurrence of the target response and "−" indicates the nonoccurrence of the target response

are targeting low-probability target responses (Fisher, Piazza, & Roane, 2011). In this agreement calculation, all agreements on the nonoccurrence of the target response are discarded. Any recorded occurrence of the target response for either observer, regardless of agreement are included in the calculation. To perform the occurrence agreement calculation, one would find the number of intervals where both observers agreed on the occurrence of the target response and divide that by the total number of intervals where either observer recorded an occurrence of the target response. For instance, in Fig. 5, there are four agreements between the observers on the occurrence of the target response and five intervals where either observer indicated there was an occurrence of the target response. This would produce the equation 4/5 = 0.8 and an occurrence IOA score of 80%.

The second variation of the interval agreement calculation is the *nonoccurrence agreement* or *nonoccurrence only*. This strategy may be most beneficial to use when targeting high-rate responses (Fisher et al., 2011). Nonoccurrence agreement is calculated in the same way as occurrence agreement; however it uses agreements of nonoccurrence as the dividend and intervals where any nonoccurrence is recorded as the divisor. For instance, in Fig. 6, there are three agreements between the two observers on the nonoccurrence of the target response and five intervals where either indicated there was a nonoccurrence of the target response. This would produce the equation 3/5 = 0.6 and a nonoccurrence IOA score of 60%.

Another strategy for IOA calculation is *frequency within interval agreement*. This IOA calculation is typically used in situations where multiple occurrences of the target response may occur within an interval. Frequency within interval agreement is very accurate but slightly more resource and time intensive, which may reduce the likelihood of use in clinical or resource-limited settings. In frequency within interval, IOA calculations are performed within each interval. Those percentages are then summed, and divided by the total number of intervals in the observation period. Figure 7 shows the data for a frequency within interval calculation. The

Nonoccurrence Agreement

Primary Observer	+	-	-	+	-	+	+	-	+	+	+	+	-	+	+
Secondary Observer	+	+	-	+	+	+	+	-	+	+	+	+	-	+	+

Note. The "+" indicates the occurrence of the target response and "-" indicates the nonoccurrence of the target response

Fig. 6 Nonoccurrence agreement. *Note.* The "+" indicates the occurrence of the target response and "−" indicates the nonoccurrence of the target response

Frequency within interval and Exact agreement

Primary Observer	||	|||	|	|||	|		|	|||	||	||	**Total**
Secondary Observer	||	||	|	||||	|		|	|||	||	|	
Frequency within interval agreement	100%	67%	100%	75%	100%	100%	100%	100%	100%	50%	892%/10 = 89.2%
Exact agreement	+	-	+	-	+	+	+	+	+	-	7/10 = 70%

Note. The "\|" indicates the occurrence of the target response in each interval.

Fig. 7 Frequency within interval and exact agreement. *Note.* The "\|" indicates the occurrence of the target response in each interval

sum of the percentages in Fig. 7 equal 892. The total number of intervals is 10. The data in Fig. 7 would produce the equation 892/10 = 89.2 and an exact agreement IOA score of 89.2%.

The final agreement strategy is *exact agreement*. In exact agreement, only intervals where the same frequency was recorded are counted as agreements. Figure 7 also shows the exact agreement analysis of the same data used for the frequency within intervals agreement calculation. The data in Fig. 7 would produce the equation 7/10 = 0.7 and an exact agreement score of 70%.

Standards and interpretation of IOA. There are several considerations around the collection of IOA data. Because the collection of IOA data may be time consuming, it is unlikely that IOA data will be collected and calculated for each session with a participant or client. Some have proposed minimum standards around IOA data collection and reporting (Horner et al., 2005). They suggest that IOA data should be collected for a minimum of 30% of sessions across all assessment and treatment phases and that the minimum agreement scores should be 80% or higher (What Works Clearinghouse, 2020).

If IOA scores are lower than 80%, it may be indicative of two problems. One issue could be that the target response is not accurately defined. If there is no consensus for what does and does not count as an instance of the target response, the independent observers will likely not record data in a manner that is similar enough to one another to produce acceptable IOA scores. One way to remedy this issue is by more thoroughly defining the operational definition for the target response. Another issue may be that the observers are not adequately trained on the data collection procedures. This again, would reduce the likelihood of agreement due to potential inaccurate recording of the occurrence of the target response. To address this issue, observers should be provided an in-depth training on the measurement strategy and the specifics of the data collection procedures.

Summarizing Data Outcomes

Thus far we have discussed various measurement techniques and the types of data they produce. Data in its raw form are simply measurements of some dimension of behavior (e.g., frequency) that provides documentation of its occurrence (Johnston & Pennypacker, 1993). Although this documentation is necessary to evaluate the effects of treatment, it alone by no means accomplishes this goal. The raw data need to be processed and analyzed after collection, in order for them to be consumed and used to make clinical decisions (Johnston & Pennypacker, 1993). Within the field of applied behavior analysis, data are most commonly depicted in graphic form (Johnston & Pennypacker, 1993; Kazdin, 2011). This is advantageous in the context of treatment for aggressive behavior because it provides an efficient way to visually analyze the treatment's effect (Fahmie & Hanley, 2008). In this section, we will discuss the ways in which data are commonly displayed, for the purposes of evaluating treatment effects. We will then go on to discuss a number of considerations t when determining the most appropriate ways to transform and summarize treatment data.

Graphic Displays and Visual Analysis

Graphs are a visual representation of data over time that can be used as an interpretative tool for evaluating the effects of treatment on a target response. Graphing data has a long history within applied behavior analysis (Kazdin, 2011) and is particularly useful for demonstrating the effects of a treatment to be monitored on a moment-by-moment basis. After target responses are recorded during an observation period, the data are transferred onto a graph that typically consists of plotting sessions on the X-axis, and the occurrences of behavior on the y-axis (Fahmie & Hanley, 2008). As data continue to be collected over time, patterns in behavior can be seen and, based on those patterns, predictions can be made regarding the effects of treatment and future probability of aggressive behavior.

Typically, treatments are evaluated within single-case experimental designs. A thorough description of single-case experimental designs is beyond the scope of this chapter (interested readers should refer to Roane, Ringdahl, Kelley, & Glover, 2011). However, for our present purposes, it is important for the reader to recognize that single-case experimental designs allow for systematic evaluation of a treatment's effect on a target response, and allow for causal inferences to be drawn. The goal is to demonstrate a functional relationship between the treatment (independent variable; IV) and target response (dependent variable; DV) by documenting changes in the DV when, and only when, there is a change in the IV.

The primary method for analyzing single-case data is visual inspection (Horner & Kratochwill, 2012). When performing visual inspection, the level, trend, and variability of behavior are critical for interpretation (Roane et al., 2011). As repeated measurements of behavior occur over time, the level of behavior refers to the overall amount of behavior measured, for example, how frequently aggressive behavior occurred. Throughout the course of treatment, behavior may remain stable, or fluctuate in level depicting variability. Behavior may also increase or decrease over time, illustrating upward and downward trends respectively. The effects of treatment are determined by comparing these elements of the data between treatment and no-treatment (i.e., baseline) conditions, within the individual. Furthermore, the efficacy of treatment is assessed by examining the immediacy of the effect (i.e., deceleration of aggressive behavior), the magnitude of the effect (i.e., the change in level), and the proportion of overlapping data points between treatment and no-treatment conditions. Thus, the effects of treatment on aggressive behavior are systematically evaluated by collecting repeated measurements of behavior over time and demonstrating a functional relation between treatment and aggressive behavior.

Although visual inspection is the preferred method for interpreting behavioral data (Horner & Kratochwill, 2012), interpretations of the data may vary across persons. Several studies, however, have suggested that when appropriate training or structured criteria are employed, interpretations tend to converge across individuals (e.g., Fisher, Kelley, & Lomas, 2003; Hagopian et al., 1997; Kahng et al., 2010; Roane, Fisher, Kelley, Mevers, & Bouxsein, 2013; Stewart, Carr, Brandt, & McHenry, 2007; Wolf & Slocum, 2015). Nevertheless, the use of statistical measures to aid in interpretation of behavioral data has also been suggested.

The use of statistical measures within the field of applied behavior analysis have historically been sparse, given that treatment decisions are based on clinical significance rather than statistical significance. That is, a small-to-moderate change in behavior may produce a statistically significant difference between treatment and no-treatment conditions, but this difference may fail to produce socially meaningful change in behavior. Therefore, within the context of treatment for aggression wherein the clinician is concerned with large reductions in aggressive behavior, a percent reduction is often calculated to quantify the effect of treatment. For example, if on average Quinn engaged in 5 aggressions per min during baseline, and engaged in only 1 aggression per min during treatment, a percent reduction would be calculated by dividing the mean of treatment by the mean of baseline and subtracting from 1 (i.e., 1/5 = 0.2; 1−0.2 = 0.8), resulting in an 80% reduction from baseline to treatment.

Another interpretive aid that can be helpful when analyzing data is to calculate the percent of overlapping data points between treatment and no-treatment conditions. Parker and Vannest (2009), for example, recommend comparing the overlap of each baseline data point with each treatment data point to provide an indication of a treatment effect. Overlaps are assigned a value of 1, non-overlaps a value of 0, and ties a value of 0.5. All overlaps and ties are then summed and subtracted from the total number of paired comparisons ($N_{\text{baseline data points}} \times N_{\text{treatment data points}}$). According to their recommendations, Parker and Vannest suggested that values of 65% or lower indicate weak effects, 66–92% indicate moderate effects, and 93–100% strong effects.

Regardless of the interpretive aid employed, data are typically transformed from the raw form and presented graphically as described above. Therefore, it is also important to consider the ways in which data may be processed and the interpretive ramifications of doing so. In the following section we will briefly describe the process for determining how to transform and display treatment data for aggressive behavior.

Data Transformations

There are numerous ways in which data may be displayed graphically, and there is no one standard way of processing the raw data before it is represented on a graph. However, the manner in which data are transformed into visual depictions of behavior can greatly influence visual analysis. For example, suppose Quinn engages in multiple topographies of aggressive behavior (e.g., hitting and kicking). During baseline, she engages in 0.5 hits per minute and 3 kicks per minute, on average. Then, during treatment, Quinn engages in 0.5 hits per minute and 0 kicks per minute, on average. If hitting were graphed in isolation, one may conclude that there was no treatment effect (0.5 hits vs. 0.5 hits). However, if the topographies were aggregated, clear differences between treatment and no-treatment conditions would be observed (3.5 aggressions per min vs. 0.5 aggressions per min). Although this is but one simple example, it serves to illustrate that as data are aggregated and transformed, visual analysis is affected.

The variations in the ways in which data are aggregated can be described along a continuum that ranges from *distant* (data are aggregated in large units) to *intimate* (raw data) representations of the data (Fahmie & Hanley, 2008; see Fig. 1). Although there is no standard rule, each variation may offer unique costs and benefits in terms of determining the effects of treatment on aggression. For example, data could be aggregated across treatment and no-treatment conditions to examine mean differences. This may be helpful in describing general changes in behavior, but any variability or trends in the data are lost. Conversely, data could be represented at a session-by-session (i.e., data is depicted across observations) or within-session level (i.e., data is depicted moment-by-moment). Here, as one moves along the continuum toward more intimate data analysis, greater detail is provided in regard to the moment-by-moment effects of treatment on behavior. The overall effects, however, may be obscured. Given that there are no clear guidelines for determining the best way to process the data for graphic display, Fahmie and Hanley offered three general rules to consider: (1) data should be depicted along the continuum that allow for interpretation of the important relations (e.g., treatment effects), (2) data should not disguise important relations, and (3) units of measurement should be combined when clinically indicated. Overall, within the context of treatment for aggressive behavior, data are best summarized and displayed such that changes in aggressive behavior can be detected in the presence of treatment, and a functional relation can be established.

Conclusion

Individuals with neurodevelopmental disabilities who also engage in aggression are at an increased risk for many negative outcomes and diminished quality of life relative to those who do not demonstrate aggressive behavior and to their neurotypical peers. Therefore, it is crucial to identify treatment strategies to diminish or eliminate aggression to improve the long-term outcomes for individuals with neurodevelopmental disabilities. Although several theories have been developed that attempt to identify the root cause of aggression, these theories fall short of identifying objective methodologies for treatment. However, the field of applied behavior analysis provides an adequate framework for the assessment and treatment of aggression (Page & Iwata, 1986).

As was highlighted throughout the current chapter, measurement of aggression is a crucial step in the treatment process. That is, without appropriately measuring the target response, one cannot conclude treatment effectiveness. Thus, we aimed at providing practitioners with guidance on the importance of and methods for selecting appropriate measures for aggressive behavior. Although we identify specific variables and processes for the selection and evaluation of relevant behavioral measures, we urge practitioners and researchers to consider variables specific to their setting (e.g., available resources) and the target response (e.g., impact of multiple dimensions of the behavior) when employing the strategies outlined here to ensure the measurement and data collection processes accurately reflect the impact of treatment on the occurrence of aggressive behavior.

Conflict of Interest We have no known conflict of interest to disclose.

References

Achenbach, T. M., & Rescorla, L. A. (2001). *Manual for the ASEBA school-age forms & profiles.* Burlington, VT: University of Vermont, Research Center for Children, Youth, & Families.

Alberto, P. A., & Troutman, A. C. (2013). *Applied behavior analysis for teachers.* London: Pearson Education.

Aman, M., & Singh, N. (1994). *The aberrant behavior checklist-community.* East Aurora, NY: Slosson Education Publications.

Brosnan, J., & Healy, O. (2011). A review of behavioral interventions for the treatment of aggression in individuals with developmental disabilities. *Research in Developmental Disabilities, 32*(2), 437–446. https://doi.org/10.1016/j.ridd.2010.12.023

Cooper, J. O., Heron, T. E., & Heward, W. L. (2020). *Applied behavior analysis.* Upper Saddle River, NJ: Merrill Publications.

Fahmie, T. A., & Hanley, G. P. (2008). Progressing toward data intimacy: A review of within-session data analysis. *Journal of Applied Behavior Analysis, 41*(3), 319–331. https://doi.org/10.1901/jaba.2008.41-319

Fisher, W. W., Kelley, M. E., & Lomas, J. E. (2003). Visual aids and structured criteria for improving visual inspection and interpretation of single-case designs. *Journal of Applied Behavior Analysis, 36*(3), 387–406. https://doi.org/10.1901/jaba.2003.36-387

Fisher, W. W., Piazza, C. C., & Roane, H. S. (Eds.). (2011). *Handbook of applied behavior analysis.* New York: Guilford Press.

Fiske, K., & Delmolino, L. (2012). Use of discontinuous methods of data collection in behavioral intervention: Guidelines for practitioners. *Behavior Analysis in Practice, 5*, 77–81. https://doi.org/10.1007/BF03391826

Fitzpatrick, S. E., Srivorakiat, L., Wink, L. K., Pedapati, E. V., & Erickson, C. A. (2016). Aggression in autism spectrum disorder: Presentation and treatment options. *Neuropsychiatric Disease and Treatment, 12*, 1525–1538. https://doi.org/10.2147/NDT.S84585

Fletcher, K. L. (2011). Neuropsychology of early childhood. In A. S. Davis (Ed.), *Handbook of pediatric neuropsychology* (pp. 31–36). New York: Springer.

Geiger, K. A., Carr, J. E., & LeBlanc, L. A. (2010). Function-based treatments for escape-maintained problem behavior: A treatment selection model for practicing behavior analysts. *Behavior Analysis in Practice, 3*, 22–32. https://doi.org/10.1007/BF03391755

Grow, L. L., Carr, J. E., & LeBlanc, L. A. (2009). Treatments for attention-maintained problem behavior: Empirical support and clinical recommendations. *Journal of Evidence-Based Practices for Schools, 10*, 70–92.

Hagopian, L. P., Fisher, W. W., Thompson, R. H., Owen-DeSchryver, J., Iwata, B. A., & Wacker, D. P. (1997). Toward the development of structured criteria for interpretation of functional analysis data. *Journal of Applied Behavior Analysis, 30*(2), 313–326. https://doi.org/10.1901/jaba.1997.30-313

Hawkins, R. P., & Dobes, R. W. (1977). Behavioral definitions in applied behavior analysis: Explicit or implicit. In B. C. Etzel, J. M. LeBlanc, & D. M. Baer (Eds.), *New developments in behavioral research: Theory, method and application. In honor of Sidney W. Bijou.* Hillsdale, NJ: Lawrence Erlbaum.

Hill, A. P., Zuckerman, K. E., Hagen, A. D., Kriz, D. J., Duvall, S. W., Van Santen, J., et al. (2014). Aggressive behavior problems in children with autism spectrum disorders: Prevalence and correlates in a large clinical sample. *Research in Autism Spectrum Disorders, 8*(9), 1121–1133. https://doi.org/10.1016/j.rasd.2014.05.006

Hirschi, T. (1969). *Causes of delinquency.* Los Angeles: University of California Press.

Horner, R. H., Carr, E. G., Halle, J., McGee, G., Odom, S., & Wolery, M. (2005). The use of single-subject research to identify evidence-based practice in special education. *Exceptional Children, 71*, 165–179. https://doi.org/10.1177/001440290507100203

Horner, R. H., & Kratochwill, T. R. (2012). Synthesizing single-case research to identify evidence-based practices: Some brief reflections. *Journal of Behavioral Education, 21*, 266–272. https://doi.org/10.1007/s10864-012-9152-2

Iwata, B. A., Pace, G. M., Kissel, R. C., Nau, P. A., & Farber, J. M. (1990). The self-injury trauma (SIT) scale: A method for quantifying surface tissue damage caused by self-injurious behavior. *Journal of Applied Behavior Analysis, 23*(1), 99–110. https://doi.org/10.1901/jaba.1990.23-99

Johnston, J. M., & Pennypacker, H. S. (1993). *Readings for strategies and tactics of behavioral research.* Hillsdale, NJ: Lawrence Erlbaum.

Kahng, S., Ingvarsson, E. T., Quigg, A. M., Seckinger, K. E., & Teichman, H. M. (2011). Defining and measuring behavior. In W. W. Fisher, C. C. Piazza, & H. S. Roane (Eds.), *The handbook of applied behavior analysis* (pp. 132–147). New York: Guilford Press.

Kahng, S. W., Chung, K. M., Gutshall, K., Pitts, S. C., Kao, J., & Girolami, K. (2010). Consistent visual analyses of intrasubject data. *Journal of Applied Behavior Analysis, 43*(1), 35–45. https://doi.org/10.1901/jaba.2010.43-35

Kanne, S. M., & Mazurek, M. O. (2011). Aggression in children and adolescents with ASD: Prevalence and risk factors. *Journal of Autism and Developmental Disorders, 41*(7), 926–937. https://doi.org/10.1007/s10803-010-1118-4

Kazdin, A. E. (2011). *Single-case research design* (2nd ed.). New York: Oxford University Press.

LeBlanc, L. A., Lund, C., Kooken, C., Lund, J. B., & Fisher, W. W. (2019). Procedures and accuracy of discontinuous measurement of problem behavior in common practice of applied behavior analysis. *Behavior Analysis in Practice, 13*, 1–10. https://doi.org/10.1007/s40617-019-00361-6

LeBlanc, L. A., Raetz, P. B., Sellers, T. P., & Carr, J. E. (2016). A proposed model for selecting measurement procedures for the assessment and treatment of problem behavior. *Behavior Analysis in Practice, 9*, 77–83. https://doi.org/10.1007/s40617-015-0063-2

Miltenberger, R. G. (2016). *Behavior modification: Principles and procedures* (6th ed.). Cengage Learning.

Mitchell, S. K. (1979). Interobserver agreement, reliability, and generalizability of data collected in observational studies. *Psychological Bulletin, 86*(2), 376–390.

National Collaborating Centre for Mental Health. (2015). Violence and aggression: Short-term Management in Mental Health. In *Health and community settings: Updated edition.* British Psychological Society. Retrieved from https://www.ncbi.nlm.nih.gov/books/NBK356335/.

Page, T. J., & Iwata, B. A. (1986). Interobserver agreement: History, theory, and current methods. In A. Poling & R. W. Fuqua (Eds.), *Research methods in applied behavior analysis* (pp. 99–126). New York: Springer.

Parenteau, R., Luiselli, J. K., & Keeley, M. (2013). Direct and collateral effects of staff-worn protective equipment on injury prevention from child aggression. *Developmental Neurorehabilitation, 16*, 73–77.

Parker, R. I., & Vannest, K. (2009). An improved effect size for single-case research: Nonoverlap of all pairs. *Behavior Therapy, 40*(4), 357–367. https://doi.org/10.1016/j.beth.2008.10.006

Reynolds, C. R., & Kamphaus, R. W. (2004). *Behavior assessment system for children* (2nd ed.). Circle Pines, MN: American Guidance Service.

Roane, H. S., Fisher, W. W., Kelley, M. E., Mevers, J. L., & Bouxsein, K. J. (2013). Using modified visual-inspection criteria to interpret functional analysis outcomes. *Journal of Applied Behavior Analysis, 46*(1), 130–146. https://doi.org/10.1002/jaba.13

Roane, H. S., & Kadey, H. J. (2011). Aggression and destruction. In J. K. Luiselli (Ed.), *Teaching and behavior support for children and adults with autism spectrum disorders: A "how to" practitioner's guide* (pp. 143–150). New York: Oxford University Press.

Roane, H. S., Ringdahl, J. E., Kelley, M. E., & Glover, A. C. (2011). Single-case experimental designs. In W. W. Fisher, C. C. Piazza, & H. S. Roane (Eds.), *The handbook of applied behavior analysis* (pp. 132–150). New York: Guilford Press.

Rojahn, J., Matson, J. L., Lott, D., Esbensen, A. J., & Smalls, Y. (2001). The Behavior Problems Inventory: An instrument for the assessment of self-injury, stereotyped behavior and aggression/destruction in individuals with developmental disabilities. *Journal of Autism and Developmental Disorders, 31*(6), 577–588. https://doi.org/10.1023/a:1013299028321

Schroeder, S. R., Marquis, J. G., Reese, R. M., Richman, D. M., Mayo-Ortega, L., Oyama-Ganiko, R., et al. (2014). Risk factors for self-injury, aggression, and stereotyped behavior among young children at risk for intellectual and developmental disabilities. *American Journal on Intellectual and Developmental Disabilities, 119*(4), 351–370. https://doi.org/10.1352/1944-7558-119.4.351

Skinner, B. F. (1938). *The behavior of organisms*. Acton, MA: Copley Publishing Group.

Stewart, K. K., Carr, J. E., Brandt, C. W., & McHenry, M. M. (2007). An evaluation of the conservative dual-criterion method for teaching university students to visually inspect AB-design graphs. *Journal of Applied Behavior Analysis, 40*(4), 713–718. https://doi.org/10.1901/jaba.2007.713-718

Underwood, M. K. (2003). *Social aggression among girls*. New York: Guilford Press.

Urban, K. D., Luiselli, J. K., Child, S. N., & Parenteau, R. (2011). Effects of protective equipment on frequency and intensity of aggression-provoked staff injury. *Journal of Developmental and Physical Disabilities, 23*, 555–562.

What Works Clearinghouse. (2020). *What works clearinghouse standards handbook, Version 4.1*. Department of Education, Institute of Education Sciences, National Center for Education Evaluation and Regional Assistance. Retrieved from https://ies.ed.gov/ncee/wwc/handbooks.

Wolf, K., & Slocum, T. A. (2015). A comparison of two approaches to training visual analysis of AB graphs. *Journal of Applied Behavior Analysis, 48*(2), 472–477. https://doi.org/10.1002/jaba.212

Functional Behavior Assessment

Jill M. Harper, Juliya Krasnopolsky, Melissa C. Theodore, Christen E. Russell, and Eris J. Dodds

Abstract This chapter discusses approaches to functional behavioral assessment (FBA) within applied settings. The chapter begins with an overview of the FBA process as best practice in the assessment and treatment of challenging behavior. The next section provides a review of FBA methods with a focus on indirect and descriptive assessments. Within this section, common FBA procedures are reviewed, considerations in the selection of FBA methods are discussed, and a summary of relevant literature is provided. The chapter ends with practice guidelines for practitioners and future areas of study for researchers.

Keywords Functional behavior assessment · Indirect · Descriptive · Experimental

Functional behavior assessment (FBA) involves gathering information about the context(s) during which an individual engages in a particular behavior (Cooper, Heron, & Heward, 2020; Hagopian, Dozier, Rooker, & Jones, 2013). During the process, behavior analysts examine how the environment and behavior interact to determine what environmental events are likely to set the occasion, or evoke the behavior, and what environmental events are likely to follow, or reinforce the behavior, lending to its continuation. The immediate goal of FBA is to identify, or at minimum, hypothesize the function of the behavior. In other words, FBA is used to

---

J. M. Harper (✉) · J. Krasnopolsky
Melmark New England, Andover, MA, USA

Van Loan School, Endicott College, Beverly, MA, USA
e-mail: jharper@melmarkne.org

M. C. Theodore · C. E. Russell · E. J. Dodds
Van Loan School, Endicott College, Beverly, MA, USA

answer the "why" question, apropos to this chapter, "Why does Jonny hit his sister, Sally"?

Answering the immediate "why" question leads to the terminal goal, the design of an effective and efficient intervention. Research has repeatedly supported the effectiveness and efficiency of function-based intervention when compared to interventions designed without consideration of the function of behavior (e.g., Iwata, Pace, Cowdery, & Miltenberger, 1994; Payne, Scott, & Conroy, 2007; Walker, Chung, & Bonnet, 2018). The identification of the function is essential not only to intervention components targeting decreases in challenging behavior but also functional replacement behaviors. For example, if through the FBA process it is identified that Jonny hits his sister Sally to gain access to Sally's toys, teaching Jonny to ask for toys, to wait for toys, or to find alternative toys is necessary to promote maintenance of treatment effects over time and across settings. Thus, FBA is a critical step in the treatment of severe challenging behavior such as aggression and violence.

The process of FBA to inform intervention is considered best practice within the field of behavior analysis (e.g., Belva, Hattier, & Matson, 2013; Gresham, Watson, & Skinner, 2001; Hagopian et al., 2013). Empirical support of this process led to its incorporation within Individuals with Disabilities Education Act (IDEA) of 1997 and the Individuals with Disabilities Education Improvement Act (IDEIA) of 2004 (Individuals With Disabilities Education Act, 20 U.S.C. § 1400, 2004). In essence, components of IDEA or IDEIA require FBAs be conducted and inform intervention within the educational system. Although the general process of FBA is considered best practice and mandated by law, the specific procedures conducted are left to the judgement of those responsible for completing the FBA.

This chapter provides an outline of the steps involved in conducting FBA, interpreting FBA outcomes, and integrating outcomes of multiple FBA tools to inform the design of function-based interventions for multiple topographies of challenging behavior including aggression and violence. Relevant research literature is reviewed, clinical recommendations offered, and future research directions proposed.

FBA as Best Practice

Gable, Quinn, Rutherford Jr, Howell, and Hoffman (1999) published a guide for FBA following the initial release of the IDEA (1997). The authors outlined a ten-step process of assessment and treatment of challenging behavior. The outline below provides a summary of the first seven steps as they relate to FBA and the use of FBA results to inform the design of a function-based intervention.

1. *Describe and verify the problem.* Compare the dimensions of behavior such as topography, frequency, and context to the behavior of peers and consider the influence of cultural variables. Reserve FBA for more severe challenging behavior (e.g., aggression and violence, property destruction, self-injurious behavior) that is not likely to be addressed by general educational or clinical practices (e.g., positive behavior supports).

2. *Define the target(s):* Consider environmental variables such as time of day, location, and context during which the behavior is and is not likely to occur. Operational definitions should include delineation of the behavior as well as examples and non-examples. For instance, instead of targeting "aggression or violence," target "hitting, kicking, or verbal threats."
3. *Select FBA methodology and collect data.* Selection of methodology should be specific to the individual and setting(s). Multiple methods of FBA will lead to more accurate results.
4. *Analyze information gathered.* Summarize information to easily identify patterns across environmental and behavior variables.
5. *Generate hypothesis statement.* Present a concise statement reflecting the observed interaction between behavior and environmental variables. For example, "When Sally has the iPad and is playing within arms-reach of Jonny, Jonny hits Sally in the arm, Sally puts the iPad down and Jonny takes it."
6. *Test hypothesis.* The hypothesized function should be tested through the systematic manipulation of relevant environmental variables. This test may be designed as a treatment analysis to decrease the likelihood of the behavior or as a functional analysis (FA) to evoke and reinforce behavior in order to verify the hypothesized function.
7. *Develop and implement behavior intervention plan.* The results of the FBA process (steps 1–6) inform the intervention plan. Both behaviors for deceleration (e.g., aggression or violence) as well as appropriate replacement behaviors (e.g., communication) are targeted.

Categories of FBA

There are many assessment procedures captured under the umbrella of FBA (Anderson, Rodriguez, & Campbell, 2015; Fryling & Baires, 2016). Different assessment procedures can be classified into three main categories of FBA which include (1) experimental (functional) analysis, (2) indirect assessment, and (3) descriptive assessment. While the goals remain the same, the methods, benefits, and limitations vary. This chapter will only briefly describe the experimental (functional) analysis method of FBA and instead concentrate on indirect and descriptive assessment.

Experimental (Functional) Analysis

One category of FBA is experimental or functional analysis (FA). The term analysis rather than assessment is used to denote the direct, systematic manipulation of environmental events rather than the discussion (indirect assessment) or observation (descriptive assessment) of environmental events (Hanley, 2012; Mayer, Sulzer-

Azaroff, & Wallace, 2014). Experimental analysis is a methodology to identify the functional, or cause–effect, relations between behavior and environment through systematic manipulation of environmental events and observation of changes in behavior (Iwata et al. 1982/Iwata, Dorsey, Slifer, Bauman, & Richman, 1994). For example, in the test condition for social-positive reinforcement (attention), the practitioner would withhold attention for a period of time to increase the value of attention as a consequence. Contingent upon the instance of a target response such as aggression, the practitioner would deliver attention for a brief period before again removing attention (test condition). Responding during this condition would be compared to a condition during which attention is delivered independent of the target response (control condition). Differential levels of behavior observed across the test condition (high levels of behavior) and control condition (low levels of behavior) would indicate that the behavior is, at least in part, maintained by social-positive reinforcement in the form of access to attention.

FA is the only FBA method that directly manipulates environmental events, and therefore, the only method that can identity, rather than hypothesize the function of behavior. As such, experimental or functional analysis has long been considered the "gold standard" of FBA methodology within the field of behavior analysis. There has been over 30 years of research conducted and hundreds of publications around FA methodology which has demonstrated its utility and flexibility (Beavers, Iwata, & Lerman, 2013; Hanley, Iwata, & McCord, 2003). Thus, the FA is often used as the "true" function when evaluating the validity of indirect or descriptive assessments.

However, FA has a distinct disadvantage when compared to indirect and descriptive assessment of aggression and violence. That is, the experimental manipulation of possible controlling variables is intended to evoke and reinforce aggressive behavior which can be dangerous and necessitate safety measures during FA sessions (Chok, Harper, Weiss, Bird, & Luiselli, 2020). FBA, on the other hand, relies on hypothesized correlations between behavior and environmental events derived from observations, interviews, and data analysis under natural conditions without changing situations that are associated with the absence and presence of aggression and violence.

Indirect Assessments

A second category of FBA is the indirect assessment, which involves the collection of information through interviews and questionnaires, most often conducted with persons who have directly observed the individual engage in the target behavior such as caregivers, teachers, or therapists, but also may be conducted with the individual themselves (Dufrene, Kazmerski, & Labrot, 2017; Floyd, Phaneuf, & Wilczynski, 2005). Interviews consist of collecting data through verbal exchanges while questionnaires and rating scales may involve collecting information through verbal or written communication.

A number of indirect assessments have been developed over time (Belva et al., 2013; Kelley, LaRue, Roane, & Gadaire, 2011). The most salient component of indirect assessments surrounds the type of questions posed. Open-ended questions, closed-ended questions, or a combination may be asked across indirect assessment procedures. Closed-ended questions are scored dichotomously (yes/no) or on some numerical rating scale (Likert scale). A few common examples of closed-ended indirect assessments are the Motivation Assessment Scale (MAS; Durand & Crimmins, 1988), Questions About Behavior Function (QABF; Matson & Vollmer, 1995), and the Functional Analysis Screening Tool (FAST; Iwata, DeLeon, & Roscoe, 2013). Open-ended questions allow for more detailed responses and follow up questions for clarification or additional information (Fryling & Baires, 2016). Common open-ended assessments are the Functional Assessment Interview (FAI; O'Neil et al., 1997) and the Open-Ended Functional Assessment Interview (Hanley, 2012).

Strengths and Limitations. Indirect assessments are considered the least-intrusive type of FBA and are often recommended as the first step in the FBA process. Major benefits of indirect assessments include ease of administration and minimization of assessment time. Because indirect assessments do not require direct observation of behavior, they are often quick to complete and can be conducted in-person, on the phone, and via teleconference. Indirect assessments can also assist practitioners in gathering initial information about the individual (e.g., diagnosis) and the frequency, duration, intensity, and topography of the target behavior.

Notwithstanding benefits, practitioners should be cautious when selecting indirect assessments and avoid using these assessments as the sole measure within an FBA (e.g., Dufrene, et al., 2017; Floyd et al., 2005). Whether through interviews or questionnaires, such assessments depend upon the recall of past events which may be inconsistent or unreliable (Belva et al., 2013; Rooker, DeLeon, Borrero, Frank-Crawford, & Roscoe, 2015). The respondent is asked not only to recall information about the behavior itself, but also recall environmental events surrounding the behavior and how these variables interact across time. This reliance on verbal reports has brought into question the reliability (agreement) and validity (accuracy) of indirect assessments (Barton-Arwood, Wehby, Gunter, & Lane, 2003; Dufrene et al., 2017; Kelley et al., 2011).

Reliability and Validity of Closed-Ended Assessments. Measures of reliability may include comparison of outcomes across time, respondents, or assessments, as well as within assessments to examine consistency of outcomes. The majority of research with respect to indirect assessment has focused on such measures of reliability and reported mixed results (Rooker et al., 2015). For example, initial reliability between respondents for the MAS was reported at moderate to high levels (Durand & Crimmins, 1988) while later studies found reliability across respondents to be in the low range (30–45%) for the MAS (e.g., Zarcone, Rodgers, Iwata, Rourke, & Dorsey, 1991).

Zaja, Moore, Van Ingen, and Rojahn (2011) compared the psychometric properties of three commonly used indirect assessments, the QABF (Matson & Vollmer, 1995), the FAST (Iwata et al., 2013), and the Functional Assessment for Multiple Casualty (FACT; Matson et al. 2003). The authors reported that across all measures of validity and reliability, the QABF and the FACT were found to have strong psychometric properties as compared to the FAST.

Iwata et al. (2013) reported on both the reliability and validity of the FAST. The FAST was administered for 196 behaviors across dyads consisting of teachers, parents, and direct-care staff. Inter-rater reliability scores ranged from moderate to high for individual items within the FAST, while moderate reliability scores were reported for overall FAST outcomes (64.8%). Overall reliability scores reported by Iwata et al. (2013) are in contrast to those previously reported by Zaja et al. (2011). In addition to reliability, Iwata et al. (2013) compared the outcomes of the FAST to FA outcomes and found moderate levels of agreement.

Within the current literature, reported reliability measures of close-ended indirect assessments are somewhat mixed (e.g., Alter, Conroy, Mancil, & Haydon, 2008; Fee, Schieber, Noble, & Valdovinos, 2016). The complexity of comparison across studies is a direct result of differences in reported measures and the inclusion and exclusion of different assessments during comparisons. However, when closely examined, the most promising close-ended indirect assessments are identified as the QABF and the FAST (e.g., Dracobly, Dozier, Briggs & Juanico 2018; Iwata et al., 2013; Paclawskyj, Matson, Rush, Smalls, & Vollmer, 2000).

Similar to the FAST, the QABF has been found to be a reliable valid measure when compared to FA outcomes. In a comparison of indirect, descriptive, and FA methods, Hall (2005) found the QABF resulted in the same identified function as the FA in three of four cases (75%). In another comparison study, Tarbox et al. (2009) reported that outcomes of the QABF exactly matched the outcomes of the FA in four out of seven cases (57.1%) and partially matched (one of multiple identified functions) in six out of seven cases (85.7%). These two studies highlight the limited validity of even the most reliable closed-ended assessments.

Despite concerns with and inconsistencies in reports of reliability and validity of indirect assessments, they continue as one of the more common forms of FBA implemented in practice (e.g., Oliver, Pratt, & Normand, 2015; Roscoe, Phillips, Kelly, Farber, & Dube, 2015). As such, both researchers and practitioners continue to examine variables that may increase their reliability and validity (Neidert, Rooker, Bayles, & Miller, 2013; Rooker et al., 2015). One factor that may contribute to the variability in reliability and validity is the number and skill set of the respondents being assessed. Emerging research may provide some hopeful direction for both researchers and practitioners alike.

For example, Smith, Smith, Dracobly, and Pace (2012) compared the agreement scores when the MAS and QABF were conducted with five respondents instead of the typical two respondents. Agreement of the function in four out of five respondents was about 50% of cases with the MAS and in almost 60% of cases with the QABF. Similar results were reported when the result of the indirect assessments were compared to FA results with a higher agreement score between the QABF and the FA (almost 85%) as compared to the agreement between the MAS and FA (about 60%). It is important to note that not only did increasing the number of respondents across indirect assessments increase reliability, but that when reliability was at acceptable levels (80%), the validity of the assessment also increased as demonstrated by agreement with FA results (Dracobly et al., 2018).

Dracobly et al. (2018) compared the results of the FAST when either caregivers or experts (board certified behavior analysts) served as respondents. Two caregivers and two experts completed the FAST followed by the completion of a standard FA (Iwata et al. 1982/Iwata, Dorsey, et al., 1994). Experts were not actively involved in the clinical oversight and therefore conducted a short observation (1 h or less) of the individual prior to completing the indirect assessment. Even with limited observation, the values of reliability between expert respondents were higher than that of the caregiver respondents. When compared to the results of the FA, experts correctly agreed on the function of behavior for 80% of cases while caregivers correctly agreed on the function for only 20% of the cases.

Open-Ended Assessments. While a number of studies have reported on reliability and validity measures across closed-ended assessments, research on open-ended assessments is limited (Fryling & Baires, 2016). In one study, Alter et al. (2008) included one open-ended assessment, the FAI (O'Neil et al., 1997), in a comparison of the reliability and validity across multiple FBA methods including the FAI, MAS, descriptive methods, and FA. Within this study both reliability and validity of the FAI was reported at low levels. The reliability between the FAI and MAS was low (25%) as the two indirect assessments did not report the same outcome. Similarly, the outcomes of the FAI did not match the outcomes of the FAs (25%).

Saini, Ubdegrove, Biran, and Duncan (2019) examined inter-rater reliability and the validity of the Open-Ended Functional Assessment Interview (Hanley, 2012). Two raters conducted the interview with one caregiver across four clinical cases. The two raters agreed on the function of behavior in three out of four cases (75%). The hypotheses were then compared to FA outcomes and verified in two of the four cases (50%). The authors concluded that the interview demonstrated high inter-rater reliability and moderate validity. The high level of inter-rater reliability was not surprising given the recent results of the Dracobly et al. (2018) study and that raters in the current study were credentialed in the field of behavior analysis. That is, one would expect higher levels of reliability across well-trained raters.

Recent advances in FBA has initiated a comprehensive examination of the validity of closed- versus open-ended assessments to inform FA design through the accurate identification of relevant antecedents and consequences (Hanley, 2012). In light of limited comparative research on this topic, Fryling and Baires (2016) discussed some inherent strengths and weakness across closed- and open-ended indirect assessments as they relate to practical application. Closed-ended assessments are more efficient relative to open-ended assessments, in part due to the focus on common environment-behavior contingencies (e.g., positive, negative, and automatic reinforcement) leaving little room to discuss alternative or idiosyncratic sources. However, such a focused assessment may produce either false negative results through missed variables or false positive results due to the forced-choice nature of the procedure. While open-ended assessments provide the opportunity to identify a wider range of environmental variables, the relevancy of such variables to the function of the target behavior must be carefully considered in order to avoid false positive results by including an irrelevant variable in the hypothesized function.

Descriptive Assessments

The final category of FBA is the descriptive assessment. Descriptive assessments involve the direct observation of behavior across routines within settings such as classrooms, homes, and community. During observations, data are collected on the ABCs, or *antecedent* events preceding the behavior, dimensions of the targeted *behavior*, and *consequences* following the behavior. Precise definitions of both the target response and environmental events are necessary to ensure consistent recording across observations. In addition to the ABCs, data may be collected on the time of day, setting, and other people within the environment. Descriptive data are commonly collected by individuals within the daily setting including teachers, paraprofessionals, clinicians, or parents.

Strengths and Limitations. A general strength across descriptive assessment methods is direct observation of the behavior. Descriptive assessment is improved by real-time data collection around antecedent and consequences as opposed to reliance on verbal reports of past events during indirect assessments (Sloman, 2010). Although there are no standard criteria for termination of descriptive assessments, it is likely that assessment length will vary depending on the frequency of the targeted behavior. For example, assessments may be brief if aggressive behavior occurs several times per day, while extended assessment time may be required to collect sufficient data samples for low-rate aggressive behavior. There are several descriptive assessment procedures outlined in the literature (Belva et al., 2013; Hagopian et al., 2013; Mayer et al., 2014; Sloman, 2010) and described below.

Narrative Assessments. Similar to open-ended indirect assessments, narrative descriptive assessments (Bijou, Peterson, & Ault, 1968) are conducted when an observer records the events that occur before and after the behavior including as many details as possible. Narrative assessments allow for the recording of idiosyncratic yet relevant variables contiguous to and following the target behavior.

Scatterplot. A scatterplot (Touchette, MacDonald, & Langer, 1985) involves collecting data on the temporal distribution of the target response. For example, the school day may be split into 15-min intervals and the occurrence/nonoccurrence or frequency of aggression noted during each interval. This type of assessment allows for the detection of patterns of behavior as it relates to time of day, but does not provide information around the specific environmental events that may co-occur during these time periods unless noted.

Antecedent-Behavior-Consequence (ABC) Methods. Another category of descriptive assessments involves observing and recording antecedent and consequence conditions that precede and follow the target behavior, respectively (Mayer et al., 2014). For example, anytime Jonny hits his sister Sally, the observer would record what happened immediately before and after the aggressive behavior. Data collection on antecedents and consequences may be recorded in a narrative format or may be more structured to include checklists.

Conditional and Background Probabilities. As first described by Bijou et al. (1968), continuous or interval data collection is often used as a descriptive assessment method within research (Sloman, 2010). During this type of assessment, the observer records occurrence of the target behavior and environmental events separately. Following some predetermined observation period, environment-behavior relations are analyzed. For conditional probabilities, data analysis involves calculating the probability of the environmental events given the occurrence of the behavior (e.g., Lerman & Iwata, 1993). In addition, the conditional and background probability (e.g., Vollmer, Borrero, Wright, Camp, & Lalli, 2001) involves both calculations of the probability of environmental events given behavior *and* the probability of environmental events across time. The addition of the background, or unconditional probability allows for the comparison of the probability of the correlation between environmental events and behavior to the general occurrence of the environment. For example, to determine if access to the iPad follows aggression, the conditional probability would be derived by dividing the number of times the iPad followed aggression by the total number of times the behavior occurred *and* comparing this proportion to the number of times the iPad was presented.

Validity of Descriptive Assessments

While there remain some mixed results, the majority of previous research concluded poor validity between descriptive assessments when compared to FA results (Camp, Iwata, Hammond, & Bloom, 2009; Hall, 2005; Lerman & Iwata, 1993; Sloman, 2010; Tarbox et al., 2009). Further, while some studies reported observation of behavioral patterns with a scatterplot analysis (Maas, Didden, Bouts, Smits, & Curfs, 2009; Touchette et al., 1985) others reported no clear patterns across analyses (English & Anderson, 2004; Kahng et al., 1998). The reliability and validity of other common descriptive assessments such as the ABC method have produced similar results.

Pence, Roscoe, Bourret, and Ahearn (2009) compared the results of the ABC method, conditional probability method, and conditional- and background probability methods to each other and to FA outcomes. The three different descriptive methods resulted in similar or identical outcomes while the comparisons between the descriptive assessments and the FA only matched in one of six cases (16.7%). Although not the focus of the study, Pence et al. included an additional analysis during which only antecedents or consequences of the ABC data were compared to FA outcomes. For some cases, antecedent but not consequences aligned with the FA outcomes while in other cases, the consequences but not the antecedent aligned with FA outcomes.

Camp et al. (2009) examined the predictive nature of antecedents alone, consequences alone, and antecedent and consequences identified by descriptive observation and conditional and background probabilities. The results of the combined antecedent and consequence analysis replicated previous studies showing the limited agreement between descriptive assessment and FA. In this case, when both antecedents and consequences were included, outcomes of the descriptive assessment matched outcomes of the FA in four of seven cases (57.1%). In addition, the results of the antecedent only and consequence only descriptive assessments replicated the Pence et al. findings that examining antecedent or consequences alone did not consistently increase the predictive validity of the descriptive assessment.

Both Hall (2005) and Tarbox et al. (2009) included descriptive assessments within a three-way comparison of indirect, descriptive, and FA methods. The results of Hall (2005) replicated Lerman and Iwata (1993) in that conditional probabilities, as a descriptive assessment produced low levels of agreement with FA outcomes (25%). Tarbox et al. used ABC data within their comparison and found agreement with FA outcomes in only one of seven cases (14.3%).

In summary, these recent studies have continued to demonstrate poor validity across descriptive assessment methods even when results of descriptive assessments are compared using antecedents only, consequences only, or both antecedents and consequences. Although descriptive assessments may lack validity with reference to behavior-function hypothesis formulation, practitioners and researchers should not abandon them all together. Rather, a shift in focus around the utility of descriptive assessment within the FBA process seems more appropriate.

Use of FBA Methods by Practitioners

An important area of the FBA literature is descriptive research on the use of FBA methods within applied settings such as clinics, schools, homes, and the community. Notably, there is limited research on implementing FBA methodology within applied settings (Oliver et al., 2015; Roscoe et al., 2015).

Ellingson, Miltenberger, and Long (1999) reported the results of a survey on the use and perceptions of FBA methodology. Thirty-six respondents throughout the state of North Dakota reported that they most often used indirect assessments (interviews and FAST) followed by FA within the natural setting and descriptive assessment (ABC). Commonly reported perceptions of FBA were that closed-ended indirect assessments were easy to use, descriptive assessments provided information about function, while FA in the natural setting informed intervention. In their discussion, the authors qualified that the definition of "functional analysis within the natural setting" used in this study was broad and may have been interpreted as including treatment analysis.

In 2015, two separate surveys on the use of FBA methodology were published by Roscoe et al. and Oliver et al. Roscoe et al. limited their survey to practitioners within the state of Massachusetts (205 respondents) while Oliver et al. used an electronic survey without limits to demographic area (724 initial respondents). Across both studies, practitioners reported most commonly using descriptive assessment methodology (62%–Roscoe et al.; 75%–Oliver et al.) while only about one-third of respondents reported using FA methodology. The survey results were more discrepant with respect to indirect assessment. While indirect assessments were commonly used by just over 75% of respondents in the Oliver et al. study, only 2% of respondents in the Roscoe et al. reported using this assessment method.

Professions outside of behavior analysis are often responsible for conducting FBA, therefore it is important to extend the evaluation of FBA practices to those disciplines. In illustration, Johnson, Goldberg, Hinant, and Couch (2019) conducted a survey across 199 school psychologists and found that indirect assessments were used most often followed by descriptive assessments, while only 25% of respondents had utilized FA methods within the last school year.

From the current surveys, it is evident that indirect and descriptive assessments are used more commonly compared to FA within the FBA process. None of the aforementioned surveys resulted in the exact agreement of FBA implementation practices. Oliver et al. (2015) and Roscoe et al. (2015) both identified descriptive assessments as the most common but differed on the rankings between indirect assessments and FA. Similarly, Ellingson et al. (1999) and Johnson et al. (2019) both identified indirect assessments as the most common but differed on the rakings of descriptive and assessment and FA. Thus, although assessment procedures were found to be most commonly implemented across all surveys, more research is needed to tease out the specific variables that determine what type of FBA will be selected, effective, and efficient.

Practice Recommendations: Evidence Based Practice in FBA

Although the general process of FBA is well outlined (Cooper et al., 2020), practitioners must individualize the specific content of the process to best fit the clinical case at hand. That is, FBA is a multistep process involving many decision points along the way. Decisions based on the framework of evidence-based practice incorporate three variables (1) the best available literature that is most relevant to the particular case, (2) professional judgement, and (3) client/setting characteristics (Slocum et al., 2014; Spencer, Detrich, & Slocum, 2012).

The first seven steps of the FBA process as outlined by Gable et al. (1999) are again outlined below. However, steps three through seven have been modified to now include practice recommendations based on the "best available literature" as presented throughout the previous sections of this chapter. Although these recommendations should be considered during the FBA process, it is important to individualize each step using professional judgement and client/setting characteristics. In the example of aggression and violence, practitioners should follow the steps below.

1. *Describe and verify the problem.* Compare the dimensions of behavior such as topography, frequency, and context to the behavior of peers and consider the influence of cultural variables. Reserve FBA for more severe challenging behavior (e.g., aggression and violence, property destruction, self-injurious behavior) that is not likely to be addressed by general educational or clinical practices (e.g., positive behavior supports).
2. *Define the target(s):* Consider environmental variables such as time of day, location, and context during which the behavior is and is not likely to occur. Operational definitions should include delineation of the behavior as well as examples and non-examples. For example, instead of targeting "aggression or violence" target "hitting, kicking, or verbal threats."
3. *Select FBA methodology and collect data.* Practitioners should be familiar with the strengths and limitations of different FBA methods. Indirect methods, as they are currently designed, have low reliability and validity measures (Hagopian et al., 2013; Mayer et al., 2014; Rooker et al., 2015). Similarly, hypotheses about the function of behavior derived by descriptive assessments do not often match outcomes of FA (Rooker et al., 2015; Sloman, 2010). Thus, it is recommended that practitioners utilize multiple FBA methods and simultaneously compare outcomes to help guide next steps (Gable et al., 1999). Further, if FBA methods must be restricted to indirect assessment, practitioners should consider conducting both closed-ended and open-ended formats to balance the strengths and limitations of these two sub-categories of indirect assessments (Fryling & Baires, 2016).

There are several considerations with respect to respondent selection that may increase the reliability and validity of indirect FBA outcomes. First, consider a respondent's or observer's level of training and experience around behavior-environment interactions and their understanding of basic learning principles (Dracobly et al., 2018). Second, multiple respondents should be used whenever possible (Smith et al., 2012). Third, reliability of the assessment outcomes is best when respondents are from the same environment and have observed the behavior over time (Borgmeier, Horner, & Koegel, 2006).
4. *Analyze information gathered.* The analysis of information collected during the FBA process will, in part, be driven by the selected method. However, practitioners should consider several guidelines across methods. First, data analysis

methods should be sensitive. Although behavior analysts often prefer visual analysis, additional measures should be considered to better capture the complex, and sometimes subtle interaction between multiple environmental variables. For example, during descriptive assessments, data should be collected in a way to allow computation of conditional and background probabilities (Rooker et al., 2015; Vollmer et al., 2001). Second, data analysis should be easy to interpret. When FBAs involve multiple assessment methods, practitioners should consider supplementing written summaries with data triangulation to highlight consistencies and discrepancies across sources of information (Gable et al., 1999).

5. *Generate hypothesis statement.* Present a concise statement reflecting the observed interaction between behavior and environmental variables. Include all relevant variables within the hypothesis. If necessary, practitioners should conduct additional FBA to either replicate outcomes from previous respondents, thus increasing the confidence in the hypothesis (Smith et al., 2012), or conduct additional methods of FBA to ensure all potentially relevant variables are examined before making the final hypothesis (Fryling & Baires, 2016; Gable et al., 1999). For example, a scatterplot might be recommended following an ABC descriptive assessment that identified denial of food as a common antecedent to aggression. The addition of the scatterplot might identify a correlation between time of day (e.g., right before meals) and problem behavior.

6. *Test hypothesis.* The hypothesized function should be tested through the systematic manipulation of variables that precede and/or follow the behavior. This test may be designed as a treatment analysis during which variables are manipulated to decrease the likelihood of the behavior or as an FA during which variables are manipulated to either increase (test conditions) or decrease (control conditions) behavior.

7. *Develop and implement behavior intervention plan.* The results of the FBA process (steps 1–6) inform the intervention plan. Both behaviors for deceleration (e.g., aggression or violence) as well as appropriate replacement behaviors (e.g., communication) are targeted.

Future Research Directions

Some common themes emerge from recent literature around FBA. Although best practice continues to highlight FA as the gold standard, current reviews of the literature on FBA practices across applied settings coupled with recent surveys of practitioners indicate greater use of indirect and descriptive assessment methods. Future research directions in the area of FBA must focus on ways in which the reliability and validity of indirect and descriptive assessments can be maximized when experimental methods are not preferred or not available (Neidert et al., 2013; Rooker et al., 2015). Some emerging research in this area was reviewed throughout this chapter and an extension of these topics is reviewed here.

The first proposed area of future research surrounds the behavior of those responsible for participating in the FBA process, whether it be behavior analysts, school psychologists, teachers, parents, or therapists. To maximize effectiveness and efficiency of FBA methods, we must first expand the current literature on practitioner behavior as it relates to the FBA process.

Recent surveys examined practitioner's selection of FBA methods (Ellingson et al., 1999; Johnson et al., 2019; Oliver et al., 2015; Roscoe et al., 2015). When asked about the function of their behavior, respondents across both the Oliver et al. (2015) and Roscoe et al. (2015) studies reported common barriers to the implementation of FA as lack of time and resources. Such responses suggest that setting characteristics affect FBA selection. Future research should examine additional variables that may influence FBA selection such as client characteristics and topography, frequency, magnitude, and duration of the target response. For example, are practitioners more likely to select indirect assessments over descriptive assessments or FA when the target behavior is severe aggression or violence?

It will be important to examine current practices across all aspects of the FBA process including system of data collection (e.g., Lerman, Hovanetz, Strobel, & Tetreault, 2009) and analysis, generation of hypotheses, and integration of FBA information into function-based interventions (e.g., Blood & Neel, 2007; Scott et al., 2005; Sugai, Lewis-Palmer, & Hagan, 1998). Such assessments of practitioner behavior as it relates to FBA will serve as a baseline measure to which comparisons can be made.

For example, Lerman et al. (2009) examined the accuracy with which school teachers and paraprofessionals collected either narrative or structured descriptive data. Participants received a group training (lecture) and then were instructed to score video-taped scenarios using narrative and structured ABC data collection methods. Not only were participants more accurate with the structured format they also reported a preference for this format. It is important to note that Lerman et al. (2009) did not collect baseline data as the purpose of this study was to compare accuracy of data collection across assessment formats.

Other studies have examined the effects of training on the accuracy of data collection during the FBA process (Luna, Petri, Palmier, & Rapp, 2018; Mayer & DiGennaro Reed, 2013). Luna et al. (2018) examined the effects of training on accuracy of data collection across narrative and structured descriptive assessments. The authors reported improved accuracy of data collection on narrative and structured descriptive data following intervention which consisted of a verbal review and group feedback. Ten of 14 teachers/paraprofessionals increased accuracy to mastery levels across both recording formats following the training.

These studies highlight the need for additional research on the necessary and sufficient training practices across different components of the FBA process. Several authors have suggested training, experience, and knowledge of the respondents may lead to more reliable and valid assessment outcomes (Borgmeier et al., 2006; Dracobly et al., 2018). Simple trainings such as those described may reduce the need for more restrictive assessments, therefore reducing the potential risk for all involved, particularly if the target behavior is aggressive or violent in nature.

One other direction of future research should set out to systematically evaluate how aspects of the environment and behavior affect FBA outcomes within the natural setting. The results of several studies have implied that different aspects of the environment (e.g., Thompson & Iwata, 2007), behavior (e.g., Matson & Wilkins, 2008), or interaction between environment and behavior may influence outcomes of indirect and descriptive assessments. For example, what are the effects of rate or intensity of behavior on outcomes of indirect assessments? Does reliability of indirect assessments increase with more opportunities to observe behavior-environment interactions? Such a research agenda might include a combination of controlled, translational experiments followed by more applied, systematic replications. This will certainly be a formidable task that has taken somewhat of a back seat to the continued refinement of FA methodology (Beavers et al., 2013; Hanley et al., 2003).

Finally, acceptance of such research agendas to refine indirect and descriptive assessments does not negate the continued search for adoption of the gold standard, FA. However, data from recent surveys implies that there are contexts for which the FA is not preferred or not available. Research agendas should be driven by such data particularly with reference to persons who have neurodevelopmental disabilities and demonstrate aggressive and violent behavior.

References

Alter, P. J., Conroy, M. A., Mancil, G. R., & Haydon, T. (2008). A comparison of functional behavior assessment methodologies with young children: Descriptive methods and functional analysis. *Journal of Behavioral Education, 17*(2), 200–219.

Anderson, C. M., Rodriguez, B. J., & Campbell, A. (2015). Functional behavior assessment in schools: Current status and future directions. *Journal of Behavioral Education, 24*(3), 338–371.

Barton-Arwood, S. M., Wehby, J. H., Gunter, P. L., & Lane, K. L. (2003). Functional behavior assessment rating scales: Intrarater reliability with students with emotional or behavioral disorders. *Behavioral Disorders, 28*(4), 386–400.

Beavers, G. A., Iwata, B. A., & Lerman, D. C. (2013). Thirty years of research on the functional analysis of problem behavior. *Journal of Applied Behavior Analysis, 46*(1), 1–21.

Belva, B. C., Hattier, M. A., & Matson, J. L. (2013). Assessment of problem behavior. In *Handbook of crisis intervention and developmental disabilities* (pp. 123–146). New York: Springer.

Bijou, S. W., Peterson, R. F., & Ault, M. H. (1968). A method to integrate descriptive and experimental field studies at the level of data and empirical concepts 1. *Journal of Applied Behavior Analysis, 1*(2), 175–191.

Blood, E., & Neel, R. S. (2007). From FBA to implementation: A look at what is actually being delivered. *Education and Treatment of Children, 30*, 67–80.

Borgmeier, C., Horner, R. H., & Koegel, R. L. (2006). An evaluation of the predictive validity of confidence ratings in identifying functional behavioral assessment hypothesis statements. *Journal of Positive Behavior Interventions, 8*(2), 100–105.

Camp, E. M., Iwata, B. A., Hammond, J. L., & Bloom, S. E. (2009). Antecedent versus consequent events as predictors of problem behavior. *Journal of Applied Behavior Analysis, 42*(2), 469–483.

Chok, J. T., Harper, J. M., Weiss, M. J., Bird, F. L., & Luiselli, J. K. (2020). *Functional analysis: A practitioner's guide to implementation and training*. New York: Elsevier/Academic Press.

Cooper, J. O., Heron, T. E., & Heward, W. L. (2020). *Applied behavior analysis* (3rd ed.). Hoboken, NJ: Pearson.

Dracobly, J. D., Dozier, C. L., Briggs, A. M., & Juanico, J. F. (2018). Reliability and validity of indirect assessment outcomes: Experts versus caregivers. *Learning and Motivation, 62*, 77–90.

Dufrene, B. A., Kazmerski, J. S., & Labrot, Z. (2017). The current status of indirect functional assessment instruments. *Psychology in the Schools, 54*(4), 331–350.

Durand, V. M., & Crimmins, D. B. (1988). Identifying the variables maintaining self-injurious behavior. *Journal of Autism and Developmental Disorders, 18*(1), 99–117.

Ellingson, S. A., Miltenberger, R. G., & Long, E. S. (1999). A survey of the use of functional assessment procedures in agencies serving individuals with developmental disabilities. *Behavioral Interventions: Theory & Practice in Residential & Community-Based Clinical Programs, 14*(4), 187–198.

English, C. L., & Anderson, C. M. (2004). Effects of familiar versus unfamiliar therapists on responding in the analog functional analysis. *Research in Developmental Disabilities, 25*(1), 39–55.

Fee, A., Schieber, E., Noble, N., & Valdovinos, M. G. (2016). Agreement between questions about behavior function, the motivation assessment scale, functional assessment interview, and brief functional analysis of children's challenging behaviors. *Behavior Analysis: Research and Practice, 16*(2), 94.

Floyd, R. G., Phaneuf, R. L., & Wilczynski, S. M. (2005). Measurement properties of indirect assessment methods for functional behavioral assessment: A review of research. *School Psychology Review, 34*(1), 58–73.

Fryling, M. J., & Baires, N. A. (2016). The practical importance of the distinction between open and closed-ended indirect assessments. *Behavior Analysis in Practice, 9*(2), 146–151. https://doi.org/10.1007/s40617-016-0115-2

Gable, R. A., Quinn, M. M., Rutherford Jr., R. B., Howell, K. W., & Hoffman, C. C. (1999). *Addressing student problem behavior: Part 2. Conducting a functional behavioral assessment* (3rd ed.). Washington, DC: Center for Effective Collaboration and Practice.

Gresham, F. M., Watson, T. S., & Skinner, C. H. (2001). Functional behavioral assessment: Principles, procedures, and future directions. *School Psychology Review, 30*(2), 156–172.

Hagopian, L. P., Dozier, C. L., Rooker, G. W., & Jones, B. A. (2013). Assessment and treatment of severe problem behavior. In *APA handbook of behavior analysis* (Translating principles into practice) (Vol. 2, pp. 353–386). Washington, DC: American Psychological Association.

Hall, S. S. (2005). Comparing descriptive, experimental and informant-based assessments of problem behaviors. *Research in Developmental Disabilities, 26*(6), 514–526.

Hanley, G. P. (2012). Functional assessment of problem behavior: Dispelling myths, overcoming implementation obstacles, and developing new lore. *Behavior Analysis in Practice, 5*(1), 54–72.

Hanley, G. P., Iwata, B. A., & McCord, B. E. (2003). Functional analysis of problem behavior: A review. *Journal of Applied Behavior Analysis, 36*(2), 147–185.

Iwata, B. A., DeLeon, I. G., & Roscoe, E. M. (2013). Reliability and validity of the functional analysis screening tool. *Journal of Applied Behavior Analysis, 46*(1), 271–284.

Iwata, B. A., Dorsey, M. F., Slifer, K. J., Bauman, K. E., & Richman, G. S. (1994). Toward a functional analysis of self-injury. *Journal of Applied Behavior Analysis, 27*(2), 197–209.

Iwata, B. A., Pace, G. M., Cowdery, G. E., & Miltenberger, R. G. (1994). What makes extinction work: An analysis of procedural form and function. *Journal of Applied Behavior Analysis, 27*(1), 131–144.

Johnson, A. H., Goldberg, T. S., Hinant, R. L., & Couch, L. K. (2019). Trends and practices in functional behavior assessments completed by school psychologists. *Psychology in the Schools, 56*(3), 360–377.

Kahng, S., Iwata, B. A., Fischer, S. M., Page, T. J., Treadwell, K. R., Williams, D. E., et al. (1998). Temporal distributions of problem behavior based on scatter plot analysis. *Journal of Applied Behavior Analysis, 31*(4), 593–604.

Kelley, M. E., LaRue, R., Roane, H. S., & Gadaire, D. M. (2011). Indirect behavioral assessments: Interviews and rating scales. In W. W. Fisher, C. C. Piazza, & H. S. Roane (Eds.), *Handbook of applied behavior analysis* (pp.182–190). New York, NY: Guilford.

Lerman, D. C., Hovanetz, A., Strobel, M., & Tetreault, A. (2009). Accuracy of teacher-collected descriptive analysis data: A comparison of narrative and structured recording formats. *Journal of Behavioral Education, 18*(2), 157–172.

Lerman, D. C., & Iwata, B. A. (1993). Descriptive and experimental analyses of variables maintaining self-injurious behavior. *Journal of Applied Behavior Analysis, 26*(3), 293–319.

Luna, O., Petri, J. M., Palmier, J., & Rapp, J. T. (2018). Comparing accuracy of descriptive assessment methods following a group training and feedback. *Journal of Behavioral Education, 27*(4), 488–508.

Maas, A. P., Didden, R., Bouts, L., Smits, M. G., & Curfs, L. M. (2009). Scatter plot analysis of excessive daytime sleepiness and severe disruptive behavior in adults with Prader-Willi syndrome: A pilot study. *Research in Developmental Disabilities, 30*(3), 529–537.

Matson, J. L., & Vollmer, T. R. (1995). *The questions about behavioral function (QABF) user's guide*. Baton Rouge, LA: Scientific Publishers.

Matson, J. L., Kuhn, D. E., Dixon, D. R., Mayville, S. B., Laud, R. B., Cooper, C. L., et al. (2003). The development and factor structure of the Functional Assessment for multiple CausaliTy (FACT). *Research in Developmental Disabilities, 24*(6), 485–495.

Matson, J. L., & Wilkins, J. (2008). Reliability of the autism spectrum disorders-comorbid for children (ASD-CC). *Journal of Developmental and Physical Disabilities, 20*(4), 327–336.

Mayer, G. R., Sulzer-Azaroff, B., & Wallace, M. (2014). *Behavior analysis for lasting change* (3rd ed.). Cornwall-on-Hudson, NY: Sloan Publishing.

Mayer, K. L., & DiGennaro Reed, F. D. (2013). Effects of a training package to improve the accuracy of descriptive analysis data recording. *Journal of Organizational Behavior Management, 33*(4), 226–243.

Neidert, P. L., Rooker, G. W., Bayles, M. W., & Miller, J. R. (2013). Functional analysis of problem behavior. In *Handbook of crisis intervention and developmental disabilities* (pp. 147–167). New York: Springer.

O'Neil, R. E., Horner, R. H., Ablin, R. W., Sprague, J. R., Storey, K., & Newton, J. S. (1997). *Functional assessment and program development for problem behaviors: A practical handbook*. New York: Brooks/Cole.

Oliver, A. C., Pratt, L. A., & Normand, M. P. (2015). A survey of functional behavior assessment methods used by behavior analysts in practice. *Journal of Applied Behavior Analysis, 48*(4), 817–829.

Paclawskyj, T. R., Matson, J. L., Rush, K. S., Smalls, Y., & Vollmer, T. R. (2000). Questions about behavioral function (QABF): A behavioral checklist for functional assessment of aberrant behavior. *Research in Developmental Disabilities, 21*(3), 223–229.

Payne, L. D., Scott, T. M., & Conroy, M. (2007). A school-based examination of the efficacy of function-based intervention. *Behavioral Disorders, 32*(3), 158–174.

Pence, S. T., Roscoe, E. M., Bourret, J. C., & Ahearn, W. H. (2009). Relative contributions of three descriptive methods: Implications for behavioral assessment. *Journal of Applied Behavior Analysis, 42*(2), 425–446.

Rooker, G. W., DeLeon, I. G., Borrero, C. S., Frank-Crawford, M. A., & Roscoe, E. M. (2015). Reducing ambiguity in the functional assessment of problem behavior. *Behavioral Interventions, 30*(1), 1–35.

Roscoe, E. M., Phillips, K. M., Kelly, M. A., Farber, R., & Dube, W. V. (2015). A statewide survey assessing practitioners' use and perceived utility of functional assessment. *Journal of Applied Behavior Analysis, 48*(4), 830–844.

Saini, V., Ubdegrove, K., Biran, S., & Duncan, R. (2019). A preliminary evaluation of interrater reliability and concurrent validity of open-ended indirect assessment. *Behavior Analysis in Practice, 13*(1), 114–125. https://doi.org/10.1007/s40617-019-00364-3

Scott, T. M., McIntyre, J., Liaupsin, C., Nelson, C. M., Conroy, M., & Payne, L. D. (2005). An examination of the relation between functional behavior assessment and selected intervention strategies with school-based teams. *Journal of Positive Behavior Interventions, 7*(4), 205–215.

Slocum, T. A., Detrich, R., Wilczynski, S. M., Spencer, T. D., Lewis, T., & Wolfe, K. (2014). The evidence-based practice of applied behavior analysis. *The Behavior Analyst, 37*(1), 41–56.

Sloman, K. N. (2010). Research trends in descriptive analysis. *The Behavior Analyst Today, 11*(1), 20.

Smith, C. M., Smith, R. G., Dracobly, J. D., & Pace, A. P. (2012). Multiple-respondent anecdotal assessments: An analysis of interrater agreement and correspondence with analogue assessment outcomes. *Journal of Applied Behavior Analysis, 45*(4), 779–795.

Spencer, T. D., Detrich, R., & Slocum, T. A. (2012). Evidence-based practice: A framework for making effective decisions. *Education and Treatment of Children, 35*(2), 127–151.

Sugai, G., Lewis-Palmer, T., & Hagan, S. (1998). Using functional assessments to develop behavior support plans. *Preventing School Failure: Alternative Education for Children and Youth, 43*(1), 6–13.

Tarbox, J., Wilke, A. E., Najdowski, A. C., Findel-Pyles, R. S., Balasanyan, S., Caveney, A. C., et al. (2009). Comparing indirect, descriptive, and experimental functional assessments of challenging behavior in children with autism. *Journal of Developmental and Physical Disabilities, 21*(6), 493.

Thompson, R. H., & Iwata, B. A. (2007). A comparison of outcomes from descriptive and functional analyses of problem behavior. *Journal of Applied Behavior Analysis, 40*(2), 333–338.

Touchette, P. E., MacDonald, R. F., & Langer, S. N. (1985). A scatter plot for identifying stimulus control of problem behavior. *Journal of Applied Behavior Analysis, 18*(4), 343–351.

Vollmer, T. R., Borrero, J. C., Wright, C. S., Camp, C. V., & Lalli, J. S. (2001). Identifying possible contingencies during descriptive analyses of severe behavior disorders. *Journal of Applied Behavior Analysis, 34*(3), 269–287.

Walker, V. L., Chung, Y. C., & Bonnet, L. K. (2018). Function-based intervention in inclusive school settings: A meta-analysis. *Journal of Positive Behavior Interventions, 20*(4), 203–216.

Zaja, R. H., Moore, L., Van Ingen, D. J., & Rojahn, J. (2011). Psychometric comparison of the functional assessment instruments QABF, FACT and FAST for self-injurious, stereotypic and aggressive/destructive behaviour. *Journal of Applied Research in Intellectual Disabilities, 24*(1), 18–28.

Zarcone, J. R., Rodgers, T. A., Iwata, B. A., Rourke, D. A., & Dorsey, M. F. (1991). Reliability analysis of the Motivation Assessment Scale: A failure to replicate. *Research in Developmental Disabilities, 12*(4), 349–360.

Functional Analysis of Violence–Aggression

Ashley M. Fuhrman, Brian D. Greer, and Wayne W. Fisher

Abstract A functional analysis is a set of procedures in which a behavior analyst uses single-case designs to systematically manipulate antecedent and consequent stimuli hypothesized to influence problem behavior and measures the effects of those manipulations using reliable, direct observation methods. The information gleaned from a functional analysis can often be used to prescribe effective treatments for violent and aggressive behavior. In this chapter, we describe the essential components of a standard functional analysis of violent and aggressive behavior and how those components can be altered to address unique or idiosyncratic functions of problem behavior. We also discuss recent advances and alterations to a standard functional analysis, provide practical suggestions for practitioners who may wish to incorporate functional analyses into their clinical work, and recommend directions for future research on functional analysis.

Keywords Aggression · Establishing operation · Functional analysis · Synthesized contingencies · Safety precautions · Trial-based functional analysis · Violent behavior

---

A. M. Fuhrman (✉) · B. D. Greer · W. W. Fisher
Children's Specialized Hospital–Rutgers University, Center for Autism Research, Education, and Services (CSH–RUCARES), New Brunswick, NJ, USA

Rutgers Robert Wood Johnson Medical School, New Brunswick, NJ, USA
e-mail: ashley.fuhrman@rutgers.edu

© Springer Nature Switzerland AG 2021
J. K. Luiselli (ed.), *Applied Behavior Analysis Treatment of Violence and Aggression in Persons with Neurodevelopmental Disabilities*, Advances in Preventing and Treating Violence and Aggression,
https://doi.org/10.1007/978-3-030-68549-2_3

Most disciplines categorize behavioral health disorders based on their structural characteristics and the extent to which symptoms cluster or covary (e.g., American Psychiatric Association, 2013), such as when a child shows delayed or peculiar language and social skills in combination with repetitive or ritualistic behavior and receives a diagnosis of autism spectrum disorder (ASD). By contrast, behavior analysts attempt to assess and categorize behavior disorders in terms of the environmental variables of which the behavior is a function. Skinner (1953) coopted the term *functional analysis* (FA) from the field of mathematics to describe the process through which behavior analysts identify the environmental variables that control behavior. According to Skinner, a *functional relation* exists between an environmental variable and a target response when a change in the former produces a consistent and expected change in the latter.

Essential Components of FA

Just as a basic scientist might investigate the variables responsible for the timing, magnitude, and persistence of behavioral relapse in the laboratory, applied behavior analysts must often uncover the environmental variables responsible for the occurrence of socially significant behavior in order to treat a problematic response. The approaches taken by both the basic scientist and the applied behavior analyst are highly similar. The basic scientist might systematically arrange different training histories to determine their effect on relapse, just as the applied behavior analyst might systematically arrange different situations or conditions that do and do not evoke problem behavior. The systematic approach to identifying why a response or effect occurs is a hallmark of FA. Equally important is identifying why responding does not occur. Thus, a major goal of any FA is the demonstration of experimental control over responding—producing the response or effect only when the necessary and sufficient variables are present.

Although reliably producing a target response is necessary when conducting an FA of problem behavior, rarely is it sufficient. This is to say that one needs to have a firm understanding of the critical differences between those situations in which responding reliably occurs and those in which responding reliably does not occur (or reliably occurs, albeit at a lower level). The more similar two conditions are that do and do not produce the response of interest, the more confident one can be that he or she has isolated at least one variable responsible for the response. Likewise, test and control conditions that differ along a number of potentially important dimensions may reliably turn behavior "on" and "off," but the results may be insufficiently precise so as to inform treatment strategies that are not overly complicated or burdensome. Thus, a major purpose of FA, at least as it pertains to application, is that it identifies only those variables of which behavior is a function. As a result, careful manipulation of the antecedent (e.g., motivating operations, discriminative stimuli) and consequent (e.g., reinforcing) events that define the test and control conditions of an FA will help in isolating those variables responsible for the occurrence and maintenance of problem behavior (see Fisher, Greer, & Bouxsein, in press, for elaboration on programming antecedent and consequent events within an FA).

Although a major purpose of conducting an FA is to identify only those variables of which behavior is a function, rarely do applied behavior analysts uncover all of the variables responsible for a socially significant response. Unlike our basic brethren, who might rightfully spend an entire career conducting a thoroughgoing FA of relapse, critically analyzing all variables responsible for each dimension of the behavioral phenomenon, applied behavior analysts are typically satisfied with uncovering only those variables most often responsible for problem behavior. The balance between conducting a thoroughgoing FA of individual contingencies maintaining problem behavior and the need to treat problem behavior typically requires a tradeoff between sufficiency and thoroughness. In fact, the proportion of time spent conducting an FA versus evaluating and then refining treatment procedures for problem behavior depends on a variety of factors, including the complexity of the case, the importance of the information that additional analyses may provide, as well as time constraints that may expedite the service timeline.

Early studies on the function of problem behavior focused on single, socially mediated variables, such as the effects of attention on self-injurious behavior (Lovaas, Freitag, Gold, & Kassorla, 1965) or the effects of escape on aggression (Carr, Newsom, & Binkoff, 1980). As the field of behavior analysis has matured, researchers have also evaluated the effects of nonsocial consequences, such as automatic reinforcement. In fact, Beavers, Iwata, and Lerman (2013) found that 16.3% of published FAs indicated that problem behavior was automatically reinforced, meaning that the problematic response persisted in the absence of therapist or caregiver behavior and/or that responding occurred despite the provision of social interaction. As Vollmer (1994) noted, the concept of automatic reinforcement implies that responding is maintained by operant mechanisms that are independent of the social environment, and indeed evidence has grown for a neurochemical interpretation of automatically reinforced self-injury (see Thompson, Symons, Delaney, & England, 1995, for an overview). Rarely, however, is violence–aggression maintained by automatic reinforcement (Beavers et al., 2013; see Ringdahl, Call, Mews, Boelter, & Christensen, 2008; Saini, Greer, & Fisher, 2015; Thompson, Fisher, Piazza, & Kuhn, 1998, for exceptions). Therefore, when violence–aggression is the only referral concern, it is common to restrict the test and control conditions of an FA to only those that implicate social functions of problem behavior.

Because the purpose of conducting an FA is to uncover those variables that control responding, applied behavior analysts working with individuals who engage in problem behavior are typically interested in determining such functional relations at the level of the individual. This is an important point to emphasize because the variables that evoke and maintain problem behavior can differ within (see Beavers & Iwata 2011, for information on prevalence) and across (e.g., Greer, Fisher, Saini, Owen, & Jones, 2016) individuals. Incorrectly identifying the variables that control problem behavior can lead to ineffective or contraindicated treatment procedures (Iwata, Pace, Cowdery, & Miltenberger, 1994). Thus, FAs of problem behavior often rely on within-subject experimental (e.g., reversal, multielement, pairwise) designs that permit the identification of controlling variables at the level of the individual and sometimes at the level of a specific problematic response within an individual (e.g., targeting pica but not aggression within an FA).

Within-subject experimental designs provide another benefit to applied behavior analysts conducting FAs of problem behavior—they allow for repeated measures of the problematic response. The reliable production of problem behavior each time, and only when, the necessary and sufficient variables are present is highly desirable when conducting an FA of problem behavior. Each additional replication of response differentiation increases the believability that those variables that differ across the test and control conditions are indeed responsible for the maintenance of problem behavior.

Variations in FA Design

In the sections that follow, we provide information on common FA designs. These include more "traditional" approaches to FA, latency- and trial-based analyses, precursor FAs, FAs of idiosyncratic functions, as well as information on synthesized contingency analyses. Any one of these could be the topic of an entire chapter or review unto itself. However, our goal in the sections that follow is not to provide detailed information on any specific FA design, nor is our goal to provide an overview of all variations of FA. Rather, we aim to provide examples of the high flexibility that FA methodology provides. We arranged the sections below around common types of changes one might make to an FA, changes that may be necessary for a variety of reasons. We discuss variations in FA design in the context of these overarching categories of FA modifications. As you will see, FA methodology is highly flexible, with aspects of the analysis adaptable to a host of different constraints, including more severe topographies of problem behavior, as well as setting and time limitations. But before diving into common FA modifications, we first provide a brief overview of the seminal study on FA conducted by Iwata, Dorsey, Slifer, Bauman, and Richman (1982/1994).

Traditional FA

In their landmark study, Iwata, Dorsey, Slifer, et al. (1982/1994) exposed the self-injurious behavior of nine patients diagnosed with a developmental disability to four conditions that alternated according to a multielement design. In the social-disproval condition, a therapist provided brief statements of concern (e.g., "Don't do that, you're going to hurt yourself") and physical contact (e.g., a hand on the shoulder) following each instance of problem behavior. This condition tested for problem behavior reinforced by access to therapist attention. In the academic-demand condition, the therapist presented academic instructions (e.g., to set puzzle pieces in a puzzle) using a three-step prompting procedure that increased in level of prompt intrusiveness until compliance occurred. Problem behavior in this condition resulted in a 30-s break from demands. The academic-demand condition tested for problem behavior reinforced by escape from academic demands. In the alone condition, the individual remained in a barren room without the therapist present. This condition tested for problem behavior maintained by automatic reinforcement. Finally, in the unstructured-play condition, the individual had access to a variety of toys, and the therapist remained in close proximity to the individual and provided praise and physical contact for appropriate behavior and for the absence of problem behavior and issued no demands. This condition served as a control from which to compare rates of self-injury occurring in the other (test) conditions.

The results of Iwata, Dorsey, Slifer, et al. (1982/1994) were illuminating not just for the study itself but for our collective understanding of problem behavior and the environmental variables that maintain it. Across participants, the FA procedures produced markedly different patterns of responding. Because the researchers were careful in constructing the test and control conditions of the FA, different patterns of responding within and across the FA conditions suggested different maintaining variables for problem behavior. For instance, Child 1 engaged in problem behavior only in the academic-demand condition, which was the only FA condition in which (a) demands were present and (b) problem behavior produced a break from those demands. Problem behavior never occurred in the absence of demands and escape, which suggests that Child 1 engaged in problem behavior to escape academic demands. One highly interesting finding of Iwata et al. was that this interpretation of behavior being maintained by social escape did not apply to all participants. For example, Child 2 and Child 4 also engaged in problem behavior in the academic-demand condition of the FA; however, problem behavior for Child 4 was most frequent in the alone condition, and levels of problem behavior for Child 2 were elevated across all conditions. Both of these patterns of responding suggest that problem behavior was maintained by automatic sources of reinforcement. The results for Child 4, whose problem behavior occurred at lower levels in those conditions in which a therapist was present, suggest that although problem behavior for this individual was automatically reinforced, the social environment modulated the automatically reinforcing process. Finally, patterns of responding for other children (e.g., Child 5) suggested that brief attention from the therapist reinforced problem behavior.

Changes to Experimental Design

The multielement design used by Iwata, Dorsey, Slifer, et al. (1982/1994) is advantageous for a number of reasons, including its brevity and robust demonstration of experimental control when responding is differentiated across conditions. However, the rapid alternation of conditions characteristic of the multielement design can be problematic when responding in one condition continues into the start of a subsequent condition and when differentiation across conditions declines with increasing numbers of conditions. Thus, researchers have evaluated alternative experimental designs suitable for use in an FA (e.g., pairwise design (Iwata, Duncan, Zarcone, Lerman, & Shore, 1994); see also Vollmer, Marcus, Ringdahl, & Roane, 1995). As a result of this work and because of the simplicity of design modifications, changing the experimental design of an FA is often a first step when responding within a multielement FA is undifferentiated (Hagopian, Rooker, Jessel, & DeLeon, 2013).

Changes to Test and Control Conditions

Functional analysis test and control conditions have also received empirical scrutiny from researchers over the years. For instance, Conners et al. (2000) showed that incorporating distinct discriminative stimuli (e.g., a specific therapist and room color) across each FA condition helped produce differentiated patterns of responding for half of their participants. Although making no changes to the test and control conditions per se, Hammond, Iwata, Rooker, Fritz, and Bloom (2013) conducted FAs in either a fixed or random order of conditions. For the fixed order, conditions progressed in a manner such that each preceding condition set up for the subsequent condition so that responding maintained by any given social reinforcer would be more likely to occur following the events that transpired in the prior session. The fixed order of conditions produced differentiated responding for three of their seven participants and had no detrimental effect for any of the participants. Other researchers have shown promising results when examining the correspondence in outcomes produced by full and abbreviated FAs (e.g., shortened session duration (Wallace & Iwata, 1999), a "brief FA" (Northup et al., 1991) designed for an outpatient setting (Kahng & Iwata, 1999)).

Other researchers have modified the test and/or control conditions of the FA in other ways. For instance, Day, Rea, Schussler, Larsen, and Johnson (1988) tested for problem behavior maintained by social positive reinforcement via access to preferred tangible items. Fisher, Piazza, and Chiang (1996) showed that setting a fixed duration of reinforcer delivery across conditions may improve the interpretation of FA results by better equating rates of problem behavior across the test conditions. As a final example, Bowman, Fisher, Thompson, and Piazza (1997) modified the FA test and control conditions for two children such that in the test condition, problem behavior produced therapist compliance with child mands for 30 s. In the control condition, the therapist complied with all mands and reminded the child that they were indeed complying. These modifications produced differentiated responding across the test and control conditions for both children when a more traditional FA was inconclusive (see Owen et al., 2020, for a replication of these procedures across 16 participants).

Changes to Format

Some FA modifications can be considered changes to the format of the FA. These modifications preserve many of the features of more "traditional" FAs while adapting the FA format to overcome various constraints, including when working in outpatient settings where appointments are brief and infrequent and when working with severe topographies of problem behavior or problem behavior that does not occur readily in a clinical setting. The so-called *brief FA* first described by Northup et al. (1991) and then replicated quickly thereafter by Derby et al. (1992) was an answer to a difficult question—how does one adapt the multielement FA for use in a 90-min outpatient appointment while preserving repeated measures and the ability to determine behavioral function? The brief FA achieved these goals while producing outcomes similar to those produced by a more extended FA (Kahng & Iwata, 1999).

Latency-based FAs are useful when working with severe topographies of problem behavior or any topography of problem behavior you wish to limit in occurrence throughout the assessment process. In a latency-based FA, the first instance of problem behavior produces the programmed reinforcer in the test condition, and it also terminates that session. When problem behavior does not occur (e.g., in the control condition), the session terminates at a predetermined time. Thus, the amount of time until the session terminates (i.e., latency) is the critical comparison across test and control conditions in a latency-based FA. Thomason-Sassi, Iwata, Neidert, and Roscoe (2011) showed that latency-based FAs produce an inverse relation when comparing latency of problem behavior to the rate of problem behavior from a more "traditional" FA and the results of the two FA formats generally show correspondence.

As a final example of changing the format of an FA, the trial-based FA described by Sigafoos and Saggers (1995) allows the behavior analyst to capitalize on naturally occurring stimulus events by bringing the test and control methodology of the FA into those settings in which problem behavior is already occurring (e.g., in a classroom). Each trial consisted of a 1-min test segment, followed by a 1-min control segment. During the test segment, an establishing operation and the associated reinforcement contingency were present, whereas both were absent during the control segment. Responding that is reliably higher in the test segment than in the corresponding control segment is suggestive of a reinforcing contingency. Such trial-based FAs are particularly useful when problem behavior is unlikely to occur in a more well-controlled environment (e.g., in a clinic).

Changes to Approach

At least two other variations of FA methodology can be considered changes to the approach of more "traditional" FAs. The first is called a *precursor FA*, and it differs from other FAs in that its goal is to minimize the occurrence of problem behavior throughout the assessment process (similar to other FA variations) but to do so by first defining the response class that includes problem behavior and then by placing FA test and control contingencies onto earlier responses within that response-class hierarchy (Smith & Churchill, 2002). The idea here is that if some responses reliably precede instances of problem behavior (i.e., are precursors to problem behavior), and they rarely occur unless problem behavior is soon to follow, then delivering the functional reinforcer for a precursor to problem behavior should minimize the occurrence of problem behavior while also determining its function. This approach to FA can be helpful when severe topographies of problem behavior have clear precursors.

A second example of changing the approach to FA is called *synthesized contingency analysis*. Variations of synthesized contingency analysis have also been called the *Interview-Informed Synthesized Contingency Analysis* (IISCA; Jessel, Hanley, & Ghaemmaghami, 2016) and the *Practical Functional Assessment*. The synthesized contingency analysis differs from more "traditional" approaches to FA in that it screens for combinations of contingencies that together reinforce problem behavior. Unlike more "traditional" FAs, which isolate individual reinforcement contingencies within and across the test and control conditions, synthesized contingency analyses incorporate all suggested or reported contingencies that surround the occurrence of problem behavior.

Research Findings and Implications

Comparisons of Synthesized and Individual Contingency Analyses

Hanley, Jin, Vanselow, and Hanratty (2014) described an assessment procedure in which they conducted an open-ended interview with a caregiver and a structured observation with the participant to identify the putative establishing operations and reinforcers for problem behavior. Based on the information gleaned from the interview and observation, they then conducted a pairwise assessment in which they combined all of the putative establishing operations and reinforcers identified by the interview and observation into a single test condition, which they compared with a single control condition in which they provided those same putative reinforcers on a response-independent basis. In subsequent publications, Hanley and colleagues called this assessment procedure the IISCA (e.g., Ghaemmaghami, Hanley, Jin, & Vanselow, 2016).

The primary purposes of basing the analysis on the open-ended interview and structured observation are to improve the efficiency and ecological validity of the analysis (Ghaemmaghami et al. 2016). The IISCA is clearly one of the most efficient assessments designed to assess the function(s) of problem behavior (Saini, Fisher, Retzlaff & Keevy, 2020). In fact, the IISCA typically produces differentiated results between the test and control condition in five sessions (three test and two control sessions; Jessel et al., 2016). In addition, treatments based on the IISCA have generally reduced problem behavior by more than 90% (Jessel, Ingvarsson, Metras, Kirk, & Whipple, 2018).

However, although researchers have conceptually presented the IISCA as a more ecologically valid functional assessment, because it purportedly identifies the ecologically relevant context in which problem behavior typically occurs in the natural environment (Coffey, 2019), research has yet to establish the ecological validity of the IISCA empirically. That is, researchers have not compared the results of the open-ended interview with direct observations in the natural environment (e.g., Thompson & Iwata, 2001) to determine whether problem behavior reliably occurs in the context(s) identified by the interview and not in other contexts not identified by the interview.

Nevertheless, research has established that the validity of an assessment procedure depends on its reliability. That is, instruments with low reliability necessarily also have low validity, because the variability resulting from measurement error also affects the instrument's validity (Nunnally, 1978). Saini, Ubdegrove, Biran, and Duncan (2019) examined the interrater agreement of the structured interview used in the IISCA and its concurrent validity with traditional functional analyses and found moderate agreement between raters (75%) and low agreement with a traditional FA (50%) that analyzes individual reinforcement contingencies (Iwata, Dorsey, Slifer, et al., 1982/1994).

A traditional FA assumes that each putative reinforcer (e.g., attention, escape) operates on the target response independently, and consistent with this assumption, it analyzes each putative reinforcer in its own test condition to evaluate its independent effects. By contrast, the IISCA assumes that when the open-ended interview and the structured observation identifies multiple putative reinforcers, the IISCA assumes that all of the identified consequences act together in an interactive fashion to reinforce problem behavior. Unfortunately, the IISCA almost never tests whether all of the identified consequences act together to reinforce problem behavior. To test for an interactive effect, the researcher must evaluate the effects of each putative reinforcer in isolation and combined with the other putative reinforcers to determine whether combined consequences produce a different effect on behavior than each consequence presented alone. Only when the combined consequences produce a differential effect on behavior relative to isolated contingencies can the researcher conclude that the combined putative reinforcers produce an interactive effect.

Fisher, Greer, Romani, Zangrillo, and Owen (2016) compared the results of the IISCA with a traditional FA on a within-subject basis to evaluate whether the putative reinforcers operate on problem behavior individually, as assumed by a traditional FA, or interactively, as assumed by the IISCA. These investigators found that the traditional FA and the IISCA produced differentiated results for four of the five participants. And in each of the four cases with differentiated results, the findings were consistent with the assumption of the traditional FA that the putative reinforcers operated independently, and contrary to the assumption of the IISCA, that the putative reinforcers interacted to produce a different effect on problem behavior.

That is, in each case, the level of differentiation between the test and control conditions and the overall level of responding maintained by the identified contingency or contingencies were equivalent for the traditional FA and the IISCA, thus providing no evidence for an interactive effect. Furthermore, six (54.5%) of the 11 contingencies the IISCA identified and included in the synthesized contingency seemed irrelevant, as they did not add to the effects on problem behavior produced by the individual contingency identified by the traditional FA. Greer, Mitteer, Briggs, Fisher, and Sodawasser (2020) replicated and extended the findings of Fisher et al. with a larger cohort and produced equivalent findings to Fisher et al.

One limitation of studies by Fisher et al. (2016) and Greer et al. (2020) is that the "true" function of problem behavior in the individual's natural environment is inferred based on the results of the analyses but is not known with absolute certainty. Therefore, when the IISCA and a traditional FA lead to different interpretations regarding the function of problem behavior, one cannot be absolutely sure which one is correct. Retzlaff, Fisher, Akers, and Greer (2020) addressed this limitation in a translational investigation in which they trained a function (e.g., escape) for a benign response that they called *surrogate destructive response* (i.e., hitting a cushioned pad) that had no history of reinforcement. For example, to teach an escape function, they presented nonpreferred demands and used a progressive prompt delay to train the participant to emit the surrogate destructive response, which terminated the demands. Once the participant mastered this new response, the investigators conducted: (a) a traditional FA; (b) then a synthesized contingency analysis (based on, but not identical to the IISCA); and (c) then another traditional FA for this newly established response. Retzlaff et al. found that the traditional FA correctly identified the function of the surrogate destructive behavior for every participant, thereby providing strong support for the validity of the traditional FA. The synthesized contingency analysis also produced differentiated results for every participant, but the investigators could not determine the specific function of the target behavior because the synthesized contingency confounded nonfunctional consequences (e.g., attention, tangible) with the *true* functional reinforcer (e.g., escape). More importantly, after applying the synthesized contingency to the surrogate destructive behavior, three of the six participants showed a new function of this target response during the second traditional FA, thereby showing that applying synthesized contingencies in a manner similar to the IISCA may induce new functions of problem behavior. As such, we recommend that practitioners implement synthesized contingencies with their clients only after conducting a traditional FA that produces undifferentiated results.

Flexibility and Versatility of FA Methods

Though Iwata, Dorsey, Slifer, et al. (1982/1994) developed the FA method specifically for analyzing the function of self-injurious behavior, their basic approach has proven to be remarkably flexible and versatile. Researchers have used these methods with a wide variety of patient populations, such as Asperger syndrome (Fisher, Rodriguez, & Owen, 2013), schizophrenia (Wilder, Masuda, O'Connor, & Baham, 2001), and traumatic brain injury (Treadwell & Page, 1996). Similarly, investigators have used these methods to analyze the function of many different response topographies, such as inappropriate sexual behavior (Fyffe, Kahng, Fittro, & Russell, 2004), hallucinations (Fisher, Piazza, & Page, 1989), and pica (Piazza et al. 1998), to name a few. In addition, this FA method has been adapted to identify a variety of idiosyncratic functions of problem behavior (e.g., Fisher, Adelinis, Thompson, Worsdell, & Zarcone, 1998; Hood, Rodriguez, Luczynski, & Fisher, 2019; Roscoe, Schlichenmeyer, & Dube, 2015). Finally, FA methods have been used to more precisely determine the epidemiology of problem behavior (Iwata et al., 1994).

Practice Recommendations

The previous sections of this chapter provided an overview of FA and a summary of recent research findings. This section will provide practitioners with recommendations on how to effectively and safely implement an FA, as well as provide a brief overview of FA research directions.

Safety Precautions

Because an FA allows individuals to engage in destructive behavior, it can present a number of safety risks that warrant discussion. For example, a patient can pose risks to (a) themselves, by engaging in self-injurious behavior (e.g., head banging), (b) therapists, if they engage in aggression (e.g., hitting and kicking), or (c) property, by engaging in property destruction (e.g., throwing objects). Possible injuries produced by self-injurious behavior and aggression can range from minor redness and swelling to breaks in the skin that leave scars or trauma resulting in broken bones or lasting tissue damage. Damage to property can range from minor scratches and marks on furniture to structural damage to furniture, cars, and walls.

Before beginning an FA, practitioners should consider what precautions they need to take to minimize risks and ensure patient and therapist safety during the analysis. Iwata, Dorsey, Slifer, et al. (1982/1994) conducted studies in an inpatient setting and had access to physicians and nurses that many practitioners implementing FAs today do not have access to. Thus, we will provide recommendations based on practices that we or other behavior analysts have used in outpatient settings. It is important to note that practitioners should refer to their company policies and procedures when developing safety precautions and contact specialists when unanticipated medical or safety issues arise.

Medical screening. First, it is essential to speak with the patient's caregivers and medical providers to gather information about the topographies and intensity of destructive behavior and any medical considerations that the practitioners need to take into account. We recommend speaking with the caregivers and medical provider(s) well in advance of FA implementation, or even before the patient's admission, to ensure enough time to modify arrangements if needed (e.g., purchase additional protective equipment; described more below).

In the interview with caregivers, we recommend conducting the Destructive Behavior Severity Scale (Appendix; Fisher, Rodriguez, Luczynski, & Kelley, 2013) developed in the Center for Autism Spectrum Disorders at the University of Nebraska Medical Center's Munroe-Meyer Institute.[1] The severity scale allows practitioners to gather information on the topography, frequency, and intensity of each category of destructive behavior (i.e., injury risk behavior, aggression, pica, self-injurious behavior, and property destruction). In the conversation with the patient's caregivers and medical provider(s), practitioners should request any information required to provide safe outpatient care for the patient's destructive behavior (e.g., any ambulatory, vision, or hearing deficits, allergies, history of seizures). After completing the severity scale and interviews, practitioners can better determine what types of precautions they should put in place to minimize risk to patients and therapists. For example, if a patient has a gastrostomy tube, a practitioner may need to take a number of precautions such as blocking patient attempts to remove the tube and developing a plan for how therapists need to respond should the patient successfully remove the tube.

Setting modifications. One antecedent manipulation that can improve patient and therapist safety during an FA is to make modifications to the setting in which a practitioner will conduct the analysis. Making modifications to the FA setting can minimize risk for self-injurious behavior, aggression, and destructive behavior. First, making the setting as barren as possible can reduce many possible safety risks. Creating a barren setting can range from removing all unnecessary small materials in the room (e.g., pencils, storage bins, etc.) to removing every possible item that could be used as a tool for self-injurious behavior, aggression, or destructive behavior, including but not limited to all furniture, rugs, and the patient's shoes.

In settings in which practitioners implement FAs regularly, installing a one-way observation window and protective padding on the treatment-room walls and floors can greatly improve patient and therapist safety. Figure 1 displays photograph examples of padded treatment rooms. As can be seen in the figure, the padding can accommodate standard room essentials (e.g., fire alarm, electrical outlets, door handles). Room padding can protect patients from certain topographies of self-injurious behavior, such as head banging, as well as protect therapists from falls that can

---

[1] Use of this scale should include a citation of both the Fisher et al. chapter, this chapter, and a statement acknowledging that the scale was developed by the Center for Autism Spectrum Disorders.

result from certain forms of aggression, such as pushing. The one-way observation window allows for the data collector(s) to be separated from the patient, which in turn, results in fewer materials in the room and more space for the patient and session therapist. Figure 2 displays photographs of the construction of the wall padding and how it secures to the wall with a metal slat. Floor pads are similar to the wall pads, but they do not have plywood or slats on the back and instead secure to one another with Velcro flaps to allow for removal for cleaning.

In settings in which practitioners cannot create a completely barren room or install protective padding on the walls and floors, such as in a classroom or a patient's home, practitioners can use temporary padding and have personal protective equipment (PPE; described below) available to decrease risks to the patient and therapists. For example, we have used toddler nap mats secured to desks or tables with patients who engage in head banging. We have also used foldable gymnastic mats to place vertically against non-padded walls.

Personal protective equipment. In addition to medical screening and modifications to the setting, providing PPE for therapists and patients can decrease the risk of injury. We will provide a brief overview of the use of PPE in this chapter but refer

Fig. 1 Photographs of a one-way observation window and protective padding installed on treatment-room walls and floors

Fig. 2 Photographs of the design and construction of the protective padding for treatment-room walls. A slat system adheres each pad to a corresponding strip on the wall

readers to Fisher, Rodriguez, Luczynski, et al. (2013) for more information, including details about the rules and regulations surrounding the use of PPE.

Therapist PPE. Therapists often use padded sports equipment as PPE. Figure 3 displays photograph examples of PPE. For example, we have utilized shoulder and chest pads often used by lacrosse players, as well as various pieces of martial-arts sparring gear (e.g., hand and arm guards, helmet, blocking pads) to protect therapists from patient hits, kicks, and bites. When patients are able to bite through the hand and arm guard, we place children's soccer shin guards underneath the hand

and arm guard, such that there is an extra layer of protection against the therapists skin while the exterior remains soft so that it does not pose a risk to the patient when they aggress (e.g., if a patient were to bite the hard exterior of the shin guard, it could produce damage to their teeth, gums, or mouth). To decrease patients' ability to grab and remove the therapists' PPE and to make the PPE less conspicuous, we have worn long-sleeved compression shirts over the equipment (see Fig. 3). It is worth noting, however, that there are few experimental analyses of the effects of therapist PPE on aggression, including evaluation of response allocation during and subsequent to wearing different types of protective equipment (Lin, Luiselli, Gilligan, & Dacosta, 2012; Parenteau, Luiselli, & Keeley, 2013; Urban, Luiselli, Child, & Parenteau, 2011).

Patient PPE. When patients engage in self-injurious behavior that could produce severe or permanent bodily harm (e.g., self-injurious behavior scored as Level 3 or 4 on the Destructive Behavior Severity Scale), practitioners might use PPE on the patient to reduce the risk of injury during an FA. Before using PPE on patients, practitioners must be aware of company policies and take the steps mentioned above in the medical screening and setting-modification sections. It is important to provide the patient with breaks from the PPE and monitor them for possible adverse effects (e.g., heat rash underneath arm splints). Practitioners should also get consent and social-validity measures from the patient's caregivers before selecting and using the PPE. Also, it is important to fade the PPE throughout the course of treatment following the FA if possible (e.g., Fisher, Piazza, Bowman, Hanley, & Adelinis, 1997).

The bottom right photographs in Fig. 3 display examples of PPE that we have used to protect patients from self-injurious behavior. It is important to remember that in many states, a prescription from a physician may be required for any type of patient PPE that limits an individual's movement. For example, we have often incorporated the use of arm splints with patients who engage in high-intensity, hand-to-head self-injurious behavior or hand biting, in which case insurance has required a prescription from a physician. Other possible forms of patient PPE include padded mittens, which we have used with patients who engage in severe hand biting or helmets, which we often use with patients who engage in severe head banging. Practitioners can use other types of patient PPE as needed based on the topography of the target behavior such as gloves when the target behavior is hand mouthing and a hat if the target behavior is hair pulling.

When using patient PPE during an FA, there are a few considerations that practitioners should remember. First, it is possible that patient PPE can mask an automatic function of the target behavior. That is, if it eliminates or decreases the automatic reinforcer produced by the target behavior, the PPE may function as extinction (Iwata, Pace, Cowdery, & Miltenberger, 1994). For example, Moore, Fisher, and Pennington (2004) conducted an FA of self-injurious behavior with and without patient PPE and observed suppressed levels of self-injurious behavior in all FA conditions when the patient was wearing PPE but identified an automatic function of self-injurious behavior when they conducted an FA without patient PPE. In these situations, practitioners should also be prepared to see novel topographies of destructive behavior emerge as a function of extinction-induced variability (Goh &

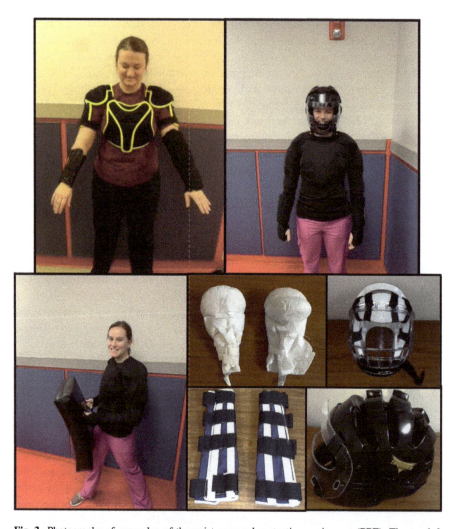

Fig. 3 Photographs of examples of therapist personal protective equipment (PPE). The top left photograph displays lacrosse pads and how shin guards can fit underneath hand and arm guards. The top right photograph shows how therapists can use martial-arts pads to block aggression. The bottom left photograph shows an example of a helmet that practitioners can wear to protect against head-directed aggression and how to make PPE less conspicuous by covering it with a compression shirt. The bottom right photographs display examples of PPE that can protect patients from self-injurious behavior

Iwata, 1994). For example, if a patient's referral concern is hand-to-head self-injurious behavior, and a practitioner uses arm splints to prevent the behavior, the patient may then begin to engage in head-to-surface self-injurious behavior or aggression if the arm splints function as extinction. Thus, practitioners should always have additional PPE (e.g., a blocking pad) in reach to block other dangerous topographies of destructive behavior.

In some cases, patient PPE may also help practitioners identify target behavior that is multiply controlled by both automatic reinforcement and social contingencies. For example, Contrucci Kuhn and Triggs (2009) conducted two FAs of head-directed self-injurious behavior with and without a helmet. In the FA in which the patient did not wear the helmet, they observed high and undifferentiated levels of self-injurious behavior, suggesting an automatic function. In the FA with the helmet, they observed elevated levels of self-injurious behavior in the attention condition, which suggested that the self-injurious behavior was multiply maintained by automatic reinforcement and attention.

It is worth noting that some settings that provide services to patients with high-intensity and high-frequency destructive behavior may also allow for the use of emergency or programmatic mechanical (e.g., arm splints, helmet) or physical (e.g., baskethold) restraint and seclusion. Practitioners should implement restraint and seclusion procedures only if the destructive behavior places the patient or therapists at imminent risk of harm, company policies and procedures allow, and the supervisors and therapists are adequately trained. Policies on restraint and seclusion should include requirements for constant supervision while in the procedure, as well as precise documentation during and following the procedure (e.g., description of antecedent events and destructive behavior[s], time and duration of implementation, name of implementor[s], and documentation of any adverse effects).

Research Directions

Recent research on the topic of FA has focused on identifying ways to increase the efficiency and feasibility of the analysis in an attempt to make it easier for practitioners to carry out. It is critical for researchers to maintain the reliability and validity of FA when conducting this type of research. In this section, we provide information on developing lines of research on this topic for practitioners to consider.

One way to increase the efficiency and feasibility of the FA is to evaluate procedures for training practitioners how to effectively and efficiently (a) implement an FA, (b) analyze its outcomes, and (c) develop effective treatments based on those outcomes. That is, by finding ways to train practitioners on how to accurately and proficiently implement an FA instead of modifying its fundamental procedures, we do not risk altering the reliability and validity of the already effective and empirically validated traditional FA. For example, Saini, Fisher, and Retzlaff (2018) evaluated the predictive validity and efficiency of applying structured criteria for visually inspecting FA results on an ongoing basis. Saini et al. applied the ongoing visual inspection (OVI) criteria to published FA results and found that OVI resulted in a 41% increase in FA efficiency compared to post-hoc visual inspection and author's post-hoc interpretations. Retzlaff, Phillips, Fisher, Hardee, and Fuhrman (2020) then developed and evaluated e-learning modules to train staff to conduct OVI of FA data accurately. Researchers could expand upon this research by evaluating the degree to which OVI increases FA efficiency during routine clinical practice.

It is also important for research to continue to evaluate and attenuate possible barriers to FA implementation to increase practitioners' use of the technology. For example, Oliver, Pratt, and Normand (2015) conducted a survey to gather data on functional-behavior-assessment methods used by behavior analysts and found that a majority of respondents reported rarely using FAs to identify the function of destructive behavior. When asked why they rarely used FAs, respondents indicated that lack of time was the biggest reason and that lack of space and resources also served as barriers to FA implementation. Similarly, Roscoe, Phillips, Kelly, Farber, and Dube (2015) found that survey respondents noted lack of (a) trained staff, (b) space, and (c) acceptance of FA procedures were the top three barriers to implementing FAs. Thus, it is critical to conduct and disseminate studies that demonstrate how practitioners can address these barriers. For example, when practitioners have limited time, they could consider conducting brief FAs (e.g., Iwata & Dozier, 2008). The field would benefit from additional research on implementing FAs in naturalistic settings and with limited resources (e.g., Mueller, Nkosi, & Hine, 2011). Continuing to identify methods for training practitioners to safely and effectively implement FAs and analyze FA outcomes is critical for future research (Chok, Harper, Weiss, Bird, & Luiselli, 2019).

In summary, FA is a well-established and effective experimental methodology for isolating the function of destructive behavior, including violence-aggression (Hanley, Iwata, & McCord, 2003). Researchers have demonstrated that practitioners can use different experimental designs or arrangements to assess a variety of maladaptive behavior in controlled or naturalistic settings. Prior to implementing FAs, practitioners should consider several safety precautions, including but not limited to medical screening, padded treatment rooms, and therapist and patient PPE. Decades of research provide empirical support for the use of FAs and directions for future research include identifying valid and reliable methods for increasing the efficiency and feasibility of FA implementation.

Acknowledgments Grants 5R01HD093734, 5R01HD079113, and 5R01HD083214 from The National Institute of Child Health and Human Development provided partial support for this work.

Appendix: Destructive Behavior Severity Scale

UNMC-MMI's Center for Autism Spectrum Disorders
   Destructive Behavior Severity Scale
      Child's   Initials:_____   Date   Of Birth:____/____/_____
      Date:____/____/_____

INJURY RISK BEHAVIOR involves frequently engaging in destructive behavior without recognizing the potential hazards, such as: (a) climbing on objects where falling is probable; (b) running into a street without watching for cars; (c) pulling down objects onto oneself; (d) touching electrical wires, stoves or other dangerous

Functional Analysis of Violence–Aggression

items; (e) drinking or eating dangerous fluids or items (e.g., cleaners, medicines, fertilizer); (f) placing a bag over one's head; or (g) getting ropes or cords tangled around one's neck.

For each of the four levels of injury risk behavior listed below, circle how often this type of behavior occurs, ranging from never (N) to over ten times per hour (+10).

N = Never   M = Monthly   W = Weekly   H = Hourly   +5 = Over 5 per hour   +10 = Over 10 per hour

FREQUENCY:

N	M	W	H	+5	+10	Level 1 = INJURY RISK BEHAVIOR resulting in: (a) no marks on body, (b) no burns, (c) no gagging, (d) no vomiting, or (e) no choking.
N	M	W	H	+5	+10	Level 2 = INJURY RISK BEHAVIOR resulting in: (a) reddening of skin or mild swelling; (b) a first degree burn; and/or (c) mild gagging.
N	M	W	H	+5	+10	Level 3 = INJURY RISK BEHAVIOR resulting in: (a) light scratches, small or shallow breaks in skin, moderate to severe swelling; (b) a second degree burn; (c) vomiting or significant choking.
N	M	W	H	+5	+10	Level 4 = INJURY RISK BEHAVIOR resulting in: (a) scars, lasting tissue damage, disfigurement; (b) a third degree burn; (c) poisoning; or (d) loss of consciousness.

AGGRESSION involves forceful pushing or striking others with body parts (e.g., pushing, hitting, kicking, head-butting); hitting others with objects; or scratching, pinching or biting others.

For each of the four levels of aggression listed below, circle how often this type of behavior occurs, ranging from never (N) to over ten times per hour (+10).

N = Never   M = Monthly   W = Weekly   H = Hourly   +5 = Over 5 per hour   +10 = Over 10 per hour

FREQUENCY

N	M	W	H	+5	+10	Level 1 = AGGRESSION resulting in (a) no marks on body and (b) no blows close to or contacting the eyes.
N	M	W	H	+5	+10	Level 2 = AGGRESSION resulting in (a) reddening of skin, and/or (b) mild swelling.
N	M	W	H	+5	+10	Level 3 = AGGRESSION resulting in (a) light scratches, (b) small or shallow breaks in skin, and/or (c) moderate to severe swelling.
N	M	W	H	+5	+10	Level 4 = AGGRESSION involving blows close to or contacting the eyes or resulting in (a) scratches that leave scars, (b) breaks in skin that leave scars, and/or (c) trauma resulting in broken bones or lasting tissue damage or disfigurement.

PICA involves the repetitive and persistent ingestion of inedible items (i.e., items that should not be eaten) such as bark, bugs, cigarette butts, clothing, coins, dirt, food dropped on the floor or ground, grass, leaves, paint chips, pet hair, etc.

For each of the four levels of pica listed below, circle how often this type of behavior occurs, ranging from never (N) to over ten times per hour (+10).

N = Never   M = Monthly   W = Weekly   H = Hourly   +5 = Over 5 per hour   +10 = Over 10 per hour

FREQUENCY

N M W H +5 +10	Level 1 = PICA involving: (a) no solid items larger than 1/2 in. in diameter (e.g., coins, large buttons), (b) no sharp items (e.g., pins, staples), (c) no contaminated items (e.g., items from garbage can or ash tray, paint chips), and (d) no toxic or poisonous items (e.g., medicines, glue).
N M W H +5 +10	Level 2 = PICA involving (a) solid items larger than 1/2 in. in diameter (e.g., coins, large buttons), but not sharp, contaminated, or toxic or poisonous items.
N M W H +5 +10	Level 3 = PICA involving sharp, contaminated, or toxic or poisonous items, but not requiring emergency medical attention (e.g., called physician for advice).
N M W H +5 +10	Level 4 = PICA involving sharp, contaminated, or toxic or poisonous items and requiring emergency medical attention.

PROPERTY DESTRUCTION involves banging, kicking, throwing, overturning, tearing, cutting, defacing, burning or stomping on objects not made for that purpose.

For each of the four levels of property destruction listed below, circle how often this type of behavior occurs, ranging from never (N) to over ten times per hour (+10).

N = Never   M = Monthly   W = Weekly   H = Hourly   +5 = Over 5 per hour   +10 = Over 10 per hour

FREQUENCY

N M W H +5 +10	Level 1 = PROPERTY DESTRUCTION resulting in disruption of property but no permanent damage to paper items, toys, teaching materials, furniture, vehicles or buildings.
N M W H +5 +10	Level 2 = PROPERTY DESTRUCTION resulting in damage to paper items or other light objects.
N M W H +5 +10	Level 3 = PROPERTY DESTRUCTION resulting in (a) breakage of pencils, plastic toys, glassware, or other breakable items, and/or (b) scratches or permanent marks on furniture, walls, cars, etc.
N M W H +5 +10	Level 4 = PROPERTY DESTRUCTION resulting in structural damage to furniture, cars, walls, etc.

SELF-INJURIOUS BEHAVIOR (SIB)–forceful striking, scratching, rubbing, poking or biting own body parts such that repetition of the behavior over time has or will cause bodily injury (e.g., hitting, kicking, pinching, scratching or biting self; eye-poking); banging body parts against objects (e.g., head banging).

For each of the four levels of SIB listed below, circle how often this type of behavior occurs, ranging from never (N) to over ten times per hour (+10).

N = Never   M = Monthly   W = Weekly   H = Hourly   +5 = Over 5 per hour   +10 = Over 10 per hour
FREQUENCY

N	M	W	H	+5	+10	Level 1 = SIB resulting in (a) <u>no</u> visible marks on body and (b) <u>no</u> blows close to or contacting the eyes.
N	M	W	H	+5	+10	Level 2 = SIB resulting in (a) reddening of skin, and/or (b) mild swelling.
N	M	W	H	+5	+10	Level 3 = SIB resulting in (a) light scratches, (b) small or shallow breaks in skin, and/or (c) moderate to severe swelling.
N	M	W	H	+5	+10	Level 4 = SIB involving blows close to or contacting the eyes or resulting in (a) scratches that leave scars, (b) breaks in skin that leave scars, and/or (c) trauma involving broken bones or lasting tissue damage or disfigurement.

References

American Psychiatric Association (2013). *Diagnostic and statistical manual of mental disorders* (5th ed.). Arlington, VA: Author.

Beavers, G. A., & Iwata, B. A. (2011). Prevalence of multiply controlled problem behavior. *Journal of Applied Behavior Analysis, 44*, 593–597. https://doi.org/10.1901/jaba.2011.44-593

Beavers, G. A., Iwata, B. A., & Lerman, D. C. (2013). Thirty years of research on the functional analysis of problem behavior. *Journal of Applied Behavior Analysis, 46*, 1–21. https://doi.org/10.1002/jaba.30

Bowman, L. G., Fisher, W. W., Thompson, R. H., & Piazza, C. C. (1997). On the relation of mands and the function of destructive behavior. *Journal of Applied Behavior Analysis, 30*, 251–265. https://doi.org/10.1901/jaba.1997.30-251

Carr, E. G., Newsom, C. D., & Binkoff, J. A. (1980). Escape as a factor in the aggressive behavior of two retarded children. *Journal of Applied Behavior Analysis, 13*, 101–117. https://doi.org/10.1901/jaba.1980.13-101

Chok, J., Harper, J. M., Weiss, M. J., Bird, F., & Luiselli, J. K. (2019). *Functional analysis: A practitioner's guide to implementation and training*. New York: Elsevier/Academic Press.

Coffey, A. L., Shawler, L. A., Jessel, J., Nye, M. L., Bain, T. A., & Dorsey, M. F. (2019). Interview-Informed Synthesized Contingency Analysis (IISCA): Novel Interpretations and Future Directions. *Behavior Analysis in Practice, 13*, 217–225. https://doi.org/10.1007/s40617-019-00348-3

Conners, J., Iwata, B. A., Kahng, S., Hanley, G. P., Worsdell, A. S., & Thompson, R. H. (2000). Differential responding in the presence and absence of discriminative stimuli during multielement functional analyses. *Journal of Applied Behavior Analysis, 33*, 299–308. https://doi.org/10.1901/jaba.2000.33-299

Contrucci Kuhn, S. A., & Triggs, M. (2009). Analysis of social variables when an initial functional analysis indicates automatic reinforcement as the maintaining variable for SIB. *Journal of Applied Behavior Analysis, 42*, 679–683. https://doi.org/10.1901/jaba.2009.42-679

Day, R. M., Rea, J. A., Schussler, N. G., Larsen, S. E., & Johnson, W. L. (1988). A functionally based approach to the treatment of self-injurious behavior. *Behavior Modification, 12*, 565–589. https://doi.org/10.1177/01454455880124005

Derby, K. M., Wacker, D. P., Sasso, G., Steege, M., Northup, J., Cigrand, K., et al. (1992). Brief functional assessment techniques to evaluate aberrant behavior in an outpatient setting: A summary of 79 cases. *Journal of Applied Behavior Analysis, 25,* 713–721. https://doi.org/10.1901/jaba.1992.25-713

Fisher, W. W., Adelinis, J. D., Thompson, R. H., Worsdell, A. S., & Zarcone, J. R. (1998). Functional analysis and treatment of destructive behavior maintained by termination of "don't" (and symmetrical "do") requests. *Journal of Applied Behavior Analysis, 31,* 339–356. https://doi.org/10.1901/jaba.1998.31-339

Fisher, W. W., Greer, B. D., & Bouxsein, K. J. (in press). Developing function-based reinforcement procedures for problem behavior. In W. W. Fisher, C. C. Piazza, & H. S. Roane (Eds.), *Handbook of applied behavior analysis* (2nd ed., pp. X–Y). New York: Guilford.

Fisher, W. W., Greer, B. D., Romani, P. W., Zangrillo, A. N., & Owen, T. M. (2016). Comparisons of synthesized and individual reinforcement contingencies during functional analysis. *Journal of Applied Behavior Analysis, 49,* 596–616. https://doi.org/10.1002/jaba.314

Fisher, W. W., Piazza, C. C., Bowman, L. G., Hanley, G. P., & Adelinis, J. D. (1997). Direct and collateral effects of restraints and restraint fading. *Journal of Applied Behavior Analysis, 30,* 105–120. https://doi.org/10.1901/jaba.1997.30-105

Fisher, W. W., Piazza, C. C., & Chiang, C. L. (1996). Effects of equal and unequal reinforcer duration during functional analysis. *Journal of Applied Behavior Analysis, 29,* 117–120. https://doi.org/10.1901/jaba.1996.29-117

Fisher, W., Piazza, C. C., & Page, T. J. (1989). Assessing independent and interactive effects of behavioral and pharmacologic interventions for a client with dual diagnoses. *Journal of Behavior Therapy and Experimental Psychiatry, 20*(3), 241–250.

Fisher, W. W., Rodriguez, N. M., Luczynski, K. C., & Kelley, M. E. (2013). The use of protective equipment in the management of severe behavior disorders. In D. Reed, F. DiGennaro Reed, & J. Luiselli (Eds.), *Handbook of crisis intervention for individuals with developmental disabilities* (pp. 87–105). New York: Springer.

Fisher, W. W., Rodriguez, N. M., & Owen, T. M. (2013). Functional assessment and treatment of perseverative speech about restricted topics in an adolescent with Asperger syndrome. *Journal of Applied Behavior Analysis, 46,* 307–311.

Fyffe, C. E., Kahng, S., Fittro, E., & Russell, D. (2004). Functional analysis and treatment of inappropriate sexual behavior. *Journal of Applied Behavior Analysis, 37,* 401–404.

Ghaemmaghami, M., Hanley, G. P., Jin, S. C., & Vanselow, N. R. (2016). Affirming control by multiple reinforcers via progressive treatment analysis. *Behavioral Interventions, 31,* 70–86. https://doi.org/10.1002/bin.1425

Goh, H. L., & Iwata, B. A. (1994). Behavioral persistence and variability during extinction of self-injury maintained by escape. *Journal of Applied Behavior Analysis, 27,* 173–174. https://doi.org/10.1901/jaba.1994.27-173

Greer, B. D., Fisher, W. W., Saini, V., Owen, T. M., & Jones, J. K. (2016). Functional communication training during reinforcement schedule thinning: An analysis of 25 applications. *Journal of Applied Behavior Analysis, 49,* 105–121. https://doi.org/10.1002/jaba.265

Greer, B. D., Mitteer, D. R., Briggs, A. M., Fisher, W. W., & Sodawasser, A. J. (2020). Comparisons of standardized and interview-informed synthesized reinforcement contingencies relative to functional analysis. *Journal of Applied Behavior Analysis, 53,* 82–101.

Hagopian, L. P., Rooker, G. W., Jessel, J., & DeLeon, I. G. (2013). Initial functional analysis outcomes and modifications in pursuit of differentiation: A summary of 176 inpatient cases. *Journal of Applied Behavior Analysis, 46,* 88–100. https://doi.org/10.1002/jaba.25

Hammond, J. L., Iwata, B. A., Rooker, G. W., Fritz, J. N., & Bloom, S. E. (2013). Effects of fixed versus random condition sequencing during multielement functional analyses. *Journal of Applied Behavior Analysis, 46,* 22–30. https://doi.org/10.1002/jaba.7

Hanley, G. P., Iwata, B. A., & McCord, B. E. (2003). Functional analysis of destructive behavior: A review. *Journal of Applied Behavior Analysis, 36,* 147–186. https://doi.org/10.1901/jaba.2003.36-147

Hanley, G. P., Jin, C. S., Vanselow, N. R., & Hanratty, L. A. (2014). Producing meaningful improvements in problem behavior of children with autism via synthesized analyses and treatments. *Journal of Applied Behavior Analysis, 47,* 16–36. https://doi.org/10.1002/jaba.106

Hood, S. A., Rodriguez, N. M., Luczynski, K. C., & Fisher, W. W. (2019). Evaluating the effects of physical reactions on aggression via concurrent-operant analyses. *Journal of Applied Behavior Analysis, 52*, 642–651.

Iwata, B. A., Dorsey, M. F., Slifer, K. J., Bauman, K. E., & Richman, G. S. (1994). Toward a functional analysis of self-injury. *Analysis and Intervention in Developmental Disabilities, 2*, 3–20. (Reprinted from Analysis and Intervention in Developmental Disabilities, 2, 3–20, 1982).. https://doi.org/10.1901/jaba.1994.27-197

Iwata, B. A., & Dozier, C. L. (2008). Clinical application of functional analysis methodology. *Behavior Analysis in Practice, 1*, 3–9. https://doi.org/10.1007/BF03391714

Iwata, B. A., Duncan, B. A., Zarcone, J. R., Lerman, D. C., & Shore, B. A. (1994). A sequential, test-control methodology for conducting functional analyses of self-injurious behavior. *Behavior Modification, 18*, 289–306. https://doi.org/10.1177/01454455940183003

Iwata, B. A., Pace, G. M., Cowdery, G. E., & Miltenberger, R. G. (1994). What makes extinction work: An analysis of procedural form and function. *Journal of Applied Behavior Analysis, 27*, 131–144. https://doi.org/10.1901/jaba.1994.27-131

Iwata, B. A., Pace, G. M., Dorsey, M. F., Zarcone, J. R., Vollmer, T. R., Smith, R. G., et al. (1994). The functions of self-injurious behavior: An experimental-epidemiological analysis. *Journal of Applied Behavior Analysis, 27*, 215–240.

Jessel, J., Hanley, G. P., & Ghaemmaghami, M. (2016). Interview-informed synthesized contingency analyses: Thirty replications and reanalysis. *Journal of Applied Behavior Analysis, 49*, 576–595.

Jessel, J., Ingvarsson, E. T., Metras, R., Kirk, H., & Whipple, R. (2018). Achieving socially significant reductions in problem behavior following the interview-informed synthesized contingency analysis: A summary of 25 outpatient applications. *Journal of Applied Behavior Analysis, 51*, 130–157.

Kahng, S., & Iwata, B. A. (1999). Correspondence between outcomes of brief and extended functional analyses. *Journal of Applied Behavior Analysis, 32*, 149–160. https://doi.org/10.1901/jaba.1999.32-149

Lin, T., Luiselli, J. K., Gilligan, K., & Dacosta, S. (2012). Preventing injury from child aggression: Single-case evaluation of staff-worn protective equipment. *Developmental Neurorehabilitation, 15*, 298–303.

Lovaas, O. I., Freitag, G., Gold, V. J., & Kassorla, I. C. (1965). Experimental studies in childhood schizophrenia: Analysis of self-destructive behavior. *Journal of Experimental Child Psychology, 2*, 67–84. https://doi.org/10.1016/0022-0965(65)90016-0

Moore, J. W., Fisher, W. W., & Pennington, A. (2004). Systematic application and removal of protective equipment in the assessment of multiple topographies of self-injury. *Journal of Applied Behavior Analysis, 37*, 73–77. https://doi.org/10.1901/jaba.2004.37-73

Mueller, M. M., Nkosi, A., & Hine, J. F. (2011). Functional analysis in public schools: A summary of 90 functional analyses. *Journal of Applied Behavior Analysis, 44*, 807–818. https://doi.org/10.1901/jaba.2011.44-807

Northup, J., Wacker, D., Sasso, G., Steege, M., Cigrand, K., Cook, J., et al. (1991). A brief functional analysis of aggressive and alternative behavior in an outclinic setting. *Journal of Applied Behavior Analysis, 24*, 509–522. https://doi.org/10.1901/jaba.1991.24-509

Nunnally, J. (1978). *Psychometric theory*. New York: McGraw-Hill.

Oliver, A. C., Pratt, L. A., & Normand, M. P. (2015). A survey of functional behavior assessment methods used by behavior analysts in practice. *Journal of Applied Behavior Analysis, 48*, 817–829. https://doi.org/10.1002/jaba.256

Owen, T. M., Fisher, W. W., Akers, J. A., Sullivan, W. E., Falcomata, T. S., Greer, B. D., et al. (2020). Treating destructive behavior reinforced by increased caregiver compliance with the participant's mands. *Journal of Applied Behavior Analysis, 53*, 1494–1513. https://doi.org/10.1002/jaba.674

Parenteau, R., Luiselli, J. K., & Keeley, M. (2013). Direct and collateral effects of staff-worn protective equipment on injury prevention from child aggression. *Developmental Neurorehabilitation, 16*, 73.

Piazza, C. C., Fisher, W. W., Hanley, G. P., LeBlanc, L. A., Worsdell, A. S., Lindauer, S. E., & Keeney, K. M. (1998). Treatment of pica through multiple analyses of its reinforcing functions. *Journal of Applied Behavior Analysis, 31*, 165–189. https://doi.org/10.1901/jaba.1998.31-165

Retzlaff, B. J., Fisher, W. W., Akers, J. S., & Greer, B. D. (2020). A translational evaluation of potential iatrogenic effects of single and combined contingencies during functional analysis. *Journal of Applied Behavior Analysis, 53*, 67–81.

Retzlaff, B. J., Phillips, L. A., Fisher, W. W., Hardee, A. M., & Fuhrman, A. M. (2020). Using e-learning modules to train registered behavior technicians to accurately conduct ongoing visual inspection of functional analyses. *Journal of Applied Behavior Analysis, 53*, 2126–2138. https://doi.org/10.1002/jaba.719

Ringdahl, J. E., Call, N. A., Mews, J. B., Boelter, E. W., & Christensen, T. J. (2008). Assessment and treatment of aggressive behavior without a clear social function. *Research in Developmental Disabilities, 29*, 351–362. https://doi.org/10.1016/j.ridd.2007.06.003

Roscoe, E. M., Phillips, K. M., Kelly, M. A., Farber, R., & Dube, W. V. (2015). A statewide survey assessing practitioners' use and perceived utility of functional assessment. *Journal of Applied Behavior Analysis, 48*, 830–844. https://doi.org/10.1002/jaba.259

Roscoe, E. M., Schlichenmeyer, K. J., & Dube, W. V. (2015). Functional analysis of problem behavior: A systematic approach for identifying idiosyncratic variables. *Journal of Applied Behavior Analysis, 48*, 289–314.

Saini, V., Fisher, W. W., & Retzlaff, B. J. (2018). Predictive validity and efficiency of ongoing visual-inspection criteria for interpreting functional analyses. *Journal of Applied Behavior Analysis, 51*, 303–320. https://doi.org/10.1002/jaba.450

Saini, V., Fisher, W. W., Retzlaff, B. J., & Keevy, M. (2020). Efficiency in functional analysis of problem behavior: A quantitative and qualitative review. *Journal of Applied Behavior Analysis, 53*, 44–66. https://doi.org/10.1002/jaba.583

Saini, V., Greer, B. D., & Fisher, W. W. (2015). Clarifying inconclusive functional analysis results: Assessment and treatment of automatically reinforced aggression. *Journal of Applied Behavior Analysis, 48*, 315–330. https://doi.org/10.1002/jaba.203

Saini, V., Ubdegrove, K., Biran, S., & Duncan, R. (2019). A Preliminary Evaluation of Interrater Reliability and Concurrent Validity of Open-Ended Indirect Assessment. *Behavior Analysis in Practice, 13*, 114–125. https://doi.org/10.1007/s40617-019-00364-3

Sigafoos, J., & Saggers, E. (1995). A discrete-trial approach to the functional analysis of aggressive behavior in two boys with autism. *Australia & New Zealand Journal of Developmental Disabilities, 20*, 287–297. https://doi.org/10.1080/07263869500035621

Skinner, B. F. (1953). *Science and human behavior*. New York: Macmillan.

Smith, R. G., & Churchill, R. M. (2002). Identification of environmental determinants of behavior disorders through functional analysis of precursor behaviors. *Journal of Applied Behavior Analysis, 35*, 125–136. https://doi.org/10.1901/jaba.2002.35-125

Thomason-Sassi, J. L., Iwata, B. A., Neidert, P. L., & Roscoe, E. M. (2011). Response latency as an index of response strength during functional analyses of problem behavior. *Journal of Applied Behavior Analysis, 44*, 51–67. https://doi.org/10.1901/jaba.2011.44-51

Thompson, R. H., Fisher, W. W., Piazza, C. C., & Kuhn, D. E. (1998). The evaluation and treatment of aggression maintained by attention and automatic reinforcement. *Journal of Applied Behavior Analysis, 31*, 103–116. https://doi.org/10.1901/jaba.1998.31-103

Thompson, R. H., & Iwata, B. A. (2001). A descriptive analysis of social consequences following problem behavior. *Journal of Applied Behavior Analysis, 34*, 169–178. https://doi.org/10.1901/jaba.2001.34-169

Thompson, T., Symons, F., Delaney, D., & England, C. (1995). Self-injurious behavior as endogenous neurochemical self-administration. *Mental Retardation and Developmental Disabilities Research Reviews, 1*, 137–148. https://doi.org/10.1002/mrdd.1410010210

Treadwell, K., & Page, T. J. (1996). Functional analysis: Identifying the environmental determinants of severe behavior disorders. *The Journal of Head Trauma Rehabilitation., 11*(1), 62–74. https://doi.org/10.1097/00001199-199602000-00008

Urban, K. D., Luiselli, J. K., Child, S. N., & Parenteau, R. (2011). Effects of protective equipment on frequency and intensity of aggression-provoked staff injury. *Journal of Developmental and Physical Disabilities, 23*, 555–562.

Vollmer, T. R. (1994). The concept of automatic reinforcement: Implications for behavioral research in developmental disabilities. *Research in Developmental Disabilities, 15*, 187–207. https://doi.org/10.1016/0891-4222(94)90011-6

Vollmer, T. R., Marcus, B. A., Ringdahl, J. E., & Roane, H. S. (1995). Progressing from brief assessments to extended experimental analyses in the evaluation of aberrant behavior. *Journal of Applied Behavior Analysis, 28*, 561–576. https://doi.org/10.1901/jaba.1995.28-561

Wallace, M. D., & Iwata, B. A. (1999). Effects of session duration on functional analysis outcomes. *Journal of Applied Behavior Analysis, 32*, 175–183. https://doi.org/10.1901/jaba.1999.32-175

Wilder, D. A., Masuda, A., O'Connor, C., & Baham, M. (2001). Brief functional analysis and treatment of bizarre vocalizations in an adult with schizophrenia. *Journal of Applied Behavior Analysis, 34*, 65–68.

Behavioral Risk Assessment of Violence-Aggression

Joseph N. Ricciardi

Abstract Aggression and violence are a subset of challenging behaviors seen in individuals with neurodevelopmental and intellectual disabilities, which can impact services and lifestyles of individuals. Aggressive behavior carries the risk of physical and emotional harm to caregivers, family members, self, and community. This chapter focuses on aggression in the form of physical acts against self, others, and property, excluding specialty areas such as suicide and criminal or sexual violence. We review the prevalence of violence-aggression in the IDD population, the adverse impact on services, safety, health and well-being to self and others, and quality of life. The chapter introduces behavioral risk assessment, distinguished from other forensic assessment practices, and as a complement to functional behavior assessment suitable for cases with risk for violence and aggression. Behavioral risk assessment evaluates factors such as (a) unusual forms of aggression (topography), (b) the intensity and frequency of aggression, (c) the potential targets and location of occurrences, and (d) the presence of any complicating features that increase risk. Understanding these variables helps clinicians and agencies develop more options for risk prevention or mitigation than functional assessment alone. A comprehensive approach to assessment based on record review and clinical interview is described. Findings can be used to develop individualized risk reduction strategies, prevention, and staffing decisions.

Keywords Aggression · Assessment · Challenging behavior · Intellectual disability · Risk management · Violence

J. N. Ricciardi (✉)
Seven Hills NeuroCare and Seven Hills Foundation, Worcester, MA, USA
e-mail: jricciardi@sevenhills.org

© Springer Nature Switzerland AG 2021
J. K. Luiselli (ed.), *Applied Behavior Analysis Treatment of Violence and Aggression in Persons with Neurodevelopmental Disabilities*, Advances in Preventing and Treating Violence and Aggression,
https://doi.org/10.1007/978-3-030-68549-2_4

Aggression and violence are a subset of challenging behaviors seen in individuals with neurodevelopmental and intellectual disabilities, which can impact choices about services, living arrangements, staffing patterns in care settings, and treatment decisions (Didden et al., 2016). Chronic aggressive behavior may adversely affect social inclusion as well (Murphy, 2009). Strictly defined, violent or aggressive behaviors involve targeting others with threatening gestures, words, or actual physical contact (van den Bogaard, Nijman, Palmstierna, & Embregts, 2018). However, most of the public would consider intentional destruction of property and physically harmful acts against self as violent or aggressive as well. This chapter accepts this broader, more socially valid definition of aggressive behaviors (Crotty, Doody, & Lyons, 2014). Outside the scope of this chapter are unique forms of aggressive behavior which often rely on specialized clinical risk assessment such as suicidality and nonsuicidal self-harm, fire-setting, and criminal or sexual offending.

Aggressive behavior carries the risk of potential harm to others, self, and community. Other persons are at risk for direct harm from the act of aggression including professional caregivers, family members, and possibly members of the community. The harmful effects of aggression may be physical and emotional (Hensel, Lunsky, & Dewa, 2012). The aggressive person is at risk for harm as a secondary consequence of perpetration of aggression, for example, stigmatization, physical injury to self, legal consequences, loss of services, and relocation. A community can be at risk for societal complications of aggressive individuals in their communities. Notably, exposure to aggressive acts diminishes community safety, creating stress and generalized concerns for safety among all individuals. As well, communities incur the expense of providing first responder interventions for severe and repetitive aggressive episodes. General risk applies to physical and emotional harm, marginalization, legal sanctions, and disruption to services. Risk management involves detecting specific behaviors that carry these risks and the contexts that increase the likelihood of occurrence, then designing interventions to mitigate the potential for harm.

Behavior analysts frequently assess challenging behavior and assume clinical leadership roles in the safe management of aggressive individuals. This chapter describes a topography-based approach to behavioral risk assessment as an additional component of traditional behavioral assessment and intervention planning. The approach is compatible with the roles of clinical behavior analysts and the considerable expertise behavioral clinicians possess in integrating historical information about behaviors of concern with direct observation. Because behavior analysts have specialized training in operationalizing behavior and deconstructing complex events into contingencies, they may be uniquely prepared for this form of risk assessment.

Review of Pertinent Research Literature

Aggression (including property destruction) may occur in as many as 8.3% of community-dwelling adults with neurodevelopmental and intellectual disabilities, with self-directed aggression occurring in 7.5%, during a 4-month period (Bowring,

Totsika, Hastings, Toogood, & Griffith, 2017). These results were obtained from a total population prevalence study, as opposed to a population sampling method. The results replicate findings from two previous total population studies. Cooper et al. (2009) found aggressive-destructive behavior at the time of the study in 9.8% of participants and self-directed aggression in 4.9%. Lundqvist (2013) reported a 1-month point prevalence of aggressive-destructive behavior of 11.9% and self-directed aggression of 8.4%. The similarity of findings across different total populations argues that this is a trustworthy finding. Additionally, much higher rates have been reported in individuals in institutional settings (Drieschner, Marrozos, & Regenboog, 2013). Accordingly, aggressive behaviors are a significant problem for individuals with neurodevelopmental and intellectual disabilities living in the community and in institutional settings. Likewise, when a person is referred for clinical-behavioral consultation, aggression is very likely to be a primary reason (Allen, 2000).

Aggressive behaviors increase risk for a range of adverse consequences. Both children and adults with neurodevelopmental and intellectual disabilities who demonstrate aggression are at risk for disruption of important relationships with family, peers, and important caregivers. Caregivers react emotionally to aggression (Hensel et al., 2012) and repeated aggression creates an ever increasing risk for isolation and restriction, and eventual separation from home and family, loss of care placements, and transfers to settings often far from their communities (Adams et al., 2018; Allen, Lowe, Moore, & Brophy, 2007). Also, aggressive behavior is one of the primary reasons why individuals are referred to more restrictive settings (Knotter, Wissink, Moonen, Stams, & Jansen, 2013). Of course, aggressive acts can harm the perpetrator as well, for instance, self-directed aggression can result in direct tissue damage and repetitive and unhealed wounds are a risk for infection. Aggression to others and property can cause secondary injury to the perpetrator. Some property items might even be toxic such as when aggression is directed at televisions, lightbulbs, and similar objects.

Aggression toward self and others and destructive behaviors often lead to seclusion and physical restraint procedures and the risks associated with these interventions (Luiselli, Sperry, & Magee, 2011; Merineau-Cote & Morin, 2013; Urban, Luiselli, Child, & Parenteau, 2011). Over time, chronic aggressive behavior can become interpreted as "criminally offending behavior" (Holland et al., 2002) and may result in criminal charges (Raina, Arenovich, Jones, & Lunsky, 2013). As these events accumulate, the person's access to ordinary community life is limited or denied (Emerson & Bromley, 1995). Table 1 summarizes the array of risks to the person exhibiting aggression and others across various forms of aggressive behavior.

The assessment of aggressive risk in a general population has employed a static risk model (scales and measures of unchanging factors), dynamic risk model (changing factors that influence risk), and a structured professional judgment approach that combines elements of both (Lofthouse, Golding, Totsika, Hastings, & Lindsay, 2017). The intent of assessment is to predict the degree of risk to others and the method combines scales with clinical judgment. A significant problem with these approaches is that they were developed for forensic, criminal, and sexual

Table 1 Forms of aggressive behavior and risks to others and self (aggressive person)

Forms of aggressive behavior	Risks to others	Risks to aggressive person
Threats and gestures Actual physical aggression Aggressive destruction of property	Fear, acute trauma, lasting traumatization Direct injuries • Injuries requiring first aid • Injuries requiring medical care • Injuries resulting in permanent disability Restraint • Injuries due to restraint procedures Exposure to bodily fluids Exposure to blood-borne pathogens	Disrupted relationships, separation, isolation Restrictive protocols Secondary injuries Restraint • Injuries due to restraint procedures Loss of placement and services Criminal justice referral
Aggressive acts toward self	Secondary traumatization Injuries during interruption procedures or application of protective devices Exposure to bodily fluids Exposure to blood-borne pathogens	Direct injuries • Injuries requiring first aid • Injuries requiring medical care • Injuries resulting in permanent disability • Repetitive and unhealed wounds: Infection and disfigurement Restraint • Injuries due to restraint procedures Imposition of protective devices

offender populations and do not apply to individuals with neurodevelopmental and intellectual disabilities (Hounsome, Whittington, Brown, Greenhill, & McGuire, 2018; Lofthouse et al., 2017). The applicability of these approaches is only now beginning to show promise with this population (Lofthouse et al., 2017). These approaches have not demonstrated applicability to non-forensic populations, and with the wider range of forms of noncriminal aggressive behavior seen in individuals with neurodevelopmental and intellectual disabilities in care settings (Ricciardi & Rothschild, 2017). For example, an adult with moderate intellectual disability and autism who demonstrates aggression toward caregivers when denied the opportunity to purchase an item in the community is a more "typical" focus of behavior analytic clinical services. This presentation is noncriminal, yet it represents a significant risk to caregivers and the community, and the perpetrator is at risk for community restrictions and placement loss. Without change over time, in some caregiver settings, the individual might begin contacting the criminal justice system, as well.

The clinical-behavioral assessment of aggression typically centers on observation and measurement of behaviors of concern with an aim toward a hypothesis of behavioral function which is then useful for treatment planning (Lloyd & Kennedy, 2014). However, assessment of function does not necessarily include an assessment of risk to self or others posed by challenging behavior. Furthermore, the standard practice of behavioral assessment is based on direct observation. With aggression risk, it would be ideal to include a method that might be more sensitive to predicting risk before it actually occurred especially in new cases and initial intake. Later direct experiences could modify the preliminary risk assessment.

In contrast to functional assessment, the assessment of risk is more concerned about the form (topography) of behaviors, impact on safety and well-being, and predicting occurrences in various contexts. Behavioral risk assessment evaluates factors such as (a) unusual forms of aggression (topography), (b) the intensity and frequency of aggression, (c) the potential targets and location of occurrences, and (d) the presence of any complicating features that increase risk. Understanding these variables helps clinicians and agencies develop more options for risk prevention or mitigation than functional assessment alone.

Synthesis of Research Findings and Implications

Behavior analysts conducting clinical-behavioral assessments of individuals with neurodevelopmental and intellectual disabilities and aggression can supplement their traditional assessment with procedures intended to identify specific forms of aggression, intensity, targets, contexts of occurrence, and complicating features (Ricciardi & Rothschild, 2017). Topography-based behavioral risk assessment proceeds through a three-phase process of record review, interview with caregivers, and direct observation which can be efficiently integrated into typical functional assessment procedures.

The review of the record is critical because the evaluator may find evidence of prior aggression that is unknown or omitted by caregiver informants during the interview phase. When reviewed before clinical interviews, record review helps the clinician know specific behaviors to ask about or follow-up on, and then what to watch for when conducting direct observations. A clinician who has access to a clinical record is obligated by ethics and standards of practice to review pertinent documents and make note of a history of behaviors that place the individual, others, and the community at risk. Further, having become aware of the history, a clinician may be further obligated to assess the likelihood of actual aggression risk at the current time and setting and, if necessary, develop strategies for risk reduction as a reasonable clinical expectation (Sheldon & Sheldon-Sherman, 2013).

When conducting a clinical interview of caregivers, a standard of practice includes asking about behaviors of concern usually in an open-ended manner. In a risk assessment, clinicians should ask about the range of aggressive behaviors even if not mentioned at first, since informants may not be comprehensive in describing the presenting problem. There is a tendency for caregivers to focus on the most immediate concerns instead of problems from the past. For example, the family and caregivers for an adult with intellectual disability entering a new program share information about sleep problems, screaming, and excessive food consumption. They should also be asked, "Is there any history of aggressive behaviors?" as a prudent check for risk. It is not surprising to find the informant saying, "Well yes, he will try to scratch your face and eyes, but usually not with us." Caregivers report what is most salient, their opinion of what is most concerning, but not necessarily everything that others might anticipate when receiving a person into care. The problem arises then, how does a clinician ensure she or he is asking *all the right questions*?

Rather than approach the behavioral risk assessment in an entirely open-ended fashion with identification of risk topographies as they happen to be revealed during the process, the clinician should identify in advance potential forms of aggressive behavior, which represent serious risk to others, self, or the community. Ideally, this is a list of behavioral topographies to help the clinician be thorough and comprehensive during the interview. With this preparation, the clinician would approach the record and clinical interviews with an organized list of what to look for during record review and during these tasks.

A behavioral rating scale can be adapted for use as a risk assessment interview tool. The Behavior Problems Inventory (BPI) (Rojahn, Matson, Lott, Esbensen, & Smalls, 2001) is a 49-item clinician administered structured interview covering self-injury, stereotypy, and aggression/destruction. The BPI also provides a clinician with a systematic approach to estimating frequency and severity during the structured interview. The psychometric properties of the instrument have been studied extensively with favorable results (Mascitelli et al., 2015). The BPI was also used in two previously referenced total population studies (i.e., Bowring et al., 2017 and Lundqvist, 2013).

The topographies assessed in the BPI include stereotyped behaviors (24 items) and other low-risk topographies such as teeth grinding, and "being mean or cruel." However, other items include more pertinent high-risk topographies for physical aggression toward others, property, and self. Clinicians would use this instrument as a starting point for a record review, reading the record with an eye for the items listed on the scale. The list would be used later as a structured interview with caregivers who know the person well and aid the clinician when reviewing the record and during an interview of presenting concerns. Note that the BPI is a rating scale that was not developed for the purpose of a comprehensive assessment of risky behavioral topographies.

Ricciardi and Rothschild (2017) described The Screening Tool for Behaviors of Concern, Adult Risk Version, a 34-item semi-structured interview tool for topography-based risk assessment (a child version has been developed as well, unpublished: Ricciardi & Weiss, 2014). The items represent a wide range of behaviors that are associated with risk to others, self, and community. Items are listed as distinct topographies, for example, "actual physical aggression" is distinguished from "threat of physical aggression" (without actual occurrence) and an additional item is "physical aggression using an object as weapon." The value of this format is that each topography is important to know about when determining actual risk. A person who threatens aggression often but never exhibits actual physical aggression is a lower risk to professional caregivers in a treatment setting than a person who exhibits actual physical aggression in the same setting. However, the same topography may be perceived as a threat to community members and places the individual at risk if the behavior is anticipated to occur in public settings. Similarly, an individual with a history of using objects as weapons during aggressive episodes may be at greater risk for harm to others than an individual who does not brandish such objects. In the Screening Tool, each behavior is listed as a separate topography, which allows for a separate clinical judgment of risk, per topography.

For some topographies, clinicians should inquire about additional risk markers. The Screening Tool for Behaviors of Concern lists several follow-up questions during the interview. For example, with an individual who exhibits physical aggression, it would be valuable to ask about high injury risk forms of physical aggression such as spitting, scratching/gouging, targeting eyes, and pulling hair. Notably, biting caries unique pain intensity and health risks for others and can be very difficult to block or release. Having biting as a part of the topographies of aggression for an individual increases the risk of harm to others in a unique way. Further, identifying that biting is a possible topography during aggressive episodes suggests use of protective equipment as a possible risk mitigation intervention with the added benefit of possible reductive effect on the behavior itself (Urban et al., 2011). Likewise, if the clinician confirms the presence of aggressive behavior using objects as a weapon, it would be important to know what the typical objects are and if access to them can be limited.

As another illustration, if an individual in a group home is known to use knives during aggressive episodes, then perhaps a restrictive procedure involving sharps counts and locked storage is warranted. If an individual has a history of hiding objects for later use during an aggressive episode, a clinician may recommend seeking permissions for room checks as a protective factor. Discovering positive findings for these questions leads to some obvious crisis prevention strategies. Similarly, asking about items a person might throw during an aggressive episode and learning that furniture is typical might lead to individualized de-escalation strategies that involve moving to a room where certain furnishings are not present or having caregivers step between furnishings and the individual in crisis. In summary, a thorough process to identify very specific topographies of aggression and any special high-risk concerns can lead to individualized prevention and risk mitigation strategies that may not otherwise have been considered. It is this level of detail that distinguishes identification of target behaviors in risk assessment from the objectives of conventional behavioral assessment.

Probable targets should be determined for all identified aggressive topographies. For example, clinicians and staff should know the persons who might be the victim of aggression and violence. Family members, professional support staff, vulnerable or fragile peers, visitors to care settings, and strangers in the community are possible targets. Consider that aggression in individuals with neurodevelopmental and intellectual disabilities may be displayed exclusively toward caregivers but not peers or only at persons who do not retaliate. Each target finding represents a different level of risk to others and to the individual, and may require a specialized plan to reduce risk.

Professional staff may have advanced training in self-protective strategies and the risk plan would be periodic refreshers or competency-based checks on their skills (Lennox, Geren, & Rourke, 2011). Alternatively, if the individual targets especially vulnerable peers, there may be a higher risk of harm to others, and a special plan might be required to avoid proximity to peers during crises, or prevent occurrence entirely by assigning a milieu without vulnerable targets. Likewise, when community members are known to be targets, there are heightened risks of harm to others plus potential for criminal justice involvement. Knowing a history of targets in advance gives a clinician the opportunity to recommend options for risk reduction through enhanced staffing and implementation of antecedent-based strategies for risk mitigation in the community. Thus, establishing a history of predictable targets will suggest additional options for risk reduction and protecting others.

Having identified aggressive topographies and targets, a clinician will want to assess the intensity of aggressive behaviors. The definition of intensity would be capacity for harmful effects on others or self. For threats and aggressive gestures, the intensity might be the duration and frequency of these episodes, while also considering the probable targets. For instance, aggressive threats that are directed at professional staff might be less of a risk to the person and others than those directed at vulnerable peers, peers prone to react aggressively in retaliation, or the general public.

Intensity of physical aggression may be the history of injuries and required treatments to the aggressive person and others, namely bruising and scratches requiring first aid, injuries that require medical treatment, and medical trauma that results in permanent disability. Relatedly, the clinician should ask about unusual forms of aggression with unique injury risks, for example, biting, hair pulling, or hitting face/head. In cases of self-directed aggression, intensity would be estimated similarly from injuries that result in reddening, bruising, open wounds first aid, medical treatment, and potential for permanent disability. As noted, injuries resulting in open wounds further increase infection risk for the person with aggressive behavior. Intensity of aggression in the form of property destruction might be determined by special targets for destruction. That is, kicking or punching walls can harm the person but less likely so than punching windows. Intensity can also be estimated by potential cost of destructive episodes, noting that high-cost destructive behaviors might increase the individual's risk of relocation and the loss of home or services. By estimating the intensity of aggressive behaviors, comprehensive behavioral risk assessment can predict harm to the others or to the individual being evaluated.

When the intensity of aggression results in tissue damage, other complicating factors should be considered. Does the person have any blood-borne diseases, possibly hepatitis B, hepatitis C, or human immunodeficiency virus (HIV). Health history should always be documented when evaluating individuals with aggression because identification of a blood-borne pathogen significantly increases risk of harm to others, especially when aggression produces an open wound or bleeding in the perpetrator or victim. These situations increase the need for preventative practices, which might include wearing of protective equipment and padding.

Discovering the potential for high-intensity aggression can inform risk reduction options, intensive staffing ratios, or specialized practices to mitigate risk. Take the case of a student with autism who aggresses toward teachers during classroom instruction and to teachers and peers during hallway transitions. The form of aggression is hair pulling with the peculiar habit of pulling the person to the ground by their own hair. Teachers followed a risk reduction protocol for wearing long hair pulled back, and wearing hats during close instruction. In addition, risk during the hallway context was managed by clearing the hallway of others during transitions and adding a second staff person to increase vigilance and support.

The topography-based model of behavioral risk assessment has some overlap with dynamic risk assessment models. At the core of dynamic risk assessment is the understanding that certain variables that come and go can influence risk for exhibiting at risk behaviors. In the forensic risk literature these are variable and situation conditions such as a change in mood and behavior such as anger, unkemptness, substance use, and acute challenges in significant relationships which are associated with increased risk (McGrath, Livingston, & Falk, 2007). Applying behavior analytic concepts these dynamic variables refer to motivating operations (MOs) which are events and stimuli that, when present or absent, establish the reinforcing potential for historic challenging behaviors (McGill, 1999). In the clinical literature, MOs include physiological (illnesses and overall health and well-being), environmental (contexts and recurrent activities), and social (particular persons) variables (Brosnan & Healy, 2011). Recurrent health problems particularly important for clinicians to note would be chronic illnesses, which recur as acute episodes. Seasonal allergies, periodic insomnia, repeated infections, and persistent constipation are but a few chronic-acute course conditions known to increase risk for aggression when present and diminish risk when acuity recedes (De Winter, Jansen, & Evenhuis, 2011; May & Kennedy, 2010; O'Reilly, 1995). Acute psychiatric symptoms and co-occurring mental health conditions have also been shown to increase risk for challenging behavior such as aggression (Allen, 2008; Ricciardi, 2013).

Other dynamic variables that influence aggression in individuals with neurodevelopmental and intellectual disabilities might include transfer into new settings, specific activities that occur/reoccur, and loss of established routines. Specific staff or unfamiliar caregivers might be identified as setting events associated with increased risk for aggressive behaviors. Each of these factors can come and go but once identified and known to the care team, risk mitigation can be employed. For example, an individual with a history of severe physical aggression (kicking, punching, and biting) who appears frightened by and has targeted new caregivers might be provided with opportunity to work side-by-side with novel and familiar staff before fully transferring care. Or, new staff might only support the person during low or no occurrence contexts such as highly preferred activities initially. Once again, assessing for the presence of physiological, environmental, and social variables and their influence on risk for aggressive behavior provides clinicians with additional opportunities for risk reduction or mitigation.

Summary and Conclusions

The principles of behavioral risk assessment and illustrations presented in the chapter suggest several practice recommendations as well as suggestions for future research, summarized below.

For advanced preparation, a clinician should establish a comprehensive list of aggressive behavior topographies. The clinician can generate a list based on her or his experience with aggressive behavior, be drawn from existing problem behavior inventories, or follow an established topography-based method (Ricciardi & Rothschild, 2017).

The clinician should review any available records using the comprehensive list of aggressive topographies as a guide to spotting past indictors of aggression. During the record review, the clinician should note any reports of medical problems, which have demonstrated influence on the occurrence of aggression. The clinician should make note of any communicable diseases, blood-borne illnesses, or chronic wounds or injuries that are the result of aggression. These findings will inform subsequent interviews with caregivers.

Interviewed caregivers should be familiar with the individual being assessed. Ideally, caregivers should be directly involved with support and care of the individual for several consecutive months to a year. Interviewing multiple caregivers is recommended and will likely yield better findings.

During the interview, the clinician should ask about each specific topography, including current and past presentation of the specific aggressive topography. Some topographies will carry special concerns: unique forms with greater risk (biting, targeting eyes and face), or unique features (using a weapon during aggressive episodes), or high risk targets (family members, vulnerable peers, strangers visiting the setting, or strangers in the community). Also, the clinician should inquire about intensity of the aggressive behavior and contexts of occurrence at home, support/care settings, community, and during transportation. This process is summarized in Table 2, "Behavioral Topography Assessment and Risk Indices."

During risk assessment, the clinician should clarify any reports of aggressive behavior or incidents from the clinical record that were not mentioned by the caregiver. In addition, the clinician should inquire about general health, the presence of any recurrent illnesses, and their relationship to aggressive behavior. No doubt, the clinician without medical training and scope of practice authority should refer to a qualified professional for any finding, or when in doubt. As previously mentioned, the literature has established that chronic-acute medical conditions such as allergies, recurrent infections, and recurrent headaches may have a relationship to aggressive behaviors. Similarly, the clinician should assess for sleep problems and refer to specialists when there are any reports of sleep difficulties.

Summarizing these practice recommendations, a comprehensive, topography-based approach can yield findings of numerous variables which, when identified, may suggest risk reduction strategies in the form of antecedent interventions, preventing exposure to at risk contexts, increased staffing ratios, enhanced staff

Table 2 Behavioral topography assessment and risk indices

Identify topographies	Identify any special concerns	Identify the typical targets	Estimate the intensity	Identify the likely contexts
Does the person exhibit threats or gestures of physical aggression, without actual aggression some of the time?	• Explicitly homicidal threats • Exhibited in public settings	• Family • Support staff • Peers • Strangers (visitors, persons in community)	• Duration of episodes • Frequency of episodes	• Home • Support settings • Community locations • While passenger in vehicle
Does the person exhibit physical aggression? (Specify the forms of physical aggression: punch, kick, grab, push, etc.)	• Biting • Spitting • Scratching/gouging • Targeting eyes • Hair pulling • Blood-borne diseases	• Family • Support staff • Peers • Vulnerable peers • Strangers (visitors) • Persons in community	• Minor injuries • Injuries requiring first aid • Injuries requiring additional medical attention • Severe injuries (specify) • Potential for lasting impairment	• Home • Support settings • Community locations • While passenger in vehicle
Does the person ever use an object as weapon during aggressive episode?	• Identify typical objects, weapons, and ability to access • Hiding weapon for later use • Fabricating a weapon for use • Throwing hard/dangerous objects at persons	• Family • Support staff • Peers • Vulnerable peers • Strangers (visitors, persons in community)	• Minor injuries • Injuries requiring first aid • Injuries requiring additional medical attention • Severe injuries (specify) • Potential for lasting impairment	• Home • Support settings • Community locations • While passenger in vehicle
Does the person ever engage in destruction of property? (Specify the forms of property destruction: punch/kick walls, break specific objects, etc.)	• Breaking glass/windows • Items with significant expense • Items with toxicity potential (televisions, lightbulbs, caustic substances, etc.)	• Identify items usually targeted, location, and access	• Single destruction in episode • Multiple destructive acts • Multiple targets • Expense of destruction • Risk of harm to others during episodes	• Home • Support settings • Community locations • While passenger in vehicle
Does the person ever exhibit aggression toward self? (Specify the forms of physical aggression to self: head to hard surface, hand to head, self-biting, etc.)	• Head as target • Eyes as target • Tissue damage • Bleeding • Using objects to injure self • Blood-borne diseases • Unhealed wounds	• Identify part of body targeted	• Force and repetition • Minor injuries • Injuries requiring first aid • Injuries requiring additional medical attention • Severe injuries (specify) • Potential for lasting impairment	• Home • Support settings • Community locations • While passenger in vehicle

training, protective equipment options, and managing health problems, among many possible options. Further, when behavioral risk assessment precedes entry into a care setting, the findings can suggest advanced strategies for risk reduction and personal safety in concert with the traditional direct observation phase of a functional behavior assessment.

More research is needed to empirically evaluate methods of behavioral risk assessment including psychometric properties of instruments and protocols. For example, the contribution of screening tool described in the chapter (Ricciardi & Rothschild, 2017) would be enhanced by establishing a measure of internal consistency (inter-rater reliability) and content validity. Another focus of research could be directed at procedures for effective training of clinicians and other treatment specialists in conducting behavioral risk assessment and formulating assessment-derived interventions. Finally, a valuable topic of future research is whether the results of behavioral risk assessment produce treatment plans and programs that successfully reduce and eliminate aggression-violence among persons with neurodevelopmental and intellectual disabilities and their caregivers.

References

Adams, D., Handley, L., Simkiss, D., Walls, E., Jones, A., Knapp, M., et al. (2018). Service use and access in young children with an intellectual disability or global developmental delay: Associations with challenging behaviour. *Journal of Intellectual & Developmental Disability, 43*(2), 232–241.

Allen, D. (2000). Recent research on physical aggression in persons with intellectual disability: An overview. *Journal of Intellectual and Developmental Disability, 25*(1), 41–57.

Allen, D. (2008). The relationship between challenging behaviour and mental ill-health in people with intellectual disabilities: A review of current theories and evidence. *Journal of Intellectual Disabilities, 12*(4), 267–294.

Allen, D. G., Lowe, K., Moore, K., & Brophy, S. (2007). Predictors, costs and characteristics of out of area placement for people with intellectual disability and challenging behaviour. *Journal of Intellectual Disability Research, 51*(6), 409–416.

Bowring, D. L., Totsika, V., Hastings, R. P., Toogood, S., & Griffith, G. M. (2017). Challenging behaviours in adults with an intellectual disability: A total population study and exploration of risk indices. *British Journal of Clinical Psychology, 56*(1), 16–32.

Brosnan, J., & Healy, O. (2011). A review of behavioral interventions for the treatment of aggression in individuals with developmental disabilities. *Research in Developmental Disabilities, 32*(2), 437–446.

Cooper, S. A., Smiley, E., Jackson, A., Finlayson, J., Allan, L., Mantry, D., et al. (2009). Adults with intellectual disabilities: Prevalence, incidence and remission of aggressive behaviour and related factors. *Journal of Intellectual Disability Research, 53*(3), 217–232.

Crotty, G., Doody, O., & Lyons, R. (2014). Aggressive behavior and its prevalence within five topographies. *Journal of Intellectual Disabilities, 18*, 76–89.

De Winter, C. F., Jansen, A. A. C., & Evenhuis, H. M. (2011). Physical conditions and challenging behaviour in people with intellectual disability: A systematic review. *Journal of Intellectual Disability Research, 55*(7), 675–698.

Didden, R., Lindsay, W. R., Lang, R., Sigafoos, J., Deb, S., Wiersma, J., et al. (2016). Aggressive behavior. In *Handbook of evidence-based practices in intellectual and developmental disabilities* (pp. 727–750). Cham, Switzerland: Springer.

Drieschner, K. H., Marrozos, I., & Regenboog, M. (2013). Prevalence and risk factors of inpatient aggression by adults with intellectual disabilities and severe challenging behaviour: A long-term prospective study in two Dutch treatment facilities. *Research in Developmental Disabilities, 34*(8), 2407–2418.

Emerson, E., & Bromley, J. (1995). The form and function of challenging behaviours. *Journal of Intellectual Disability Research, 39*(5), 388–398.

Hensel, J. M., Lunsky, Y., & Dewa, C. S. (2012). Exposure to client aggression and burnout among community staff who support adults with intellectual disabilities in Ontario, Canada. *Journal of Intellectual Disability Research, 56*(9), 910–915.

Holland, T., Clare, I. C. H., & Mukhopadhyay, T. (2002). Prevalence of 'criminal offending' by men and women with intellectual disability and the characteristics of 'offenders': Implications for research and service development. *Journal of Intellectual Disability Research, 46*, 6–20.

Hounsome, J., Whittington, R., Brown, A., Greenhill, B., & McGuire, J. (2018). The structured assessment of violence risk in adults with intellectual disability: A systematic review. *Journal of Applied Research in Intellectual Disabilities, 31*(1), e1–e17.

Knotter, M. H., Wissink, I. B., Moonen, X. M., Stams, G. J. J., & Jansen, G. J. (2013). Staff's attitudes and reactions towards aggressive behaviour of clients with intellectual disabilities: A multi-level study. *Research in Developmental Disabilities, 34*(5), 1397–1407.

Lennox, D., Geren, M., & Rourke, D. (2011). Emergency physical restraint: Considerations for staff training and supervision. In *The handbook of high-risk challenging behaviors in people with intellectual and developmental disabilities* (pp. 271–292). Paul H. Brookes Publishing Company, Baltimore, MD: Paul H. Brookes.

Lloyd, B. P., & Kennedy, C. H. (2014). Assessment and treatment of challenging behaviour for individuals with intellectual disability: A research review. *Journal of Applied Research in Intellectual Disabilities, 27*(3), 187–199.

Lofthouse, R., Golding, L., Totsika, V., Hastings, R., & Lindsay, W. (2017). How effective are risk assessments/measures for predicting future aggressive behaviour in adults with intellectual disabilities (ID): A systematic review and meta-analysis. *Clinical Psychology Review, 58*, 76–85.

Luiselli, J. K., Sperry, J. M., & Magee, C. (2011). Descriptive analysis of physical restraint (protective holding) among community living adults with intellectual disability. *Journal of Intellectual Disabilities, 15*(2), 93–99.

Lundqvist, L. O. (2013). Prevalence and risk markers of behavior problems among adults with intellectual disabilities: A total population study in Örebro County, Sweden. *Research in Developmental Disabilities, 34*(4), 1346–1356.

Mascitelli, A. N., Rojahn, J., Nicolaides, V. C., Moore, L., Hastings, R. P., & Christian-Jones, C. (2015). The behaviour problems inventory-short form: Reliability and factorial validity in adults with intellectual disabilities. *Journal of Applied Research in Intellectual Disabilities, 28*(6), 561–571.

May, M. E., & Kennedy, C. H. (2010). Health and problem behavior among people with intellectual disabilities. *Behavior Analysis in Practice, 3*(2), 4–12.

McGill, P. (1999). Establishing operations: Implications for the assessment, treatment, and prevention of problem behavior. *Journal of Applied Behavior Analysis, 32*(3), 393–418.

McGrath, R. J., Livingston, J. A., & Falk, G. (2007). A structured method of assessing dynamic risk factors among sexual abusers with intellectual disabilities. *American Journal on Mental Retardation, 112*(3), 221–229.

Merineau-Cote, J., & Morin, D. (2013). Correlates of restraint and seclusion for adults with intellectual disabilities in community services. *Journal of Intellectual Disability Research, 57*(2), 182–190.

Murphy, G. (2009). Challenging behavior: A barrier to inclusion? *Journal of Policy and Practice in Intellectual Disabilities, 6*(2), 89–90.

O'Reilly, M. F. (1995). Functional analysis and treatment of escape-maintained aggression correlated with sleep deprivation. *Journal of Applied Behavior Analysis, 28*(2), 225–226.

Raina, P., Arenovich, T., Jones, J., & Lunsky, Y. (2013). Pathways into the criminal justice system for individuals with intellectual disability. *Journal of Applied Research in Intellectual Disabilities, 26*(5), 404–409.

Ricciardi, J. N. (2013). Co-occurring psychiatric disorders in individuals with intellectual disability. In *Handbook of crisis intervention and developmental disabilities* (pp. 213–243). New York: Springer.

Ricciardi, J. N., & Rothschild, A. W. (2017). Behavioral risk assessment. In *Applied behavior analysis advanced guidebook* (pp. 93–116). London: Academic Press.

Ricciardi, J. N., & Weiss, A. (2014). *Clinical risk assessment and management of children and adolescents with intellectual and developmental disabilities*. Workshop presented at the Annual conference of the Berkshire Association for Behavior Analysis and Therapy, Amherst, MA.

Rojahn, J., Matson, J. L., Lott, D., Esbensen, A. J., & Smalls, Y. (2001). The Behavior Problems Inventory: An instrument for the assessment of self-injury, stereotyped behavior, and aggression/destruction in individuals with developmental disabilities. *Journal of Autism and Developmental Disorders, 31*, 577–588.

Sheldon, J. B., & Sheldon-Sherman, J. A. (2013). Legal and ethical issues. In *Handbook of crisis intervention and developmental disabilities* (pp. 261–279). New York: Springer.

Urban, K. D., Luiselli, J. K., Child, S. N., & Parenteau, R. J. (2011). Effects of protective equipment on frequency and intensity of aggression-provoked staff injury. *Journal of Developmental and Physical Disabilities, 23*, 555–562.

van den Bogaard, K. J., Nijman, H. L., Palmstierna, T., & Embregts, P. J. (2018). Characteristics of aggressive behavior in people with mild to borderline intellectual disability and co-occurring psychopathology. *Journal of Mental Health Research in Intellectual Disabilities, 11*(2), 124–142.

Social Validity Assessment

James K. Luiselli

Abstract Social validity concerns the acceptance and approval of intervention objectives, procedures, and outcomes among service recipients, care providers, and other consumers. This chapter addresses social validity assessment within applied behavior analysis (ABA) treatment of violence-aggression in persons who have neurodevelopmental disabilities, including an overview and historical context, description of assessment methodologies, and practice recommendations. The chapter further reviews pertinent research examples of social validity assessment and presents suggestions for application in and dissemination of ABA treatment studies.

Keywords Aggression · Applied behavior analysis · Neurodevelopmental disabilities · Social validity assessment · Violence

Social validity refers to the opinions and attitudes of service recipients, practitioners, care providers and related stakeholders about the objectives, methods, and outcomes of intervention practices and research (Foster & Mash, 1999; Kazdin, 1977; Wolf, 1978). As detailed in this chapter, social validity is typically assessed through questionnaires, surveys, and rating scales which yield quantified measures of intervention acceptance, satisfaction, and approval. Assessment methods that feature direct observation and measurement of intervention preferences are also used in clinical and research contexts (Common & Lane, 2017; Ferguson et al., 2018). The results of social validity assessment are intended to improve how treatment services are designed and implemented through comprehensive analysis

---

J. K. Luiselli (✉)
Melmark New England, Andover, MA, USA
e-mail: jluiselli@melmarkne.org

© Springer Nature Switzerland AG 2021
J. K. Luiselli (ed.), *Applied Behavior Analysis Treatment of Violence and Aggression in Persons with Neurodevelopmental Disabilities*, Advances in Preventing and Treating Violence and Aggression,
https://doi.org/10.1007/978-3-030-68549-2_5

of procedures, person values, community standards, and cultural norms among other factors. There are professional practice expectations related to social validity as well. For example, consistent with the *Professional and Ethical Compliance Code for Behavior Analysts* (Behavior Analyst Certification Board, 2017), "Social validity is an important component in aiding behavior analysts in objectively and subjectively measuring what is of social importance to facilitate the interests of their clients" (Common & Lane, 2017, p. 77).

For several reasons, social validity assessment is critically important when evaluating applied behavior analysis (ABA) treatment of violence and aggression in persons with neurodevelopmental disabilities. First, many individuals do not respond favorably to least restrictive procedures alone (e.g., differential reinforcement) and require more invasive methods of physical management (Luiselli, 2011a; Reed, Luiselli, Miller, & Kaplan, 2013). In most cases, judgements from care providers about their acceptance of restrictive procedures predict compliance with intervention recommendations. That is, care providers will usually implement procedures they approve with greater integrity as compared to procedures they do not prefer (Gresham & Lopez, 1996; Kazdin, 1980).

However, preferred interventions or those rated as highly acceptable may not represent the most *effective* procedures for treating violence and aggression. Specifically, effective intervention plans often combine multiple procedures and may be more effortful to implement than less procedurally demanding and complex alternatives. This distinction between preference and effectiveness can be addressed through social validity assessment in order to inform decisions about intervention choices of care providers and service recipients themselves (Hanley, 2010).

Yet another reason to conduct social validity assessment in cases of violence and aggression is affirming or justifying intervention procedures relative to treatment objectives. Of course, the clinical goal is to eliminate offending behavior so that physical harm to others is stopped, further risk is curtailed, and service recipients achieve a better quality of life. But intervention success may not rest exclusively with elimination, rather a *reduction* in frequency and intensity of violence and aggression for extended periods of time and within the least restrictive setting. This alignment of treatment objectives with intervention procedures should be a strong focus of social validity assessment.

Social validity assessment preceding intervention for violence and aggression can additionally query care providers about possible barriers and obstacles to effective treatment. For example, there may be concerns that a service setting does not have sufficiently trained personnel to intervene properly, lacks requisite resources, or needs supplemental supports in order to maintain safety. An appraisal of these and similar impediments contributes to risk management and prevention as vital components of violence and aggression intervention protocols.

This chapter begins with an historical overview of social validity in ABA and clinical psychology, highlighting seminal concepts and principles that have defined contemporary assessment methods. Another section of the chapter reviews research examples of social validity assessment in the area of violence and aggression among persons with neurodevelopmental disabilities. Next, I present several methodologies for conducting social validity assessment with care providers, other stakeholders, and service recipients, whenever possible. The chapter concludes with a summary of social validity assessment recommendations within ABA practice and research.

Overview and Historical Context

Wolf (1978) published a trend-setting article in the *Journal of Applied Behavior Analysis* titled, "Social Validity: The Case for Subjective Assessment or How Behavior Analysis is Finding It's Heart." Referencing ABA's dedication to problems of social significance (Baer, Wolf, & Risley, 1968), he proposed, "If we aspire to social importance, then we must develop systems that allow our consumers to provide us feedback about how our applications relate to their values, to their reinforcers" (p. 2). Wolf further stated that subjective measurement would be a reasonable approach to assess complex consumer preferences in "socially acceptable and practical ways." Put simply, his organizing message was that ABA should and could achieve its core commitments by asking consumers what they "liked" and "disliked" about the services proposed for them, how those services were delivered, and the effects of services on meaningful life measures.

Unfortunately, the proposed inclusion of social validity assessment within the objective and empirical measurement foundation of ABA was not received positively by many professionals four decades ago. Critics claimed that subjective data may not relate to observed behavior, could be inaccurate, and represented hypothetical "internal variables" that most behavior analysts discounted at the time. As counterargument, Wolf (1978) reasoned that people can learn to be more reliable reporters through correspondence ("say-do") training. Further, a person's opinions and attitudes are reasonable outcome measures when evaluating the effects of behavioral intervention, as in "I liked the program but it was hard to implement," or "Maybe not all of the procedures are necessary," or "The effects of intervention did not last." Asking-inquiring about objectives, procedures, and results also builds positive relationships and cooperation among service recipients and care providers. In summary, Wolf (1978) communicated persuasively to ABA professionals that data-based measurement of intervention effects combined with the impressions of the people receiving and implementing procedures represented the most comprehensive approach to program evaluation with individuals, groups, and systems.

Over the years, commentary about social validity assessment expanded. Finney (1991) wrote that "Wolf's (1978) paper on social validity changed most behavior analyst's views about how to judge the importance of research findings" (p. 245). Van Houten (1979) emphasized the contribution of social validity assessment "to determine the optimal levels for target behaviors" (p. 581) both preceding and following intervention. Additional points by Fawcett (1991) concentrated on the broad social goals of programs, behavioral categories subsumed by those goals, and specific procedures comprising these categories. Hawkins (1991) also discussed the social acceptability of procedures such as practicality, satisfaction, and cost-effectiveness during post-intervention assessment.

With the evolution and increasing acceptance of social validity within the ABA professional community following Wolf (1978), Schwartz and Baer (1991) published an extensive article of recommended practice standards. They summarized several key dimensions of social validity assessment methodology.

Scope and Direction. Ideally, are the goals of intervention important and relevant "to desired lifestyle changes" because they are reasonable, likely to be achieved, and norm referenced? On the same theme, acceptability should be assessed by asking whether procedures are practical, time-efficient, easy to implement, non-stigmatizing, and able to be generalized to other individuals and settings. Additional objectives for social validity assessment relate to satisfaction of intervention outcomes, absence of negative side effects from intervention, and whether intervention results persist long term.

Consumer Populations. Service recipients and their care providers are the primary targets of social validity assessment. However, Schwartz and Baer (1991) advised that "many people other than the program recipients are passive consumers of treatment programs" (p. 193). These populations include (a) indirect consumers who are responsible for program operations (e.g., administrators, center directors, school principals), (b) members of the immediate community (e.g., neighbors, restaurant staff, transportation drivers), and (c) "people who do not know or interact with direct-indirect consumers but live in the same community" (p. 194). By drawing on the broadest base of consumers, social validity assessment can capture information from collective sources and guide satisfactory and successful practices for individuals, groups, and society at large.

Accuracy. Accurate social validity assessment does not assess the opinions of the wrong community, incorrectly assess the opinions of the proper community, or correctly assess the opinions of the proper community but not incorporate the feedback to affect change. Schwartz and Baer (1991) also referenced *social invalidity* "as the behaviors of consumers who not only disapprove of some component in the ongoing program but are going to do something about their disapproval" (p. 190). Accordingly, accurate and socially valid assessment must elicit truthful reporting from consumers that encourages valued actions, does not dissuade complaints or dissatisfaction, and improves the procedures and policies governing intervention.

In addition to recommending more expansive social validity assessment that accurately addresses a greater breadth of consumers, Schwartz and Baer (1991) stressed that objectives, methods, and anticipated outcomes should be identified before intervention is introduced and throughout implementation. Construction of social validity questionnaires and surveys (detailed in a later section of the chapter) should consider wide variation of consumer responses, require differential responding, specify the period of time being assessed, and "address all the dimensions pertinent to the acceptability and viability of a program" (p. 198). Finally, it is expected that accurate social validity ratings of satisfaction or disapproval will correlate with direct intervention measures and effects. In illustration, care providers would likely report high approval of ABA intervention that eliminated aggressive behavior of adults at a residential treatment setting.

Acknowledging the "roots" of social validity within the discipline of ABA, Foster and Mash (1999) reviewed assessment of intervention goals, procedures, and results in clinical treatment research. Judgements about the goals of intervention can be derived from normative comparisons and subjective evaluations by the consumers of treatment services. Common social validity assessments of intervention acceptability have included ratings of hypothetical case vignettes and self-report satisfaction questionnaires. Foster and Mash (1999) included many informative and fine-grained analyses of what social validity represented at the time of publication, concluding that "Although social validity assessments began with behavior analysts struggling with issues involving the acceptability and importance of treatment goals, procedures and outcomes in clinical outcome research will help investigators both to explore how various aspects of social validity of interventions can be enhanced and to narrow the gap between research information and practice needs" (p. 17). This appraisal certainly has relevance for ABA treatment of violence and aggression in persons with neurodevelopmental disabilities as many behavior analysts routinely collaborate with non-behavioral clinicians when formulating, implementing, and evaluating treatment plans (Luiselli, 2018).

Apropos to research, Horner et al. (2005) advised that social validity assessment should include dependent measures deemed socially important and interventions must be practical as well as produce socially relevant outcomes. Other criteria applied to social validity in a research context are that natural care providers implement the intervention procedures within typical (i.e., non-simulated) settings and during lengthy periods of time. The implication from these guidelines is that socially valid research must produce practices that are not only effective but can be applied with fidelity within conventional settings that treat service recipients.

Finally, a fairly robust research literature has accumulated on social validity, primarily treatment acceptability, of behavior reduction procedures within ABA (Carter, 2007; Elliott, 1998; Kazdin, 1981; Reimers & Wacker, 1988; Witt & Martens, 1983). Social validity assessment in these studies has featured non-professional respondents to written case illustrations and fewer instances of raters who actually implemented intervention procedures. Yet, it is noteworthy that several consistent findings emerged from this research and reflect contemporary conclusions about treatment acceptability, especially for care providers intervening with persons who are violent and aggressive:

1. Reinforcement-based intervention procedures rather than punishment procedures are rated as more acceptable for decreasing challenging behaviors. The consensus is that respondents more readily accept intervention procedures that rely on pleasurable consequences to increase appropriate behaviors compared to negative consequences applied to challenging behaviors.
2. Simple, time-efficient, and non-stigmatizing intervention procedures are rated as more acceptable than multicomponent and effortful behavior reduction plans.

These acceptable intervention procedures also require less time to train and have "good fit" within service settings.
3. Acceptability ratings are often influenced by the severity of the behavior requiring treatment. In effect, respondents judge invasive and restrictive interventions procedures as acceptable if such treatment is directed at dangerous and harmful challenging behaviors.
4. The effectiveness of treatment can impact ratings of acceptability. That is, treatment success independent of the types of intervention procedures strongly impacts acceptance.
5. Treatment acceptability ratings by care providers before intervention may not correlate with or predict their preference for intervention procedures during and following implementation.
6. The occurrence of adverse side effects from intervention is associated with less favorable ratings of treatment acceptability.

However, notwithstanding the evolving prominence of social validity assessment and resulting practice recommendations, articles in peer-reviewed journals reporting social validation remain low, in the range of 12–25% (Carr, Austin, Britton, Kellum, & Bailey, 1999; Ferguson et al., 2018; Kennedy, 1992). This situation is unfortunate because research should inform practice and guide decisions about many facets of intervention, including assessment and evaluation. It can be fairly concluded that research descriptions of how social validity assessment was formulated and implemented on a clinical level are overlooked in the extant literature and in need of correction.

Research Review

As it pertains to social validity assessment in neurodevelopmental disabilities, the only substantive research within ABA treatment of violence and aggression has concerned attitudes and opinions about physical restraint, herein defined as manual and behavior-contingent immobilization of a person's voluntary movement. Of course, physical restraint is customarily reserved as an emergency or planned intervention for seriously challenging behavior, should be clinically justified based on demonstrated ineffectiveness of less restrictive procedures, and must always be applied concurrently with methods to teach adaptive skills (Luiselli, 2011b; Reed et al., 2013; Sturmey, 2009). Notably, treatment acceptability of physical restraint remains a controversial topic within the community of neurodevelopmental disabilities service providers and policy makers and accordingly, should be a priority for social validity assessment among many consumer groups (Chan, Webber, & French, 2014; Rickard, Chan, & Merriam, 2013).

McDonnell and Sturmey (2000) evaluated the social validity of physical restraint among three consumer groups composed of special education staff at two schools for students with developmental disabilities ($N = 41$), residential care providers in hospital and community settings for persons with intellectual disability ($N = 47$), and professionally inexperienced high school pupils ($N = 74$). The participants in this research viewed three brief (18 s) video recordings of an adult male attempting to pull the hair of a care provider who was assisted by a second care provider in applying two methods of floor restraint and one method of chair restraint. After watching each video recording, the research participants completed the Treatment Evaluation Inventory (TEI: Kazdin, 1980) to document their acceptability of the three restraint methods. All three groups rated the chair restraint more favorably than floor restraint with no statistically significant differences found between the two methods of applying physical restraint on the floor.

Cunningham, McDonnell, Easton, and Sturmey (2003) assessed the opinions of undergraduate students ($N = 24$), residential care staff ($N = 21$), and adults with intellectual disability ($N = 18$) concerning the same three methods of physical restraint depicted in the McDonnell and Sturmey (2000) study. Social validity ratings were derived by asking the research participants two questions following their viewing of the video recordings: (1) "How would you feel if you saw this happening," and (2) "How would you feel if this happened to you?" Ratings were quantified on a 5-point satisfaction scale in which "1" indicated high satisfaction and "5" indicated dissatisfaction. Additionally, the research participants rated paired comparisons of the physical restraint methods such that acceptability could be ranked ordered. Results were that chair restraint was rated as more acceptable than floor restraint among the three participant groups, thus replicating the findings reported by McDonnell and Sturmey (2000).

In a study with care providers ($N = 25$) of adults who had intellectual disability and challenging behavior including aggression, Luiselli, Sperry, and Draper (2015) designed a social validity questionnaire to solicit opinions about rationale-justification, training, safety, and implementation effectiveness of physical restraint. The questionnaire included 12 statements that the research participants responded to on a 5-point rating scale (1: strongly disagree, 2: disagree, 3; neither disagree or agree, 4: agree, 5: strongly agree). The study results, shown in Table 1, revealed generally high ratings of approval, satisfaction, and effectiveness. Factors to consider in interpreting these findings are that all but one of the 25 research participants were experienced implementers of physical restraint who worked in an adult-care setting that had comprehensive and carefully supervised standards for applying physical intervention with service recipients. The same or similar results might not be obtained among less experienced care providers and in settings with less rigorous policies and procedures.

Related research by Luiselli, Sperry, Draper, and Richards (2017) surveyed parents-guardians ($N = 27$) of adults who had intellectual disability about physical restraint implementation for aggression and other challenging behaviors at a community-based habilitation setting. This social validity assessment featured a questionnaire similar to Luiselli et al. (2015) which sampled opinions about the rationale-justification, training, implementation, and effectiveness of physical restraint. The consumer sample was also divided into parent-guardian groups who reported that their daughter/son had or had not experienced physical restraint. Both

Table 1 Average ratings on social validity questionnaire completed by care providers of adults with intellectual and developmental disabilities ($N = 25$)

Statement	Average rating
Physical restraint should only be used if less intensive intervention procedures have failed	4.5
I am able to implement physical restraint safely without harming the person being held	4.4
I am confident implementing physical restraint	4.4
Physical restraint is sometimes needed to ensure safety of the adults we serve	4.3
Physical restraint is an effective intervention procedure	4.3
The training I received taught me how to properly implement physical restraint	4.3
I am able to implement physical restraint safely without harming myself	4.3
The training I received taught me to use physical restraint as one component of a comprehensive behavior support plan	4.2
If needed, physical restraint can be adapted to ensure safety and minimal to no risk	4.2
The training I received taught me methods to avoid using physical restraint	4.0
Physical restraint is an acceptable procedure for behavior support	3.9
Effective use of physical restraint makes it possible for clients to make progress and achieve a better quality of life	3.6

From Luiselli, J. K., Sperry, J. S., & Draper, C. (2015). Social validity assessment of physical restraint intervention by care-providers of adults with intellectual and developmental disabilities. *Behavior Analysis in Practice*, 8, 170–175
1 = strongly disagree, 2 = disagree, 3 = neither disagree or agree, 4 = agree, 5 = strongly agree

groups agreed that physical restraint should only be used if less restrictive procedures had failed and physical restraint can be adapted to ensure safety during application. The two groups were less convinced that physical restraint is effective and that such intervention makes it possible to achieve a better quality of life.

The research concerned with physical restraint represents one direction of social validity assessment in the treatment of violence and aggression in persons with neurodevelopmental disabilities. As described, studies have emphasized acceptability of different physical restraint procedures, intervention objectives, risk-benefit analysis, and effectiveness. These same areas can and should be assessed for other behavioral interventions that are commonly implemented in service settings, for example, response blocking, redirection, and escape extinction (Vollmer, Peters, & Slocum, 2015). It is also true that social validity assessment of ABA training methods can inform content and instruction with care provider trainees (Luiselli, Bass, & Whitcomb, 2010) and would be especially valuable guiding physical management and prevention training that concentrates on violence and aggression (Lennox, Green, & Rourke, 2011).

A related area of social validity research has considered the procedures ABA professionals use when conducting clinical assessment and supervision of care providers. Langthorne and McGill (2011) examined the acceptability of functional analysis procedures (Chok, Weiss, Harper, Bird, & Luiselli, 2019) with children who had developmental disabilities and displayed aggression, self-injury, and other challenging behaviors. Teachers and parents ($N = 13$) recorded social validity ratings on a modified version of the Treatment Acceptability Rating Form-Revised (TARF-R: Reimers and Wacker 1988) according to a 5-point scale ranging from "strongly disagree" to "strongly agree." Average ratings by the respondents endorsed functional analysis as an acceptable, effective, and recommended assessment method. These findings are particularly relevant for clinicians, consultants, and other ABA practitioners responsible for intervention planning in cases of violence and aggression, namely approval of functional analysis by a primary consumer group of treatment services.

Yet another example of social validity assessment applied with care providers is acceptance of performance management interventions conducted by supervisors. Codding, Feinberg, Dunn, and Pace (2005) recorded procedural fidelity of teachers ($N = 5$) implementing behavior support plans with students who had brain injuries, aggression, property destruction, and related challenging behaviors. A combination of scheduled observations, performance feedback, praise, and correction by a supervisor improved procedural fidelity among all teachers. Crucial to this study was a post-intervention social validity assessment and results indicating that "the teachers strongly agreed with items related to the purposes and procedures as well as the benefits of the intervention outcomes on their skills and subsequent impact on their students" (p. 213).

Similar assessments have been conducted with care providers to identify performance improvement procedures they perceive as being most effective and appealing *preceding* implementation of a supervisory intervention. Strohmeier, Mule, and Luiselli (2014) completed such evaluation with special education care providers ($N = 44$) at a school for children with neurodevelopmental disabilities. Supervisors at the school were interested in identifying training methods the care providers believed would improve their implementation integrity of student behavior support plans. The social validity assessment consisted of a rating questionnaire about perceived effectiveness, satisfaction, and acceptability of four strategies: (a) receiving performance feedback, (b) completing online training modules, (c) working toward a financial incentive, and (d) avoiding future meetings with a supervisor. Among these choices, performance feedback was rated as the most effective and acceptable strategy, suggesting that the supervisors should adopt this method to improve intervention integrity. Following performance feedback, the supervisors could directly observe the care providers implementing behavior support plans to ascertain whether performance reflects their assessed preferences.

Assessment Methodologies

Various *subjective* measures of social validity have dominated ABA practice. Interviews with single individuals or more than one person in a group are relatively easy to arrange in most circumstances (Carter, Moss, Hoffman, Chung, & Sisco,

2011). However, there may be procedural inconsistency between and among interviewers, especially if they do not follow a standard script or engage in dissimilar conversation with respondents. Another limitation is that face-to-face interaction with an interviewer could bias or otherwise affect the objectivity of respondents. Similarly, some people may be reluctant to discuss their attitudes and opinions during individual and group interviews.

There are several empirically researched rating scales and forms for assessing social validity, typically constructed with behavior-specific indicators and respective numerical ratings. Measures of treatment acceptability include the Treatment Evaluation Inventory (TEI: Kazdin, 1980), Intervention Rating Profile-20 (IRP-20: Witt, Martens, & Elliot, 1984), and Treatment Acceptability Rating Form-Revised (TARF-R: Reimers, Wacker, & Cooper, 1991). These and related instruments were developed principally to acquire acceptability ratings of child-focused treatments from teachers and parents. The strong psychometric properties (internal consistency, factor structure) and relative ease of administration and scoring are notable advantages of such protocols. These forms and inventories produce global ratings and may have to be adapted for greater sensitivity to intervention concerns that arise in ABA treatment of violence and aggression in neurodevelopmental disabilities.

Unlike the TEI, ITR-20, and TARF-R, the social validity assessments conducted by Cunningham et al. (2003), Luiselli et al. (2015, 2017), and Strohmeier et al. (2014) are examples of non-empirically researched methods that were designed for explicit areas of clinical interest in those studies. Figure 1 illustrates such a form that can be used at the intervention planning stage for a child or adult who demonstrates violence and aggression. Specifically, the form asks care providers to confirm intervention objectives and recommendations as well as propose procedural alternatives, suggest additional program resources, and cite potential implementation barriers that need to be overcome. For a clinician or consultant involved with intervention formulation, this assessment tool is invaluable in gathering information with high social validity from the persons who will be conducting treatment.

Figure 2 is another clinically specific social validity assessment form, in this case to evaluate care provider reactions to a behavior support plan they implemented with an aggressive student at school. The care providers endorse one of five numerical ratings that quantify acceptance and satisfaction with different elements of the behavior support plan (e.g., comprehension, training, effectiveness). The form also requests that the care providers briefly explain any unfavorable ratings and provide additional comments at their discretion. This feedback informs decisions about intervention, for example, simplifying procedures or revising training strategies in situations where care providers consistently record lower acceptance ratings. The ability to tailor social validity assessment to unique clinical challenges and exigencies is perhaps the chief advantage of these forms.

One *direct* measure of social validity is observing the behavior of normative populations to determine reasonable intervention objectives and outcomes with service recipients. Comparative measurement applies well to several performance indicators such as communication, interpersonal, and leisure skills. However, the same

Child-Adult:	
Setting:	
Intervention Target: AGGRESSION: Physical contact with the hands towards another person in the form of a slap, punch, grab, or hair pull	
Respondent Name:	
Date:	

Assessment Information		
Assessment Questions	YES or NO	Explanation
Do you approve of the intervention objectives?		
Are recommendations appropriate for intervention target?		
Do you suggest changing any of the intervention recommendations?		
Will you require additional resources to implement intervention recommendations?		
Do you anticipate any barriers to implementing intervention recommendations?		

Proposed Intervention Recommendations
1:
2:
3:
4:
5:

Fig. 1 Pre-intervention social validity assessment form

tactic does not translate as well to the treatment of violence and aggression because the accepted social norm is the absence of such behavior.

A service recipient's preference for particular intervention procedures is another method of social validation through direct measurement. Hanley (2010) described a concurrent-chains methodology in which children are exposed to two or more behavior-change procedures that are correlated with conspicuous stimuli such as colored poster boards or interventionists wearing different colored jerseys. After the children experience the intervention procedures, (a) smaller versions of the linked stimuli (e.g., colored cards or micro-switches) are made available to them in a separate location, (b) they select the most preferred intervention procedure, and (c) that intervention procedure is subsequently implemented in the original treatment setting. With this methodology, "preference for behavior-change procedures, which

Child-Adult:
Setting:
Respondent Name (or anonymous):
Date:

Instructions: Please record your opinions about the behavior support plan (BSP) you implemented with the child-adult during September-December 2018 to treat aggression by checking one rating for each statement.

Statements	Ratings				
	1: Strongly Disagree	2: Disagree	3: No Opinion	4: Agree	5: Agree
The BSP was easy to learn and I understood all of the procedures					
If you selected Rating #1 or #2, please explain:					
The BSP procedures were easy to implement					
If you selected Rating #1 or #2, please explain:					
The BSP properly addressed intervention objectives					
If you selected Rating #1 or #2, please explain:					
I was trained effectively to implement the BSP					
If you selected Rating #1 or #2, please explain:					
The child-adult responded positively to the BSP					
If you selected Rating #1 or #2, please explain:					
I would recommend the BSP for other children-adults					
If you selected Rating #1 or #2, please explain:					
Additional Comments					

Fig. 2 Intervention social validity assessment form

are difficult to describe to young children, are directly assessed by recording each child's selection of cues correlated with the behavior-change procedures" (p. 15). With this assessment methodology, intervention preference corresponds to treatment acceptance and can be compared and contrasted to demonstrated behavior change.

Intervention preference as a direct measure of social validity also extends to care providers. Davis, Reichle, and Southard (2000) evaluated the effects of a high-probability (high-p) instructional sequence and non-contingent access to preferred items as two intervention procedures to improve transition compliance of classroom students. Although both procedures were effective and the care providers rated them as acceptable, they demonstrated preference for the high-probability instructional sequence by implementing it more frequently. Similarly, Gabor, Fritz, Roath, Rothe, and Gourley (2016) trained care providers to implement non-contingent reinforcement (NCR), differential reinforcement of other behavior (DRO), and differential reinforcement of alternative behavior (DRA), then had them rate acceptability of each procedure before implementation with children. After demonstrating 90% of greater intervention integrity, the care providers were allowed to choose from among the three procedures preceding child sessions. Results of the study did not reveal a clear and consistent relationship between procedural effectiveness and acceptance among the care providers.

Identifying intervention preferences of service recipients and care providers provides objective measurement of socially valid procedures but to date, only a few studies have conducted such assessment for violence and aggression and the research has been confined to young children with autism and intellectual disability (Hanley, Piazza, Fisher, Contrucci, & Maglieri, 1997; Hanley, Piazza, Fisher, & Maglieri, 2005). Consider, too, the early admonition by Schwartz and Baer (1991) that "Valid choice requires that the consumer have extensive experience with all the alternatives, that all the alternatives are equally effective, and that all alternatives are easily available" (p. 200). In many service settings, these conditions may not be possible, arranging them could be prohibitive, and assessment with dangerous and high-risk service recipients contraindicated.

The continuation and maintenance of intervention procedures by care providers is another direct measure of social validity that can be incorporated on a practical level (Gresham & Lopez, 1996; Kennedy, 2002). The rationale for this approach is that care providers would be expected to persistently follow procedures and treatment plans they prefer compared to methods they do not like as much. However, preference by itself may not be sufficient to explain intervention longevity without considering long-term treatment success. That is, treatment success that is not sustained would appear to have a negative influence on care provider preference regardless of other desirable components of intervention.

Summary and Conclusions

Social validity assessment is a vital and mandatory component of ABA treatment for violence and aggression in persons with neurodevelopmental disabilities. Feedback about intervention objectives, methods, and outcomes from service recipients, care providers, and the larger community is influential for guiding treatment, training, and standards of care. Although integration of social validity assessment within ABA practice and research has grown (Common & Lane, 2017), implementation in the area of violence and aggression is insufficient despite the high-risk concerns posed by this clinical problem and acceptance of methods to deliver treatment effectively, safely, and ethically (Luiselli, 2011a).

On one hand, poor integration of social validity assessment in clinical settings may be the result of several factors. First, some ABA practitioners possibly lack training about how to conduct social validity assessment as a component of routine practice. Their inexperience could be further complicated by limited-to-no-direction from organizational leaders, themselves uneducated about social validity and assessment methodologies. Relative to research endeavors, efforts may be hampered by the types of studies implemented with persons who receive ABA treatment of violence and aggression. Research dissemination might also be compromised by editorial policies which do not clarify parameters applied to social validity assessment.

Several recommendations, presented in this concluding section, are intended to promote assessment of social validity in both practice and research domains.

Practice Recommendations

At the forefront of practice recommendations is behavior analysts, psychologists, and clinicians advocating for social validity assessment in their routine treatment activities with service recipients. Any properly formulated ABA intervention for violence and aggression will specify target measures and respective data recording but social validity should be assessed just as systematically. Beyond individual cases, it is also the responsibility of ABA professionals to educate operations and administrative personnel about the merits of social validity assessment as a facet of continuous quality improvement (CQI) in treatment settings serving high-risk clinical populations.

Most social validity assessment in practice relies on subjective measurement through interviews with and distribution of questionnaires and surveys to care providers. Schwartz and Baer (1991) proposed several guidelines for preparing assessment materials and Luiselli (2018) suggested steps that clinicians and consultants should take with care providers.

1. Whenever possible, conduct social validity assessment preceding, during, and following intervention. Each of these distinct time points will generate feedback from respondents unique to intervention planning, implementation, and outcome. Table 2 depicts some common assessment targets and objectives specific to pre-intervention, intervention, and post-intervention phases.
2. Design a social validity assessment questionnaire that ideally is a single page, double-spaced if needed, but not lengthier so that respondents are not overwhelmed by the format.
3. Include between 6 and 8 statements or inquiries on the questionnaire, written in behavior-specific language that is easily understood and confined to a single sentence. Some examples are "I approve the positive reinforcement procedure of the behavior support plan," and "Did the training you received teach you the necessary skills to implement intervention?"

Table 2 Social validity assessment targets and objectives

Intervention phase	Targets and objectives
Pre-intervention	• Explanation of intervention objectives
	• Description of intervention behaviors
	• Intervention risk-benefit analysis
	• Perceived obstacles and barriers to intervention
	• Preparation of written intervention guidelines
Intervention	• Implementation of intervention procedures
	• Data recording procedures
	• Intervention evaluation strategies
	• Intervention side effects
	• Intervention training and supervision
	• Service recipient(s) response to intervention
Post-intervention	• Intervention effects: generalization
	• Intervention effects: maintenance
	• Impressions of indirect consumers
	• Intervention fading

4. Have respondents record a numerical rating for each statement and inquiry on the questionnaire. Four-to-seven point Likert-type scales are usually sufficient to support differential responding, in formats such as 1: strongly disagree, 2: disagree, 3: neither disagree or agree, 4: agree, and 5: strongly agree, or 1: poor, 2: fair, 3: good, and 4: very good.
5. As illustrated in Figs. 1 and 2, ask respondents to briefly explain why they endorsed any unfavorable ratings. Also add a "comments" section to encourage narrative responses and further feedback that touches on social validity.
6. Allow the option of respondents writing their name on the questionnaire or completing the questionnaire anonymously.
7. Be specific about the time period covered by the questionnaire, for example, "Please record your ratings for the 8 months of clinical services provided to the group home."
8. Explain the social validity assessment process to respondents, emphasizing the desire to document their feedback and recommendations for improving intervention planning, implementation, and outcome. Respondents should also be advised that participation is voluntary and does not constitute a performance appraisal related to their employment.
9. Several methods for distributing a questionnaire are possible depending in part on the number of respondents, needed resources, and practical constraints:

    (a) In-person group meetings enable a clinician, supervisor, or consultant to assemble respondents, hand out the questionnaire, guarantee independent

responding, and ensure 100% return rate. A possible disadvantage is response bias or reactivity among respondents that is occasioned by the presence of the group leader.
(b) Respondents can be requested to complete a questionnaire independently and return it to a designated location (e.g., office mailbox) on or before a deadline date. This method avoids the social influences of group meetings but does not control for possible conferencing by respondents. A further limitation is respondents not returning questionnaires on time or at all.
(c) Questionnaires can be distributed via email correspondence with a requested return date. However, this approach does not guarantee the anonymity of respondents or timely completion. Using free web-based survey services is an option that is private although the issue of return remains.

10. Quantifying questionnaire ratings and categorizing respondent explanations and comments are the end products of social validity assessment that either support elements of intervention or direct necessary revisions. Post-assessment review with respondents is helpful, allowing them to elaborate on their questionnaire ratings and feedback. Absent such interactions, the professionals responsible for intervention must aggregate questionnaire responses, rank-order areas of practice that must improve, and establish a problem-solving approach to resolution. Of many possible decisions, questionnaire results may lead to changing the content of training sessions conducted with care providers, revising the format of written intervention guidelines, introducing new procedures for supervising treatments, or considering alternative evaluation methodologies.

Research Recommendations

Several recommendations are needed to promote social validity assessment research within ABA generally and specifically with treatment of violence and aggression in persons who have neurodevelopmental disabilities. First, a suggestion by Carr et al. (1999) was having editorial guidelines of peer-reviewed journals specify social validity inclusion criteria expected in studies submitted for publication. Relatedly, the importance of social validity assessment could be emphasized to editorial board members and ad hoc consultants responsible for reviewing manuscripts. Hanley (2010) also proposed several pertinent guidelines (e.g., two or more interventions are equally effective, a more effective procedure is less preferred) and Ferguson et al. (2018) cogently opined that "including guidelines such as these could potentially increase the number of articles reporting social validity measures in behavior analytic journals" (p. 8). These direct efforts by editors and reviewers would very likely heighten the awareness of social validity assessment among ABA researchers and graduate students seeking publications in reputable journals.

Ferguson et al. (2018) further commented about possible reluctance of behavior analysts to include measures of social validity when conducting research. As a valuable research project itself, surveys could be conducted to determine when, how, and why ABA professionals incorporate social validity assessment within research. Survey results could have substantive impact on inclusion of social validity assessment in future research by disseminating findings to organizations such as the Behavior Analyst Certification Board (BACB), Association for Behavior Analysis International (ABAI), and Association of Professional Behavior Analysts (APBA). In consequence, these organizations could advocate for greater representation of social validity research at annual conferences and professional training workshops.

Finally, with few exceptions, research has rarely conducted social validity assessment with the service recipients of ABA treatment. Cunningham et al. (2003) surveyed the impressions of adults with intellectual disability about physical restraint and Hanley (2010) summarized direct observation measures to assess intervention preferences of children with developmental disorders. For many persons who have neurodevelopmental disabilities, the process of assessing their acceptance of and satisfaction with treatment is not easy given the prevalence of cognitive and communication limitations in the population. Nonetheless, in keeping with the original premise of social validity Wolf (1978) introduced to ABA professionals, service recipients represent the primary consumers of treatment, their opinions, attitudes, and recommendations matter greatly, and what they have to say should guide program decisions that have greatest impact on their quality of life.

References

Baer, D. M., Wolf, M. M., & Risley, T. R. (1968). Some current dimensions of applied behavior analysis. *Journal of Applied Behavior Analysis, 1*, 91–97.

Behavior Analyst Certification Board (2017). Professional and ethical compliance code for behavior analysts. Littleton, CO: Behavior Analyst Certification Board..

Carr, J. E., Austin, J. L., Britton, L. N., Kellum, K. K., & Bailey, J. S. (1999). An assessment of social validity trends in applied behavior analysis. *Behavioral Interventions, 14*, 223–231.

Carter, E. W., Moss, C. K., Hoffman, A., Chung, Y. C., & Sisco, L. (2011). Efficacy and social validity of peer support arrangements for adolescents with disabilities. *Exceptional Children, 78*, 107–125.

Carter, S. L. (2007). Review of recent treatment acceptability research. *Education and Treatment of Children, 42*, 301–316.

Chan, J., Webber, L., & French, P. (2014). The importance of safeguarding the rights and the role of legislation: The Australian perspective. In S. Karim (Ed.), *A human rights perspective on reducing restrictive procedures in intellectual disabilities and autism spectrum disorders* (pp. 53–72). Birmingham, UK: British Institute of learning Disabilities.

Chok, J., Weiss, M. J., Harper, J. M., Bird, F., & Luiselli, J. K. (2019). *Functional analysis: A practitioner's guide to implementation and training*. New York: Elsevier/Academic Press.

Codding, R. S., Feinberg, A. B., Dunn, E. K., & Pace, G. M. (2005). Effects of immediate performance feedback on implementation of behavior support plans. *Journal of Applied Behavior Analysis, 38*, 205–219.

Common, E. A., & Lane, K. L. (2017). Social validity assessment. In J. K. Luiselli (Ed.), *Applied behavior analysis advanced guidebook: A manual for professional practice* (pp. 73–92). New York: Elsevier/Academic Press.

Cunningham, J., McDonnell, A., Easton, S., & Sturmey, P. (2003). Social validation data on three methods of physical restraint: Views of consumers, staff, and students. *Research in Developmental Disabilities, 24*, 307–316.

Davis, C. A., Reichle, J. E., & Southard, K. L. (2000). High-probability requests and a preferred item as a distractor: Increasing successful transitions in children with behavior problems. *Education and Treatment of Children, 23*, 423–440.

Elliott, S. N. (1998). Acceptability of behavioral treatments: Review of variables that influence treatment selection. *Professional Psychology: Research and Practice, 19*, 68–80.

Fawcett, S. B. (1991). Social validity: A note on methodology. *Journal of Applied Behavior Analysis, 24*, 235–239.

Ferguson, J. L., Cihon, J. H., Leaf, J. B., Van Meter, S. M., McEachin, J., & Leaf, R. (2018). Assessment of social validity trends in the journal of applied behavior analysis. *European Journal of Behavior Analysis, 29*, 146–157.

Finney, J. W. (1991). On further development of the concept of social validity. *Journal of Applied Behavior Analysis, 24*, 245–249.

Foster, S. L., & Mash, E. J. (1999). Assessing social validity in clinical treatment research: Issues and procedures. *Journal of Consulting and Clinical Psychology, 67*, 308–319.

Gabor, A. M., Fritz, J. N., Roath, C. T., Rothe, B. R., & Gourley, D. A. (2016). Caregiver preference for reinforcement-based interventions for problem behavior maintained by positive reinforcement. *Journal of Applied Behavior Analysis, 49*, 215–227.

Gresham, F. M., & Lopez, M. F. (1996). Social validation: A unifying construct for school-based consultation research and practice. *School Psychology Quarterly, 11*, 204–227.

Hanley, G. P. (2010). Toward effective and preferred programming: A case for the objective measurement of social validity with recipients of behavior-change programs. *Behavior Analysis in Practice, 3*, 13–21.

Hanley, G. P., Piazza, C. C., Fisher, W. W., Contrucci, S. A., & Maglieri, K. M. (1997). Evaluation of client preference for function-based treatments. *Journal of Applied Behavior Analysis, 30*, 459–473.

Hanley, G. P., Piazza, C. C., Fisher, W. W., & Maglieri, K. M. (2005). On the effectiveness of and preference for punishment and extinction components of function-based interventions. *Journal of Applied Behavior Analysis, 38*, 51–66.

Hawkins, R. (1991). Is social validity what we are interested in? Argument for a functional approach. *Journal of Applied Behavior Analysis, 24*, 205–213.

Horner, R. H., Carr, E. G., Halle, J., McGee, G., Odom, S., & Wolery, M. (2005). The use of single-subject research to identify evidenced-based practice in special education. *Exceptional Children, 71*, 165–179.

Kazdin, A. E. (1977). Assessing the clinical or applied importance of behavior change through social validation. *Behavior Modification, 1*, 427–452.

Kazdin, A. E. (1980). Acceptability of alternative treatments for deviant child behavior. *Journal of Applied Behavior Analysis, 13*, 259–273.

Kazdin, A. E. (1981). Acceptability of child treatment techniques: The influence of treatment efficacy and adverse side effects. *Behavior Therapy, 12*, 493–506.

Kennedy, C. H. (1992). Trends in the measurement of social validity. *The Behavior Analyst, 15*, 147–156.

Kennedy, C. H. (2002). The maintenance of behavior change as an indicator of social validity. *Behavior Modification, 26*, 594–604.

Langthorne, P., & McGill, P. (2011). Assessing the social acceptability of the functional analysis of problem behavior. *Journal of Applied Behavior Analysis, 44*, 403–407.

Lennox, D., Green, M., & Rourke, D. (2011). Emergency physical restraint: Considerations for staff training and supervision. In J. K. Luiselli (Ed.), *The handbook of high-risk challeng-*

ing behaviors in intellectual and developmental disabilities (pp. 271–134). Baltimore: Paul H. Brookes.

Luiselli, J. K. (Ed.). (2011a). *The handbook of high-risk challenging behaviors in intellectual and developmental disabilities.* Baltimore: Paul H. Brookes.

Luiselli, J. K. (2011b). Therapeutic implementation of physical restraint. In J. K. Luiselli (Ed.), *The handbook of high-risk challenging behaviors in intellectual and developmental disabilities* (pp. 243–256). Baltimore: Paul H. Brookes.

Luiselli, J. K. (2018). *Conducting behavioral consultation in educational and treatment settings.* New York: Elsevier/Academic Press.

Luiselli, J. K., Bass, J., & Whitcomb, S. (2010). Training knowledge competencies to direct-care service providers: Outcome assessment and social validation of a training program. *Behavior Modification, 34*, 403–414.

Luiselli, J. K., Sperry, J. S., & Draper, C. (2015). Social validity assessment of physical restraint intervention by care-providers of adults with intellectual and developmental disabilities. *Behavior Analysis in Practice, 8*, 170–175.

Luiselli, J. K., Sperry, J. S., Draper, C., & Richards, C. (2017). Parent-guardian evaluation of physical restraint among adults with intellectual disability: A social validity assessment. *Advances in Neurodevelopmental Disorders, 1*, 73–78.

McDonnell, A. A., & Sturmey, P. (2000). The social validation of three physical restrain procedures: A comparison of young people and professional groups. *Research in Developmental Disabilities, 21*, 85–92.

Reed, D. D., Luiselli, J. K., Miller, J. R., & Kaplan, B. A. (2013). Therapeutic restraint and protective holding. In D. D. Reed, F. DiGennaro Reed, & J. K. Luiselli (Eds.), *Handbook of crisis intervention and developmental disabilities* (pp. 107–120). New York: Springer.

Reimers, T. M., & Wacker, D. P. (1988). Parents' ratings of the acceptability of behavioral treatment recommendations made in an outpatient clinic: A preliminary analysis of the influence of treatment effectiveness. *Behavioral Disorders, 14*, 7–15.

Reimers, T. M., Wacker, D. P., & Cooper, L. J. (1991). Evaluation of the acceptability of treatments for their children's behavioral difficulties: Ratings by parents receiving services in an outpatient clinic. *Child & Family Behavior Therapy, 13*, 53–71.

Rickard, E. D., Chan, J., & Merriam, B. (2013). Issues emanating from the implementation of policies on restraint with people who have intellectual disabilities. *Journal of Policy and Practice in Intellectual Disabilities, 10*, 252–259.

Schwartz, I. S., & Baer, D. M. (1991). Social validity assessments: Is current practice state of the art? *Journal of Applied Behavior Analysis, 24*, 189–204.

Strohmeier, C., Mule, C., & Luiselli, J. K. (2014). Social validity assessment of training methods to improve treatment integrity of special education service providers. *Behavior Analysis in Practice, 7*, 15–20.

Sturmey, P. (2009). It is time to reduce and safely eliminate restrictive behavioral practices. *Journal of Applied Research in Intellectual Disabilities, 22*, 105–110.

Van Houten, R. (1979). Social validation: The evolution of standards of competency for target behaviors. *Journal of Applied Behavior Analysis, 12*, 581–591.

Vollmer, T. R., Peters, K. P., & Slocum, S. K. (2015). Treatment of severe behavior disorders. In H. S. Roane, J. E. Ringdahl, & T. S. Falcomata (Eds.), *Clinical and organizational applications of applied behavior analysis* (pp. 47–67). New York: Elsevier/Academic Press.

Witt, J. C., & Martens, B. K. (1983). Assessing the acceptability of behavioral interventions used in classrooms. *Psychology in the Schools, 20*, 510–517.

Witt, J. C., Martens, B. K., & Elliot, S. N. (1984). Factors affecting teachers' judgements of the acceptability of behavioral interventions: Time involvement, behavior problem severity, and type of intervention. *Behavior Therapy, 15*, 204–209.

Wolf, M. M. (1978). Social validity: The case for subjective measurement or how applied behavior analysis is finding its heart. *Journal of Applied Behavior Analysis, 11*, 203–214.

Part II
Intervention, Training, and Supervision

Communication-Focused Treatment of Violence-Aggression

Valdeep Saini and William E. Sullivan

Abstract Communication-focused treatments based on behavioral interventions have shown to be the most robust and efficacious in treating aggression and violence in individuals with neurodevelopmental disorders (NDD). The most commonly prescribed behavioral intervention for aggression and violence exhibited by individuals with NDD is functional communication training (FCT). According to criteria for empirically supported treatments developed by Divisions 12 and 16 of the American Psychological Association, FCT is considered a "well-established" treatment for violence and aggression exhibited by children with NDD, and is characterized as "probably efficacious" with adults. In this chapter, we discuss variables related to the effectiveness of FCT as well as provide strategies for using FCT effectively in real-world settings, including teaching communication skills and programing for generalization of those skills. Furthermore, we discuss how FCT can be incorporated into a comprehensive behavioral treatment package for aggression and violence. Last, we identify limitations to communication-focused treatments, discuss methods to mitigate relapse of aggression and violence, and provide suggestions for areas of future research.

Keywords Aggression · Behavior therapy · Behavioral treatment · Communication · Communication skills · Communication therapy · FCT · Functional communication · Violence

V. Saini (✉)
Department of Applied Disability Studies, Brock University, St. Catharines, ON, Canada
e-mail: vsaini@brocku.ca

W. E. Sullivan
State University of New York Upstate Medical University, Syracuse, NY, USA

© Springer Nature Switzerland AG 2021
J. K. Luiselli (ed.), *Applied Behavior Analysis Treatment of Violence and Aggression in Persons with Neurodevelopmental Disabilities*, Advances in Preventing and Treating Violence and Aggression,
https://doi.org/10.1007/978-3-030-68549-2_6

Introduction

Early and effective intervention is essential in order to eliminate aggressive behavior exhibited by individuals with neurodevelopmental disabilities (NDD). Horner, Carr, Strain, Todd, and Reed (2002) conducted a research synthesis of interventions for challenging behaviors and found that the early adoption of behavioral interventions can result in reductions of challenging behaviors by up to 90%. The absence of behavioral intervention can lead to more persistent aggression over time, and individuals who engage in aggression are at increased risk for denial of services, social isolation, institutionalization, over-use of medication, physical restraint, and physical abuse (Antonacci, Manuel, & Davis, 2008; Lunsky et al., 2017; McGillivray & McCabe, 2004; Murphy et al., 2005).

Anti-psychotic medication is often prescribed to manage aggressive behaviors in individuals with NDD, even when a comorbid diagnosis of mental illness is not provided (Grey & Hastings, 2005). However, the efficacy of such medications in producing long-term reductions in aggression are mixed. That is, there is scant evidence for the efficacy of pharmacotherapy for treating aggression in individuals with NDD (Matson & Wilkins, 2008; Tsiouris, 2010). Whereas medications infrequently address the factors that give rise to and maintain aggression in persons with NDD, behavioral interventions that account for these factors have been repeatedly shown to result in sustainable elimination of violence and aggression over time (Brosnan & Healy, 2011).

One of the most important outcomes of functional analysis methods (see Chapter "Functional Analysis of Violence–Aggression") has been the ability to systematically identify the putative reinforcer(s) for challenging behavior exhibited by individuals with NDD, which allows a clinician to manipulate that reinforcer to decrease aggression and replace it with an alternative, prosocial behavior (Beavers, Iwata, & Lerman, 2013). That is, a functional analysis is conducted to identify the conditions that evoke aggression and environmental events that serve as functional consequences that maintain aggression, results of which allow a clinician to provide those same consequences for adaptive behavior.

Withholding the reinforcers for aggression while simultaneously providing those reinforcers contingent upon a specific, alternative behavior is termed differential reinforcement of alternative behavior (DRA; Petscher, Rey, & Bailey, 2009). For example, if a child kicks other children at school, and a functional analysis indicates that kicking is maintained by access to adult attention, DRA would involve teaching the child an alternative response, such as sitting cross-legged, and delivering adult attention contingent upon each instances of the alternative behavior. In many cases, DRA may be the ideal treatment because it rarely produces negative side effects and it provides an appropriate option for individuals to earn valuable reinforcers once they are no longer provided for aggression. Withholding reinforcers for aggression while providing individuals an opportunity to obtain those reinforcers through appropriate behavior has shown to lead to more efficacious reductions in aggression than only withholding putative reinforcers (Shukla & Albin, 1996). DRA is considered a "well-established" empirically valid treatment for challenging behavior according to criteria established by The Division 12 Task Force on the Promotion and Dissemination of Psychological Procedures.

Review of Pertinent Research Literature

The most commonly prescribed treatment for aggression exhibited by individuals with NDD based on DRA is functional communication training (Falcomata & Wacker, 2013; Tiger, Hanley, & Bruzek, 2008). Functional communication training (FCT) is a function-based DRA procedure that involves teaching individuals to use an appropriate communication response to access the reinforcer(s) responsible for maintaining aggression (Tiger et al., 2008). Whereas traditional DRA treatments focus on *any* alternative behavior deemed to be appropriate as a method to access the reinforcer maintaining aggression, FCT seeks to establish communicative skills and create the environmental conditions under which a socially appropriate *communication response* will be used to access reinforcement. For example, consider the child that kicked other children to obtain adult attention—rather than reinforcing crossing legs, FCT would teach and reinforce an alternative communication response such as vocalizing, "Can we talk, please?" That is, FCT differs from other DRA treatments in that the alternative behavior is a form of discriminable communication that is likely to be recognized by others in the individual's social environment (e.g., speaking, sign-language).

Providing the reinforcers maintaining aggression contingent on appropriate communication instead of another, noncommunicative, alternative behavior may have therapeutic advantages because it has long been established that aggression in individuals with NDD often serves as a method for interacting socially with the environment (Durand & Moskowitz, 2019). Challenging behavior frequently serves as a form of communication for individuals with limited verbal skills or inadequate communicative repertoires (Carr & Durand, 1985). Results of theoretical and empirical studies have suggested a strong inverse relation between communication ability and severity of challenging behavior, including violence and aggression (Sigafoos, 2000). After analyzing 95 differentiated functional analyses of aggression, Beavers et al. (2013) found 97.8% indicated aggression was maintained by social reinforcement, suggesting that a high proportion of aggressive behavior is likely to have a communicative underpinning. A common conclusion from these studies is that by improving verbal abilities, challenging behavior might be eliminated. This may also be the reason why investigators of large review studies have cited FCT as the most effective treatment for challenging behavior, including aggression that is based on the results of a functional analysis (Hagopian, Fisher, Sullivan, Acquisto, & LeBlanc, 1998; Matson, Dixon, & Matson, 2005; Rooker, Jessel, Kurtz, & Hagopian, 2013).

Kurtz, Boelter, Jarmolowicz, Chin, and Hagopian (2011) applied the criteria for empirically supported treatments developed by Divisions 12 and 16 of the American

Psychological Association for evaluation of single-case research studies to examine the efficacy of FCT for treating challenging behaviors such as aggression. They found that FCT far exceeded criteria designated as a "well-established" treatment for challenging behavior exhibited by children with NDD, and could be characterized as "probably efficacious" with adults. Moreover, a meta-analysis of 36 single-case studies conducted by Heath, Ganz, Parker, Burke, and Ninci (2015) found that FCT was highly effective in reducing challenging behavior.

The two principal goals of FCT are to eliminate aggressive behavior and to establish a more acceptable, yet functionally equivalent, communication response (FCR). This intervention has been effective at treating a wide-array of aggressive and violent behaviors including kicking, hitting, biting, pinching, scratching, hair pulling, pushing, spitting, throwing objects, and other forms of forceful contact toward another individual (Brosnan & Healy, 2011). Independent of the topography of the aggressive behavior, FCT is most effective when used to treat aggression that occurs to access attention or objects from others, or to escape from aversive situations such as being asked to engage in nonpreferred task demands.

It is common for violence and aggression to be maintained by either, or both, social positive reinforcement such as gaining access to tangible items that another person in the environment has, or social negative reinforcement such as the removal of an aversive or noxious item presented by another person in the environment. In these situations FCT would involve teaching FCRs that would result in contingent access to those social reinforcers that aggression previously led to. For example, consider an adult with NDD with a limited vocal-verbal repertoire who lives in a residential setting and pulls the hair of the residence staff to gain access to food during mealtimes. In this context, FCT could involve teaching the individual an FCR such as a sign response for "food" that they could use to appropriately request food. When the FCR is emitted, the residence staff could reinforce the appropriate behavior by providing food. Under these circumstances, the individual would also be taught that hair pulling is no longer an effective way of getting food from others.

Alternatively, aggression is often maintained by the removal of aversive items or events rather than access to preferred items or events (i.e., social negative reinforcement; Beavers et al., 2013). Consider a child with NDD who communicates using 3–5 word sentences but punches his classroom teacher every time she asks him to do a math worksheet. After being punched, the teacher removes the math worksheet assuming the child needs to calm down. A functional analysis might reveal that punching is maintained by the contingent removal of an aversive task demand (i.e., math worksheet). In this context, FCT could involve teaching the child to say a vocal FCR such as, "break please" in order to communicate to the classroom teacher that he needs a break from math worksheets. The classroom teacher would reinforce this vocal FCR by providing a contingent break. The teacher would also teach the child that punching is no longer an effective way of getting breaks from math problems.

Synthesis of Research Findings and Implications

Combining Communication-Focused Treatments with Other Behavioral Treatments

It is common for FCT to be combined with other behavioral interventions as part of a comprehensive treatment package for eliminating violence and aggression. In fact, a large body of literature has suggested that FCT is most effective when combined with additional antecedent and consequence-based strategies (Brosnan & Healy, 2011). Therefore, in many circumstances it may be appropriate to determine which of these strategies would be most appropriate to supplement FCT given the severity of aggression, available clinical and environmental resources, and goals for ensuring the durability of FCT over time.

Combining Functional Communication Training with Antecedent-Based Strategies Antecedent-based strategies include intervention components that focus on (a) eliminating the motivation to engage in aggression, (b) manipulating the environment to no longer signal the availability of reinforcement for aggression, or (c) both. That is, although aggression is learned through a contingent relation between the aggressive behavior and its consequence, there may be antecedent factors that increase the motivation or probability that aggression will occur (e.g., a nonpreferred activity or unpredictable routine). Antecedent-based strategies focus on supplementing FCT by increasing the individual's motivation to engage in communication instead of aggression, as well as manipulating the physical and social environment to be discriminative for the FCR.

Many antecedent-strategies have been used in combination with FCT and include but are not limited to: (a) increasing the predictability of a schedule or routine through a visual representation of a sequence of events (Massey & Wheeler, 2000); (b) interspersing high-probability of compliance requests with new or more difficult tasks that have a low-probability of compliance and higher likelihood of evoking aggression (Horner, Day, Sprague, O'Brien, & Heathfield, 1991); (c) delivering putative reinforcers for aggression on a time-based schedule in addition to occurrences of the FCR (Hagopian, Wilson, & Wilder, 2001); and (d) increasing an individual's autonomy by providing choice and control over daily events that are meaningful to them (Dyer, Dunlap, & Winterling, 1990; Sullivan & Roane, 2018; Zelinsky & Shadish, 2018). This latter antecedent-based strategy may be particularly useful in combination with FCT given that individuals with NDD may have a limited ability to communicate with others in their social environment, which effectively reduces choice making opportunities. Choice making in combination with FCT contributes to the individual's overall communicative repertoire and is likely to complement FCT given that limited opportunities to make choices appears to result in increased occurrences of aggression (Kern et al., 1988).

Combining Functional Communication Training with Consequence-Based Strategies Consequence-based strategies include those intervention components that focus on generic classes of consequences that can be arranged for aggression and include (a) extinction of aggression, (b) punishment for aggression, and (c) ongoing reinforcement for aggression. Consequence-based strategies may be particularly useful in supplementing FCT given that they directly operate on aggressive behavior.

By far the most common intervention component combined with FCT is extinction (Lerman & Iwata, 1996). Extinction involves withholding the functional reinforcer for aggression to teach the individual that challenging behavior is no longer an effective way of communicating. The importance of extinction as a supplement to FCT has been demonstrated in numerous studies showing that FCT without extinction frequently fails to produce clinically meaningful reductions in aggression (Fisher et al., 1993; Shukla & Albin, 1996). For example, Hagopian et al. (1998) examined 27 cases of FCT, and in 11 of those cases FCT was implemented without extinction. In none of the 11 cases was challenging behavior reduced to clinically meaningful levels. In contrast, FCT with extinction was implemented in 25 cases and challenging behavior was reduced to clinically meaningfully levels in 11 of the 25 cases. It is a commonly held belief among clinicians that implementing FCT in combination with extinction whenever possible is best clinical practice (Tiger et al., 2008).

In some situations, extinction cannot be implemented and more intrusive procedures such as punishment are necessary to reduce aggression. Punishment during FCT involves the contingent application or removal of a consequence following aggression in order to eliminate challenging behavior. Research on challenging behavior has shown that adding punishment to FCT can increase the efficacy of the communication-focused treatment (Hanley, Piazza, Fisher, & Maglieri, 2005). When FCT with extinction was ineffective at reducing challenging behavior in 14 of 25 cases, Hagopian et al. (1998) added a punishment contingency and were able to reduce challenging behavior to clinically meaningful levels in 100% of cases. Similarly, Rooker et al. (2013) found that FCT plus punishment was effective at reducing challenging behavior in 5 of 9 cases. Punishment can take many forms including time-out from reinforcement, reprimands, and contingent restraint (Hagopian et al., 1998). However, efforts should be made to remove punishment completely or move to a less intrusive form of punishment over time. Negative side effects of punishment that could occur when combined with communication-based interventions can often be circumvented by continuing to deliver functional reinforcers for communication (e.g., Hagopian, Bruzek, Bowman, & Jennett, 2007).

In other situations, neither extinction nor punishment can be practically implemented, or neither are appropriate consequences for aggression (e.g., a large individual who engages in severe aggression). The concern is that challenging behavior may continue to contact reinforcement, in which case the effectiveness of FCT may depend on the competition between reinforcement obtained for communication versus aggression. Athens and Vollmer (2010) evaluated several strategies designed to increase the relative value of reinforcement for communication over aggression when extinction could not be implemented. They found that individuals with NDD chose to engage in appropriate alternative behavior such as communication when those alternative behaviors led to longer durations with a reinforcer, a greater quality reinforcer, or when the delay to reinforcement was shorter relative to aggression. Researchers have recommended that parameters of functional reinforcement such as duration, quality, and delay be manipulated to favor communication rather than aggression in situations where extinction cannot be implemented.

Increasing the Practicality of Communication-Focused Treatments

Despite the widespread effectiveness of FCT, simply teaching an FCR may not be a practical endpoint for treatment. First, the communication response could occur at too high of a rate for caregivers to reinforce naturally as illustrated by an adult with NDD who continually requests food with his or her FCR and ends up eating throughout the day. One might consider simply only reinforcing the FCR on occasion, however, if an FCR occurs at a very high rate and frequently goes unreinforced, it could extinguish and lead to the reemergence of aggression. Moreover, the FCR could occur at times during which it is inappropriate or difficult to deliver reinforcement, for example, when a parent attends to a sick child and a sibling with a NDD requests adult attention with an FCR. Therefore, establishing alternative appropriate communication to acquire putative reinforcers for aggression is considered only a starting point in a comprehensive communication-focused treatment. Researchers have increased their focus on ways of increasing the practicality of communication-focused treatments by thinning the schedule of reinforcement to more naturalistic levels while simultaneously maintaining low rates of aggression (Greer, Fisher, Saini, Owen, & Jones, 2016). Reinforcement-schedule thinning involves incorporating treatment components designed to facilitate delay to reinforcement and teach tolerance for periods in which the reinforcer cannot be delivered. Reinforcement schedule-thinning procedures are another method for programming for generalization and maintenance of a communication-focused treatment.

Hagopian, Boelter, and Jarmolowicz (2011) identified a number of different schedule-thinning procedures following FCT, including delay schedules (Hagopian et al., 1998) and response restriction (Roane, Fisher, Sgro, Falcomata, & Pabico, 2004), but suggested that multiple schedules were the ideal procedure when the goal is to delay positive reinforcement for periods greater than 1 min. Multiple schedules involve the alternation of at least two reinforcement schedules, each of which are signaled. Reinforcement components are signaled with a discriminative stimulus (S^D), and extinction components are signaled with an S-Delta (S^Δ; Ferster & Skinner, 1957). During the S^D component the FCR produces reinforcement, and during the S^Δ component the FCR does not produce reinforcement. The most common strategy for implementing multiple schedules as a schedule-thinning procedure following FCT has been to arrange short periods of extinction that alternate with longer periods of reinforcement and then gradually fading those periods so that reinforcement is available for a brief time and extinction is progressively increased for longer durations (Saini, Miller, & Fisher, 2016). Figure 1 depicts an example of FCT combined with a multiple-schedule reinforcement thinning procedure. Following the initial FCT evaluation, the duration of time in which reinforcement is delivered for the FCR (and the S^D is present) is gradually reduced from 4 min to 1 min and the duration in which extinction of the FCR is in place (and the S^Δ is present) is gradually increased from 1 min to 4 min.

Hagopian et al. (2011) suggested that chain schedules of reinforcement are the ideal strategy when aggression is maintained by negative reinforcement. Chain schedules involve increasing the number of tasks that must be completed before the opportunity to emit the FCR is made available and before the FCR produces reinforcement. When chain schedules are initially introduced with FCT, the response requirement is small (e.g., one task) and is gradually increased over time. Ghaemmaghami, Hanley, and Jessel (2016) suggested that a variation of a chain schedule could also be used for aggression maintained by positive reinforcement by teaching individuals with NDD to engage in other, appropriate behavior during periods in which the FCR would not be reinforced. An example would be a child with NDD playing with a lesser preferred toy while waiting for a tangible item that historically evoked aggression. This type of chain schedule involves delivering putative reinforcers for challenging behavior contingent on appropriate behavior and

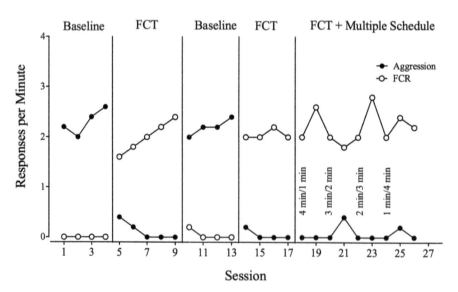

Fig. 1 Functional communication training plus multiple-schedule reinforcement thinning. The duration in which the S^D is present and the FCR is reinforced was reduced from 4 min to 1 min. The duration in which the S^Δ is present and the FCR was not reinforced was increased from 1 min to 4 min

systematically increasing the response requirements for appropriate behavior. Reductions in challenging behavior such as aggression have averaged 91–94% when FCT has been combined with reinforcement-schedule thinning such as multiple and chain schedules (Greer et al., 2016; Jessel, Ingvarsson, Metras, Kirk, & Whipple, 2018).

Practice Recommendations

Considerations When Selecting a Communication Response Topography

One of the first considerations for developing a communication-focused treatment for aggression is determining the appropriate response topography for the FCR. There have been a wide range of FCRs employed in the treatment literature for violent behavior in individuals with NDD. For example, FCRs have consisted of vocal responses (e.g., Carr & Durand, 1985), manual signs (e.g., Falcomata & Wacker, 2013), microswitch activation (Wacker et al., 2013), picture exchange or touch (Saini, Sullivan, Baxter, DeRosa, & Roane, 2018), and voice-output devices (e.g., Ringdahl et al., 2009). Although any FCR that an individual is able to emit proficiently can help to reduce the occurrence of aggression, when incorporated into FCT, there are a number of variables to consider when selecting what FCR to teach. Namely, effort associated with engaging in the FCR, the speed at which the individual can acquire the FCR, and the social validity of the FCR are important considerations. In the following sections we will describe these variables and their influence on the effects of communication-based approaches to treating violent behavior in individuals with NDD.

FCR Effort For individuals with NDDs who engage in aggression, selecting an FCR that is of lower effort than the violent behavior has been commonly recommended (e.g., Tiger et al., 2008). That is, in order for an FCR to effectively replace aggression, it needs to be more efficient than aggression in producing the functional reinforcer. For example, Horner and Day (1991) conducted a three-experiment study that examined different aspects of FCRs, and how each of these components contributed to the efficacy of FCT. In their first experiment the authors determined that a 12-year-old boy diagnosed with an NDD engaged in escape-maintained aggression. During treatment, they taught the participant to emit two different FCRs, both of which were manual signs. One of the FCRs consisted of signing one word ("break"), whereas the second FCR required the participant to sign a complete sentence ("I want to go, please") and then compared the efficacy of these two FCRs. Outcomes showed that when the higher-effort FCR was required, aggression continued to occur; whereas when the lower-effort FCR was used, aggression decreased. Given that signing a complete sentence is inherently more effortful than signing a single word, and potentially more effortful than aggression, this study highlights the role that response effort can have on the effectiveness of FCT during the treatment of violent behavior.

Speed of Learning the FCR A second variable worth consideration when selecting an FCR is the speed at which the individual will acquire the response, for example, number of teaching trials or time associated with learning. Although the training procedures will obviously affect the speed of acquisition, the topography of the FCR will also play a role. It is especially important to select a response topography that the individual is likely to acquire readily as the continuation of aggression may pose serious risk to the individual and others in their environment. First, selecting a topography-based response (e.g., manual sign) versus a selection-based response (e.g., picture exchange) should be considered. Sundberg and Sundberg (1990) suggested that individuals with NDD may acquire topography-based responses more quickly than selection-based responses. Because topography-based systems have different responses for each word (e.g., a different sign for "attention" and "toys"), compared to a selection-based system where the individual may be required to emit a topographically similar responses (e.g., touching a card), acquiring a topography-based response may be easier for individuals affected by a NDD as they will not have to discriminate amongst an array of responses as in a selection-based system. However, Vignes (2007) examined topography versus selection-based acquisition in three children with NDD and found that they were able to more readily and accurately acquire selection-based responses over topography-based responses. Individuals with NDD may struggle with fine-motor coordination and thus acquiring a manual sign can be difficult. For those individuals with fine-motor difficulties, they may acquire a simple selection-based response in a fewer number of teaching sessions. Regardless of these mixed findings, selection of the FCR should consider individual characteristics that may impact the speed of acquisition of these responses.

Proficiency A third variable to consider when selecting an FCT is the level of proficiency the individual has with emitting the FCR. Ringdahl et al. (2009) developed an assessment procedure for identifying the proficiency of FCRs, termed *mand-topography assessment*, then evaluated their relative efficacy when incorporated into FCT. Three individuals with an NDD that each engaged in some form of violent behavior (e.g., aggression) participated. The assessment began by providing each participant 10 opportunities, or trials, to use one of three or four different communication responses (i.e., microswitch activation, manual sign, card touch, or voice-output device). Throughout this assessment process, the level of prompting required for the participants to emit the various FCRs was measured as an indication of proficiency level. Those communication responses that required less prompting, relative to the other communication modalities, were considered to be more proficient.

Following the mand-topography assessment, Ringdahl et al. (2009) then conducted an FCT treatment comparison across high- and low-proficiency FCRs. Outcomes for all three participants showed that violent behavior decreased to a greater extent when the high-proficiency FCRs were incorporated into treatment, relative to the low-proficiency FCRs. Moreover, participants displayed consistently higher levels of communication with the high-proficiency FCRs, relative to the low-proficiency FCRs. These findings highlight the impact that proficiency may have of the efficacy of FCT for treating violent behavior in individuals with NDD.

Preference The individual's preference across communication modalities has also been shown to impact the efficacy of FCT (Peck et al., 1996; Richman, Wacker, & Winborn, 2001; Winborn, Wacker, Richman, Asmus, & Geier, 2002). For instance, Winborn-Kemmerer, Ringdahl, Wacker, and Kitsukawa (2009) evaluated the preference of FCR topography in two individuals diagnosed with an NDD who engaged in violent behavior. Following a functional analysis, each participant was taught two novel FCRs, which were then incorporated into an FCT evaluation. Although both topographies of FCRs reduced violent behavior, both participants showed a clear preference for one of the FCRs and allocated their responding accordingly when the FCRs were concurrently available. Thus, although both FCR modalities were effective at reducing violent behavior in the context of FCT, these findings demonstrate that the preference of these FCR will influence the individuals response allocation (i.e., choice) across communication modalities. Furthermore, Ringdahl et al. (2018) evaluated FCR preference on the persistence of communication in the face of treatment challenges (e.g., FCRs stop producing reinforcement) during FCT. Findings indicated that preferred FCRs were more likely to persists when FCT was challenged, suggesting that by selecting preferred FCRs the longevity of treatment may be enhanced.

Social Validity A final variable worth consideration when selecting an FCR is the extent to which the FCR will be recognized and reinforced by others in the individual's natural environment. Durand (1999) evaluated the role of FCR topography on the generalization of the FCT treatment effects across novel settings and caregivers with five individuals affected by an NDD. In this study, voice-output devices were used as FCRs and results suggested that these children were able to generalize their communication skills in the community (e.g., at the mall) and were able to access social reinforcement from untrained persons. Similarly, Durand and Carr (1991) demonstrated that if the FCR is reinforced in the individual's natural environment, it may improve the long-term effectiveness of FCT.

Strategies for Teaching Functional Communication Responses

Functional communication responses are under the functional control of a specific source of motivation and form of reinforcement (Skinner, 1957). That is, an FCR is a response that is used to request a particular want or need (i.e., reinforcer) and is controlled by that source of reinforcement and the individual's motivation to obtain it. This form of communication training is based on the function of the response, rather than the topography, and hinges on careful manipulation of the variables that control violent behavior, namely motivational factors and functional reinforcers.

Teaching an individual to emit an appropriate FCR is vital to the effectiveness of FCT. That is, without establishing an appropriate FCR to replace aggression, FCT will be ineffective. Thus when teaching an FCR, it is crucial for the training to take place under conditions similar to those that were determined to occasion violent behavior in the functional analysis (described in Chapter "Functional Analysis of Violence–Aggression") such that the relevant motivation is in place. This can be accomplished in one of two ways. First, the teacher may contrive the motivation by arranging a situation determined to occasion aggression. This approach often involves setting up a condition that mimics the functional analysis condition associated with elevated levels of violent behavior. A second option would be for the teacher to wait for those evocative situations to arise naturally in the individual's environment. Both options have relative benefits and disadvantages.

By contriving the motivation, the teacher can provide the learner repeated opportunities to prompt and reinforce the FCR under controlled, and presumably safer, conditions (Tiger et al., 2008). For example, suppose that that a child's violent behavior was maintained by access to preferred tangible items (e.g., toys). During training, the teacher would first allow the child to interact with the tangible items for a brief period of time (e.g., 1 min) and then restrict access to them. Restricting access to the tangible items would increase motivation for emitting a response to regain access. This situation can then be repeatedly presented to the individual to provide practice with emitting the FCR and obtaining the reinforcer determined to maintain violent behavior. However, given the contrived nature of these situations, additional steps may be needed to promote the generalization of functional communication across different contexts and treatment agents (Moes & Frea, 2002).

As for the naturalistic-training approach, this method is likely to be helpful in promoting generalization as training will take place in the natural environment. For instance, suppose a child engages in violent behavior when asked to take a shower, which was determined to be maintained by escape (i.e., does not have to shower) via functional analysis. During naturalistic training, the teacher would wait until it is time for the child to get a shower and implement the training procedures accordingly. Because the teacher must wait for these situations to arise naturally, there will be less opportunities for the learner to respond (e.g., one shower per day) resulting is slower acquisition of the FCR (Tiger et al., 2008).

After the training approach has been selected, contrived or natural, specific prompting strategies will be implemented to help the individual acquire the FCR. Acquisition-level training occurs when teaching an individual to emit a novel FCR and requires the teacher to provide enough support for the learner to emit the correct response and deliver the functional reinforcer. After the learner is able to readily emit the response with prompting in the presence of the relevant stimulus conditions, those prompts must be systematically withdrawn in order to transfer control from the prompts to the stimuli associated with the relevant motivating conditions. In order to transfer that control, it is necessary that the teacher carefully track the learners' progress and systematically withdraw those prompts as the learner begins to emit the FCR independently.

There are two common prompting strategies employed to train FCRs to individuals with NDD. These prompting strategies can be generally described as *least-to-most* and *most-to-least* sequences, where the terms "most" and "least" describe the intrusiveness of the prompt. For an example of least-to-most prompting, Ringdahl et al. (2009) taught FCRs of picture card touch, manual sign, and voice-output device to individuals with NDD who engaged in aggression. Following a functional analysis, it was determined that all participants engaged in aggression, at least in part, to gain access to preferred tangible items. As such, the authors arranged the motivation by restricting access to preferred tangible items in a trial-based format to provide repeated opportunities for the individual to emit the FCR and obtain reinforcement. During each trial (i.e., presentation of motivational variables), a least-to-most procedure was implemented. This consisted of an experimenter first prompting the participant to emit the FCR by delivering a vocal request (e.g., "If you want the toy, touch the card"). If the child emitted the correct response within 5 s of the vocal prompt, the functional reinforcer was delivered (i.e., the toy). If the participant did not emit the response, a model prompt was provided such that the experimenter demonstrated the appropriate communication response (e.g., touched the card themselves) and rephrased the initial vocal prompt ("If you want the toy, touch the card like this."). Again, if the child emitted the FCR within 5 s of the model prompt the functional reinforcer was provided; if not, physical guidance was implemented, which consisted of the experimenter using hand-over-hand physical prompting to assist the individual to emit the FCR. This process continued until the individual was able to emit the response following the vocal or model prompt on greater than 80% of trials and without aggression. For all participants, at least one FCR was acquired and reached the proficiency criteria, and was effectively incorporated into FCT.

The most-to-least procedure begins with the most intrusive prompt and fading those prompts out over time until the FCR occurs independently. Fisher et al. (1993) described this procedure, in which they termed an errorless procedure, during FCR training with four individuals diagnosed with an NDD who engaged in aggression. The authors first identified the function of each individual's aggression. Then, situations that were found to occasion violent behavior were arranged during training. As training began, the authors first immediately physically guided each participant to emit the FCR as soon as the relevant motivational variable was presented (e.g., immediately when the child's toy was taken away). Then, over successive trials, the experimenters slowly faded out the physical prompts by only providing the minimum amount of assistance necessary for the individual to emit the FCR (e.g., gentle touch to the elbow). This process continued until each participant was able to emit the FCR independently.

In similar procedure, termed *time-delay,* a controlling prompt that ensures the individual emits the correct response is immediately delivered as the relevant motivational variable is presented and is then systematically delayed over time (Charlop, Schreibman, & Thibodeau, 1985). For example, Saini et al. (2018) taught four young children with NDDs who engaged in aggression or related maladaptive behavior to emit FCRs (i.e., card touch) within the context of FCT. Ten-trial-training sessions were conducted where each trial consisted of an experimenter presenting the relevant motivation for aggression, and delivering the functional reinforcer contingent on emission of the FCR. First, the experimenters physically guided the participants to emit the FCR as soon as the motivation was presented (i.e., 0-s delay) and delivered reinforcement. Following two consecutive 10-trial sessions in which zero levels of aggression were observed, the prompt was delayed to 2 s. That is, the experimenter would present the relevant motivational variable, and waited 2 s before delivering the controlling prompt (i.e., physically guiding the FCR). Across sessions, the prompt was delayed (i.e., 2 s, 5 s, 10 s) until each participant was emitting the FCR independently and in the absence of violent behavior across two consecutive 10-trial sessions.

Increasing the Complexity of Functional Communication Responses

Over the course of treatment, it may be beneficial to systematically increase the complexity of the FCR to a response that is likely to be recognized by others. Although previous research has suggested low-effort FCRs result in large reductions of violent behavior for individuals with NDD (e.g., Horner & Day, 1991), increasingly complex responses may be more socially acceptable and perhaps more likely to recruit reinforcement from novel persons as FCT treatments are generalized to the individual's natural environment. In order to train more complex FCRs, a two-step process could be adopted (Hanley, Jin, Vanselow, & Hanratty, 2014; Santiago, Hanley, Moore, & Jin, 2016). Ghaemmaghami, Hanley, Jessel, and Landa (2018) taught and reinforced a simple FCR (e.g., "May way") to replace violent behavior with four children with NDD. After these simple FCRs were introduced into FCT and effectively reduced violent behavior, the authors taught a more complex FCR using a successive shaping process (e.g., "Excuse me? May I have my way, please?"). As the more complex FCR was introduced into treatment, the simpler response along with violent behavior were both placed on extinction so only the complex FCRs would be reinforced. In general, these studies were able to show that it is possible to move from simple FCRs to more complex FCRs, all while maintaining low-levels of violent behavior.

Guidelines for Promoting Generalization of Communication-Based Treatments

The utility of FCT depends on the extent to which treatment effects generalize to natural settings and care providers. That is, the individual with NDD must not demonstrate violent behavior but emit the FCR in the situations that previously occasioned violent behavior in the natural environment. Generalization has long been an important issue in behavioral treatment and is an essential component to effective treatment delivery targeting socially significant behavior. Stokes and Baer (1977) outlined several different tactics for promoting generalization, some of which have been outlined in the FCT literature.

To promote the generality of FCT, clinicians should train caregivers to implement the treatment procedures with high-levels of fidelity. The terminal goal of any FCT treatment is to transfer those gains into the individual's natural environment. Therefore, one of the most pertinent aspects of the transition from the training setting to the natural environment is to ensure that caregivers are able to implement the procedures as prescribed. For example, if the caregiver fails to deliver the functional reinforcer contingent on the emission of an FCR, violent behavior may recur (Mitteer, Greer, Fisher, Briggs, & Wacker, 2018). Should the caregiver deliver the functional reinforcer following the occurrence of violent behavior, inadvertently or otherwise, it is possible that violent behavior will reemerge, undermining the behavioral treatment (St. Peter Pipkin, Vollmer, & Sloman, 2010).

There have been several studies that have shown FCT can be effectively implemented by caregivers such as school teachers (Northup et al., 1994) and parents (Saini et al., 2018). Caregivers are typically taught to intervene in natural settings using behavioral skills training (BST) (Saini et al., 2018; Wacker et al., 2005) in which a trainer first provides vocal instructions to the caregiver on how to respond to occurrences of functional communication (i.e., deliver the reinforcer) and violent behavior (i.e., ignore the behavior or block if dangerous). Next, the trainer models the correct responses to the caregiver. Then, the caregiver and trainer role play such that the trainer would emit both functional communication and violent behavior as the individual targeted for intervention might. Throughout this process the trainer delivers immediate corrective feedback and praise as needed. This procedure continues until the caregiver is able to implement all the treatment procedures correctly.

Simply teaching the individual to recruit reinforcement through functional communication might not be enough to promote generalization, therefore, more explicit programming is often needed. One such tactic is to implement FCT across a variety of treatment agents and/or treatment contexts. This strategy has been termed *multiple exemplar training,* and was demonstrated by Durand and Carr (1991). In this evaluation, FCT effectively reduced aggression displayed by three individuals with NDD. During treatment, the authors trained three different therapists to implement FCT, all of which were able to eliminate violent behavior effectively. As treatment was introduced into the individuals' classroom with their teachers implementing FCT, generalization was enhanced. Thus, these findings suggest that implementing FCT across multiple caregivers can help to promote the generality of these treatment effects to the natural environment.

A second generalization strategy is to incorporate objects, items, events, or people into the treatment context that are present, or could be made present, in the individual's natural environment. This tactic is termed *programming common stimuli.* Fisher, Greer, Fuhrman, and Querim (2015) evaluated the effects of incorporating visual stimuli into FCT on generalization across contexts with individuals with

NDD who engaged in aggressive behavior participated. First, the authors identified the function of each participants' aggressive behavior via functional analysis. They then trained an FCR and implemented FCT which eliminated aggression in both participants. The authors subsequently incorporated visual signals during a schedule-thinning procedure and evaluated the effects of those visual signals as they moved FCT into various contexts (i.e., different therapy rooms). Outcomes suggested that by incorporating common visual stimuli into the treatment context and then presenting those stimuli into novel contexts, FCT readily generalized.

Research Direction

Limitations of Communication-Focused Treatments and Considerations for Future Research

Although FCT is commonly used in the treatment of violence and aggression in persons with NDD, questions have been raised about the durability of these interventions over long periods of time in naturalistic settings and when implemented by caregivers (Falcomata & Wacker, 2013; Neely, Garcia, Bankston, & Green, 2018). For example, Saini et al. (2018) showed that with 3 of 4 children with NDD, challenging behaviors relapsed when FCT was implemented in the home setting by parents, despite challenging behaviors being completely eliminated in a clinic setting. Methods to prevent relapse or reemergence of a previously reinforced behavior that occurs after the removal (or reduction) of reinforcement for an alternative response (e.g., FCR), have recently received increased attention and become the focus of translational research on FCT (Fisher et al., 2018; Greer & Shahan, 2019; Pritchard, Hoerger, Mace, Penney, & Harris, 2014).

Relapse of aggression could be due to factors including poor treatment integrity, change in contextual factors, and abrupt changes in the schedule of reinforcement (Podlesnik & Kelley, 2015). This latter factor may be of particular importance when designing communication-focused treatments as Briggs, Fisher, Greer, and Kimball (2018) found a 76% resurgence rate of challenging behaviors when reinforcement schedules for the FCR were thinned during FCT. Furthermore, they found that resurgence was more likely when caregivers implemented schedule-thinning procedures as there was a higher probability that they delivered reinforcement for challenging behavior. Mitteer et al. (2018) suggested that the focus of future FCT research should be on increasing caregiver resilience during intervention by reinforcing *caregiver* behaviors related to adherence (e.g., following through, extinction of aggression, reinforcing the FCR on the appropriate schedule; Allen & Warzak, 2000).

In addition to increasing adherence to FCT by reinforcing caregiver behavior, researchers have suggested several other strategies for mitigating the resurgence of challenging behavior following FCT including (a) increasing the duration of FCT prior to exposing the FCR to periods of extinction (Fisher, Greer, Fuhrman, Saini, & Simmons, 2018), (b) providing access to alternative activities during delays to reinforcement or periods of extinction (Fuhrman, Greer, Zangrillo, & Fisher, 2018), (c) establishing discriminative control over FCRs using multiple schedules and then transferring stimuli associated with the schedules to new contexts (Fisher et al., 2015), and (d) teaching more than one FCR to replace aggression as a means to increase the overall communicative repertoire (Lambert, Bloom, Samaha, & Dayton, 2017).

Incorporating strategies to mitigate resurgence may be a necessary step in communication-focused treatments. Wacker et al. (2017) recommended defining maintenance of FCT as the persistence of treatment effects in the face of treatment challenges such as decreased treatment integrity or the sudden and unintentional introduction of extinction for the FCR. Furthermore, Wacker et al. suggested that that treatments may need to be continued for much longer periods of time than currently reported in the literature. Namely, a communication-focused treatment should continue until data demonstrate that FCRs will persist and challenging behavior fails to show resurgence when treatment is challenged. Overall, relatively few treatment studies have evaluated the variables that affect resurgence, and those that have typically include only a few participants (Radhakrishnan, Gerow, & Weston, 2019). Future research should focus on identifying variables that reduce the resurgence of challenging behavior in order to increase the durability of FCT in typical environments.

Conclusion

Many individuals with NDD who have communication deficits often resort to violence and aggression to interact socially with their environment, either gaining access to preferred items and activities or avoiding and escaping nonpreferred conditions. A considerable number of studies have evaluated treatments of aggressive behavior exhibited by individuals with NDD and the vast majority have indicated that communication-focused treatments such as FCT are the most robust and efficacious (Durand & Moskowitz, 2015). Communication-focused treatments are generally effective when implemented with high integrity, however, future research should focus on methods to sustain intervention gains in less than ideal conditions such as when treatment integrity errors occur or when a novel context is introduced during treatment generalization. Clinicians should continue to plan for generalization and maintenance at the onset of FCT according to current best practices, which may in turn increase the social acceptability of the intervention.

References

Allen, K. D., & Warzak, W. J. (2000). The problem of parental nonadherence in clinical behavior analysis: Effective treatment is not enough. *Journal of Applied Behavior Analysis, 33*, 373–391. https://doi.org/10.1901/jaba.2000.33-373

Antonacci, D. J., Manuel, C., & Davis, E. (2008). Diagnosis and treatment of aggression in individuals with developmental disabilities. *Psychiatric Quarterly, 79*, 225–247. https://doi.org/10.1007/s11126-008-9080-4

Athens, E. S., & Vollmer, T. R. (2010). An investigation of differential reinforcement of alternative behavior without extinction. *Journal of Applied Behavior Analysis, 43*, 569–589. https://doi.org/10.1901/jaba.2010.43-569

Beavers, G. A., Iwata, B. A., & Lerman, D. C. (2013). Thirty years of research on the functional analysis of problem behavior. *Journal of Applied Behavior Analysis, 46*, 1–21. https://doi.org/10.1002/jaba.30

Briggs, A. M., Fisher, W. W., Greer, B. D., & Kimball, R. T. (2018). Prevalence of resurgence of destructive behavior when thinning reinforcement schedules during functional communication training. *Journal of Applied Behavior Analysis, 51*, 620–633. https://doi.org/10.1002/jaba.472

Brosnan, J., & Healy, O. (2011). A review of behavioral interventions for the treatment of aggression in individuals with developmental disabilities. *Research in Developmental Disabilities, 32*, 437–446. https://doi.org/10.1016/j.ridd.2010.12.023

Carr, E. G., & Durand, V. M. (1985). The social communicative basis of severe behavior problems in children. In S. Reiss & R. R. Bootzin (Eds.), *Theoretical issues in behavior therapy* (pp. 219–254). New York: Academic Press.

Charlop, M. H., Schreibman, L., & Thibodeau, M. G. (1985). Increasing spontaneous verbal responding in autistic children using a time delay procedure. *Journal of Applied Behavior Analysis, 18*, 155–166. https://doi.org/10.1901/jaba.1985.18-155

Durand, V. M. (1999). Functional communication training using assistive devices: Recruiting natural communities of reinforcement. *Journal of Applied Behavior Analysis, 32*, 247–267. https://doi.org/10.1901/jaba.1999.32-247

Durand, V., & Carr, E. G. (1991). Functional communication training to reduce challenging behavior: Maintenance and application in new settings. *Journal of Applied Behavior Analysis, 24*, 251–264. https://doi.org/10.1901/jaba.1991.24-251

Durand, V. M., & Moskowitz, L. (2015). Functional communication training: Thirty years of treating PB. *Topics in Early Childhood Special Education, 35*, 116–126. https://doi.org/10.1177/0271121415569509

Durand, V. M., & Moskowitz, L. J. (2019). The link between problem behavior and communication impairment in persons with developmental disabilities. *Current Developmental Disorders Reports*. Advanced online publication. https://doi.org/10.1007/s40474-019-00172-y

Dyer, K., Dunlap, G., & Winterling, V. (1990). Effects of choice making on the serious problem behaviors of students with severe handicaps. *Journal of Applied Behavior Analysis, 23*, 515–524. https://doi.org/10.1901/jaba.1990.23-515

Falcomata, T. S., & Wacker, D. P. (2013). On the use of strategies for programming generalization during functional communication training: A review of the literature. *Journal of Developmental and Physical Disabilities, 25*, 5–15. https://doi.org/10.1007/s10882-012-9311-3

Ferster, C. B., & Skinner, B. F. (1957). *Schedules of reinforcement*. East Norwalk, CT: Appleton-Century-Crofts.

Fisher, W. W., Greer, B. D., Craig, A. R., Retzlaff, B. J., Fuhrman, A. M., Lichtblau, K. R., et al. (2018). On the predictive validity of behavioral momentum theory for mitigating resurgence of problem behavior. *Journal of the Experimental Analysis of Behavior, 109*, 281–290. https://doi.org/10.1002/jeab.303

Fisher, W. W., Greer, B. D., Fuhrman, A. M., & Querim, A. C. (2015). Using multiple schedules during functional communication training to promote rapid transfer of treatment effects. *Journal of Applied Behavior Analysis, 48*, 713–733. https://doi.org/10.1002/jaba.254

Fisher, W. W., Greer, B. D., Fuhrman, A. M., Saini, V., & Simmons, C. A. (2018). Minimizing resurgence of destructive behavior using behavioral momentum theory. *Journal of Applied Behavior Analysis, 51*, 831–853. https://doi.org/10.1002/jaba.499

Fisher, W., Piazza, C., Cataldo, M., Harrell, R., Jefferson, G., & Conner, R. (1993). Functional communication training with and without extinction and punishment. *Journal of Applied Behavior Analysis, 26*, 23–36. https://doi.org/10.1901/jaba.1993.26-23

Fuhrman, A. M., Greer, B. D., Zangrillo, A. N., & Fisher, W. W. (2018). Evaluating competing activities to enhance functional communication training during reinforcement schedule thinning. *Journal of Applied Behavior Analysis, 51*, 931–942. https://doi.org/10.1002/jaba.486

Ghaemmaghami, M., Hanley, G. P., & Jessel, J. (2016). Contingencies promote delay tolerance. *Journal of Applied Behavior Analysis, 49*, 548–575. https://doi.org/10.1002/jaba.333

Ghaemmaghami, M., Hanley, G. P., Jessel, J., & Landa, R. (2018). Shaping complex functional communication responses. *Journal of Applied Behavior Analysis, 51*, 502–520. https://doi.org/10.1002/jaba.468

Greer, B. D., Fisher, W. W., Saini, V., Owen, T. M., & Jones, J. K. (2016). Functionalcommunication training during reinforcement schedule thinning: An analysis of 25 applications. *Journal of Applied Behavior Analysis, 49*, 105–121. https://doi.org/10.1002/jaba.265

Greer, B. D., & Shahan, T. A. (2019). Resurgence as choice: Implications for promoting durable behavior change. *Journal of Applied Behavior Analysis*. Advanced online publication. https://doi.org/10.1002/jaba.573

Grey, I. M., & Hastings, R. P. (2005). Evidence-based practices in intellectual disability and behaviour disorders. *Current Opinion in Psychiatry, 18*, 469–475. https://doi.org/10.1097/01.yco.0000179482.54767.cf

Hagopian, L. P., Boelter, E. W., & Jarmolowicz, D. P. (2011). Reinforcement schedule thinning following functional communication training: Review and recommendations. *Behavior Analysis in Practice, 4*, 4–16. https://doi.org/10.1007/BF03391770

Hagopian, L. P., Bruzek, J. L., Bowman, L. G., & Jennett, H. K. (2007). Assessment and treatment of problem behavior occasioned by interruption of free-operant behavior. *Journal of Applied Behavior Analysis, 40*, 89–103. https://doi.org/10.1901/jaba.2007.63-05

Hagopian, L. P., Fisher, W. W., Sullivan, M. T., Acquisto, J., & LeBlanc, L. A. (1998). Effectiveness of functional communication training with and without extinction and punishment: A summary of 21 inpatient cases. *Journal of Applied Behavior Analysis, 31*, 211–235. https://doi.org/10.1901/jaba.1998.31-211

Hagopian, L. P., Wilson, D. M., & Wilder, D. A. (2001). Assessment and treatment of problem behavior maintained by escape from attention and access to tangible items. *Journal of Applied Behavior Analysis, 34*, 229–232. https://doi.org/10.1901/jaba.2001.34-229

Hanley, G. P., Jin, C. S., Vanselow, N. R., & Hanratty, L. A. (2014). Producing meaningful improvements in problem behavior of children with autism via synthesized analyses and treatments. *Journal of Applied Behavior Analysis, 47*, 16–36. https://doi.org/10.1002/jaba.106

Hanley, G. P., Piazza, C. C., Fisher, W. W., & Maglieri, K. A. (2005). On the effectiveness of and preference for punishment and extinction components of function-based interventions. *Journal of Applied Behavior Analysis, 38*, 51–65. https://doi.org/10.1901/jaba.2005.6-04

Heath, A. K., Ganz, J. B., Parker, R., Burke, M., & Ninci, J. (2015). A meta-analytic review of functional communication training across mode of communication, age, and disability. *Review Journal of Autism and Developmental Disorders, 2*, 155–166. https://doi.org/10.1007/s40489-014-0044-3

Horner, R. H., Carr, E. G., Strain, P. S., Todd, A. W., & Reed, H. K. (2002). Problem behavior interventions for young children with autism: A research synthesis. *Journal of Autism and Developmental Disorders, 32*, 423–446. https://doi.org/10.1023/A:1020593922901

Horner, R. H., & Day, H. M. (1991). The effects of response efficiency on functionally equivalent competing behaviors. *Journal of Applied Behavior Analysis, 24*(4), 719–732. https://doi.org/10.1901/jaba.1991.24-719

Horner, R. H., Day, H. M., Sprague, J. R., O'Brien, M., & Heathfield, L. T. (1991). Interspersed requests: A non-aversive procedure for reducing aggression and self-injury during instruction. *Journal of Applied Behavior Analysis, 24*, 265–278. https://doi.org/10.1901/jaba.1991.24-265

Jessel, J., Ingvarsson, E. T., Metras, R., Kirk, H., & Whipple, R. (2018). Achieving socially significant reductions in problem behavior following the interview-informed synthesized contingency analysis: A summary of 25 outpatient applications. *Journal of Applied Behavior Analysis, 51*, 130–157. https://doi.org/10.1002/jaba.436

Kern, L., Vorndran, C. M., Hilt, A., Ringdahl, J. E., Adelman, B. E., & Dunlap, G. (1988). Choice as an intervention to improve behavior: A review of the literature. *Journal of Behavioral Education, 8*, 151–169. https://doi.org/10.1023/A:1022831507077

Kurtz, P. F., Boelter, E. W., Jarmolowicz, D. P., Chin, M. D., & Hagopian, L. P. (2011). An analysis of functional communication training as an empirically supported treatment for problem behavior displayed by individuals with intellectual disabilities. *Research in Developmental Disabilities, 32*(6), 2935–2942. https://doi.org/10.1016/j.ridd.2011.05.009

Lambert, J. M., Bloom, S. E., Samaha, A. L., & Dayton, E. (2017). Serial functional communication training: Extending serial DRA to mands and problem behavior. *Behavioral Interventions, 32*, 311–325. https://doi.org/10.1002/bin.1493

Lerman, D. C., & Iwata, B. A. (1996). Developing a technology for the use of operant extinction in clinical settings: An examination of basic and applied research. *Journal of Applied Behavior Analysis, 29*, 345–382. https://doi.org/10.1901/jaba.1996.29-345

Lunsky, Y., Khuu, W., Tadrous, M., Vigod, S., Cobigo, V., & Gomes, T. (2017). Antipsychotic use with and without comorbid psychiatric diagnosis among adults with intellectual and developmental disabilities. *The Canadian Journal of Psychiatry, 63*, 361–369. https://doi.org/10.1177/0706743717727240

Massey, N. G., & Wheeler, J. J. (2000). Acquisition and generalization of activity schedules and their effects on task engagement in a young child with autism in an inclusive pre-school classroom. *Education and Training in Mental Retardation and Developmental Disabilities, 35*, 326–334.

Matson, J. L., Dixon, D. R., & Matson, M. L. (2005). Assessing and treating aggression in children and adolescents with developmental disabilities: a 20-year overview. *Educational Psychology, 25*, 151–181. https://doi.org/10.1080/0144341042000301148

Matson, J. L., & Wilkins, J. (2008). Antipsychotic drugs for aggression in intellectual disability. *The Lancet, 371*, 9–10. https://doi.org/10.1016/S0140-6736(08)60046-X

McGillivray, J. A., & McCabe, M. P. (2004). Pharmacological management of challenging behaviour of individuals with intellectual disability. *Research in Developmental Disabilities, 25*, 523–537. https://doi.org/10.1016/j.ridd.2004.03.001

Mitteer, D. R., Greer, B. D., Fisher, W. W., Briggs, A. M., & Wacker, D. P. (2018). A laboratory model for evaluating relapse of undesirable caregiver behavior. *Journal of the Experimental Analysis of Behavior, 110*, 252–266. https://doi.org/10.1002/jeab.462

Moes, D. R., & Frea, W. D. (2002). Contextualized behavioral support in early intervention for children with autism and their families. *Journal of Autism and Developmental Disorders, 32*, 519–533. https://doi.org/10.1023/A:1021298729297

Murphy, G. H., Beadle-Brown, J., Wing, L., Gould, J., Shah, A., & Holmes, N. (2005). Chronicity of challenging behaviours in people with severe intellectual disabilities and/or autism: A total population sample. *Journal of Autism and Developmental Disorders, 35*, 405–418. https://doi.org/10.1007/s10803-005-5030-2

Neely, L., Garcia, E., Bankston, B., & Green, A. (2018). Generalization and maintenance of functional communication training for individuals with developmental disabilities: A systematic and quality review. *Research in Developmental Disabilities, 79*, 116–129. https://doi.org/10.1016/j.ridd.2018.02.002

Northup, J., Wacker, D. P., Berg, W. K., Kelly, L., Sasso, G. M., & DeRaad, A. (1994). The treatment of severe behavior problems in schools using a technical assistance model. *Journal of Applied Behavior Analysis, 27*, 33–47. https://doi.org/10.1901/jaba.1994.27-33

Peck, S. M., Wacker, D. P., Berg, W. K., Cooper, L. J., Brown, K. A., Richman, D., et al. (1996). Choice making treatment of young children's severe behavior problems. *Journal of Applied Behavior Analysis, 29*, 263–290. https://doi.org/10.1901/jaba.1996.29-263

Petscher, E. S., Rey, C., & Bailey, J. S. (2009). A review of empirical support for differential reinforcement of alternative behavior. *Research in Developmental Disabilities, 30*, 409–425. https://doi.org/10.1016/j.ridd.2008.08.008

Podlesnik, C. A., & Kelley, M. E. (2015). Translational research on the relapse of operant behavior. *Revista Mexicana de Análisis de la Conducta, 41*, 226–251.

Pritchard, D., Hoerger, M., Mace, F. C., Penney, H., & Harris, B. (2014). Clinical translation of animal models of treatment relapse. *Journal of the Experimental Analysis of Behavior, 101*, 442–449. https://doi.org/10.1002/jeab.87

Radhakrishnan, S., Gerow, S., & Weston, R. (2019). Resurgence of challenging behavior following functional communication training for children with disabilities: A literature review. *Journal of Developmental and Physical Disabilities*. Advanced online publication. https://doi.org/10.1007/s10882-019-09685-1

Richman, D. M., Wacker, D. P., & Winborn, L. (2001). Response efficiency during functional communication training: Effects of effort on response allocation. *Journal of Applied Behavior Analysis, 34*, 73–76. https://doi.org/10.1901/jaba.2001.34-73

Ringdahl, J. E., Berg, W. K., Wacker, D. P., Crook, K., Molony, M. A., Vargo, K. K., et al. (2018). Effects of response preference on resistance to change. *Journal of the Experimental Analysis of Behavior, 109*, 265–280. https://doi.org/10.1002/jeab.308

Ringdahl, J. E., Falcomata, T. S., Christensen, T. J., Bass-Ringdahl, S. M., Lentz, A., Dutt, A., et al. (2009). Evaluation of a pre-treatment assessment to select mand topographies for functional communication training. *Research in Developmental Disabilities, 30*, 330–341. https://doi.org/10.1016/j.ridd.2008.06.002

Roane, H. S., Fisher, W. W., Sgro, G. M., Falcomata, T. S., & Pabico, R. R. (2004). An alternative method of thinning reinforcer delivery during differential reinforcement. *Journal of Applied Behavior Analysis, 37*, 213–218. https://doi.org/10.1901/jaba.2004.37-213

Rooker, G. W., Jessel, J., Kurtz, P. F., & Hagopian, L. P. (2013). Functional communication training with and without alternative reinforcement and punishment: An analysis of 58 applications. *Journal of Applied Behavior Analysis, 46*, 708–722. https://doi.org/10.1002/jaba.76

Saini, V., Miller, S. A., & Fisher, W. W. (2016). Multiple schedules in practical application: Research trends and implications for future investigation. *Journal of Applied Behavior Analysis, 49*, 421–444. https://doi.org/10.1002/jaba.300

Saini, V., Sullivan, W. E., Baxter, E. L., DeRosa, N. M., & Roane, H. S. (2018). Renewal during functional communication training. *Journal of Applied Behavior Analysis, 51*, 603–619. https://doi.org/10.1002/jaba.471

Santiago, J. L., Hanley, G. P., Moore, K., & Jin, C. S. (2016). The generality of interview-informed functional analyses: Systematic replications in school and home. *Journal of Autism and Developmental Disorders, 46*, 797–811. https://doi.org/10.1007/s10803-015-2617-0

Shukla, S., & Albin, R. W. (1996). Effects of extinction alone and extinction plus functional communication training on covariation of problem behaviors. *Journal of Applied Behavior Analysis, 29*, 565–568. https://doi.org/10.1901/jaba.1996.29-565

Sigafoos, J. (2000). Communication development and aberrant behavior in children with developmental disabilities. *Education and Training in Mental Retardation and Developmental Disabilities, 35*, 168–176.

Skinner, B. F. (1957). *Verbal behavior*. New York: Appleton-Century-Crofts.

St. Peter Pipkin, C., Vollmer, T. R., & Sloman, K. N. (2010). Effects of treatment integrity failures during differential reinforcement of alternative behavior: A translational model. *Journal of Applied Behavior Analysis, 43*, 47–70. https://doi.org/10.1901/jaba.2010.43-47

Stokes, T. F., & Baer, D. M. (1977). An implicit technology of generalization. *Journal of Applied Behavior Analysis, 10*, 349–367. https://doi.org/10.1901/jaba.1977.10-349

Sullivan, W. E., & Roane, H. S. (2018). Incorporating choice in differential reinforcement of other behavior arrangements. *Behavioral Development, 23*(2), 130–137. https://doi.org/10.1037/bdb0000079

Sundberg, C. T., & Sundberg, M. L. (1990). Comparing topography-based verbal behavior with stimulus selection-based verbal behavior. *The Analysis of Verbal Behavior, 8*, 31–41. https://doi.org/10.1007/bf03392845

Tiger, J. H., Hanley, G. P., & Bruzek, J. (2008). Functional communication training: A review and practical guide. *Behavior Analysis in Practice, 1*, 16–23. https://doi.org/10.1007/BF03391716

Tsiouris, J. A. (2010). Pharmacotherapy for aggressive behaviours in persons with intellectual disabilities: Treatment or mistreatment? *Journal of Intellectual Disability Research, 54*, 1–16. https://doi.org/10.1111/j.1365-2788.2009.01232.x

Vignes, T. (2007). A comparison of topography-based and selection-based verbal behavior in typically developed children and developmentally disabled persons with autism. *The Analysis of Verbal Behavior, 23*, 113–122. https://doi.org/10.1007/bf03393051

Wacker, D. P., Berg, W. K., Harding, J. W., Barretto, A., Rankin, B., & Ganzer, J. (2005). Treatment effectiveness, stimulus generalization, and acceptability to parents of functional communication training. *Educational Psychology, 25*, 233–256. https://doi.org/10.1080/0144341042000301184

Wacker, D. P., Harding, J. W., Morgan, T. A., Berg, W. K., Schieltz, K. M., Lee, J. F., & Padilla, Y. C. (2013). An evaluation of resurgence during functional communication training. *The Psychological Record, 63*(1), 3–20. https://doi.org/10.11133/j.tpr.2013.63.1.001

Wacker, D. P., Schieltz, K. M., Berg, W. K., Harding, J. W., Dalmau, Y. C. P., & Lee, J. F. (2017). The long-term effects of functional communication training conducted in young children's home settings. *Education and Treatment of Children, 40*, 43–56. https://doi.org/10.1353/etc.2017.0003

Winborn, L., Wacker, D. P., Richman, D. M., Asmus, J., & Geier, D. (2002). Assessment of mand selection for functional communication training packages. *Journal of Applied Behavior Analysis, 35*, 295–298. https://doi.org/10.1901/jaba.2002.35-295

Winborn-Kemmerer, L., Ringdahl, J. E., Wacker, D. P., & Kitsukawa, K. (2009). A demonstration of individual preference for novel mands during functional communication training. *Journal of Applied Behavior Analysis, 42*, 185–189. https://doi.org/10.1901/jaba.2009.42-185

Zelinsky, N. A., & Shadish, W. (2018). A demonstration of how to do a meta-analysis that combines single-case designs with between-groups experiments: The effects of choice making on challenging behaviors performed by people with disabilities. *Developmental Neurorehabilitation, 21*, 266–278. https://doi.org/10.3109/17518423.2015.1100690

Behavioral Treatment of Sexual Offending

Duncan Pritchard, Heather Penney, Veda Richards, and Nicola Graham

Abstract In this chapter, we review assessment, treatment, risk management, and service delivery as it applies to male sexual offenders with intellectual and neurodevelopmental disabilities. Treatment relapse is discussed from the perspective of recent research showing that relapse is related to the context in which the behavior is reinforced. The chapter discusses the applied behavior analysis (ABA)-based multicomponent behavioral treatment (MCBT) that we have developed in our residential program over the last 10 years. Further, we review case studies on the young people that we have supported and have been able to follow-up since their discharge from the program. The case studies highlight the need for all agencies to work together effectively to keep everyone safe and that for some clients, current time-limited, "treat and hope" programs are not always successful in the long term. The chapter concludes with legal and ethical issues faced by behavior analysts and suggestions for future research.

Keywords Applied behavior analysis · Multicomponent behavioral treatment · Neurodevelopmental disabilities · Residential programming · Sexually offending behavior

Some persons with intellectual disabilities and other neurodevelopmental disorders (IDND) present sexual offending behavior that puts their victims at risk of serious harm. The consequences for the offender can also be serious as they may subsequently be required to live a more restricted life, sometimes far away from their families and friends. Although most sexual offending behavior literature focuses on contact behavior directed at children, sexual offending behavior presented by people with IDND is sometimes directed at their peers, staff, adult strangers and, occasionally, animals. Non-contact sexual offenses such as voyeurism, viewing or downloading illegal pornography via the Internet, and sharing images and videos via social media, can also lead to the person being arrested and charged with serious offenses.

Behavior analysts are faced with a significant challenge in treating sexual offending behavior and ensuring that treatment relapse does not occur. In this chapter, we review assessment, treatment, risk management, and service delivery as it applies to male sexual offenders with IDND. Given the persistence of sexual offending behavior, treatment relapse is discussed from the perspective of recent research showing that relapse is related to the context in which the behavior is reinforced. We also discuss the applied behavior analysis (ABA)-based multicomponent behavioral treatment (MCBT) that we have developed in our residential program over the last 10 years. Further, we review case studies on the young people that we have supported and have been able to follow-up since their discharge from the program. These case studies highlight the need for all agencies to work together effectively to keep everyone safe and that for some clients, current time-limited, 'treat and hope' programs are not always successful in the long term. Finally, the chapter also considers legal and ethical issues faced by behavior analysts and concludes with suggestions for future research.

Literature Review

Sexual offending behavior presented by a person with IDND often leads to the person being obliged to live away from their family in a segregated setting. More seriously, if the person is not diverted from prosecution due to the degree of their intellectual disability (ID), they can be imprisoned. Unfortunately for behavior analysts already working in this field, or suddenly finding themselves required to deliver treatment, the literature currently provides little in the way of evidence-based practice. For example, a mainstream sex offender treatment based on cognitive-behavioral therapy (CBT), the UK-based Core Sex Offender Treatment Program (Core-SOTP), has recently been withdrawn from UK prisons because it has been shown to increase the risk of reoffending (Mews, Di Bella, & Purver, 2017). This is worrying because over the last 20 or so years, group-based adapted-CBT treatment programs (e.g., SOTSEC-ID, 2010) have become the dominant treatment used with sexual offenders with IDND in the UK.

The SOTSEC-ID program was implemented with 46 males with IDND who were identified to be at 'risk of sexual offending' (p. 539). The treatment was implemented across nine settings, including open and secure settings and was delivered at a slower pace and over a longer time period compared to mainstream-CBT treatment. The results showed gains across a number of outcome measures such as increased sexual knowledge and victim empathy, improvements in attitudes consistent with sexual offending, and reduced cognitive distortions. However, gains in these outcome measures are not the real measure of the effectiveness of treatment for sexual offending. Rather, the critical measure is: Did reoffending occur? For example, Lindsay, Michie, Steptoe, Moore, and Haut (2011) compared a group of 15 male sexual offenders against women with a group of 15 male sexual offenders against children. The outcome measure used was the Questionnaire on Attitudes Consistent with Sexual Offending (QACSO). Both groups demonstrated improved attitudes consistent with sexual offending after 36 months in treatment, but at follow-up after 36 months, reoffending across both groups was 23%.

In the SOTSEC-ID (2010) study, of the 46 men who received treatment, three men presented harmful noncontact sexual behaviors (i.e., public masturbation, indecent exposure, stalking, and verbal sexual harassment) during the 1-year treatment period. Four men presented sexually abusive behavior during the 6-month follow-up period, two of whom had already offended during the treatment period. Heaton and Murphy (2013) later followed up 34 of the original cohort and reported that 11 of the 34 (32%) had presented 'problematic sexual behavior' and that two of these 11 men had been convicted as a result. The majority of those persons who offended were diagnosed with autism spectrum disorder (ASD).

It is concerning that the offending rate was so high for those men treated in the SOTSEC-ID program. In contrast, Craig, Stringer, and Sanders (2012) reported the results of a CBT program that treated 14 male sex offenders described as having 'intellectual limitations' rather than intellectual disability. The sample had a mean Full-Scale IQ of 74 (range, 67–79). Two participants dropped out during treatment because their probation orders came to an end, but none of the remaining 12 reoffended during treatment or during a 6-month follow-up period. Craig et al. were able to follow up six of the men for 12 months and reported that none of these men reoffended. The follow-up period was relatively brief, and only reported on six men, so claims as to the long-term effectiveness of the treatment program should be treated with caution. It may or may not be relevant that, firstly, the men attending this program were more able than the men in the SOTSEC-ID (2010) sample and, secondly, that they had already been severely punished so would have been aware of the likely consequences of any further reoffending.

In another CBT-based program implemented in the UK, 12 program completers (four of the original sample dropped out) demonstrated reductions in attitudes consistent with offending and increased sexual knowledge (Rose, Rose, Hawkins, & Anderson, 2012). The sample was assessed using the WAIS III ($M = 58$; range, 49–70). The participants had committed a range of serious sexual offences, including rape, indecent assault, and stalking. One of the 12 men reoffended during the 18-month follow-up period and had to move from his community placement to a low-secure placement.

Lindsay, Olley, Baillie, and Smith (1999) reported that of four adolescent sexual offenders who received community-based cognitive therapy over 2 years, two did not reoffend after 3 years and two did not reoffend after 4 years post-treatment. The treatment used by Lindsay et al. is worthy of further comment. Lindsay et al. clearly had the opportunity to establish a strong rapport with the participants over the treatment period, including going out for lunch as a group on a number of occasions. During the treatment period they knew of episodes where the participants had put themselves in high-risk situations such as spending time in environments where they had previously offended and talking to children the same age as their victims. They were thus able to challenge the boys and warn them of the serious consequences of any reoffending.

In a departure from CBT-based treatment, mindfulness-based therapy was reported by Singh et al. (2011) to help three adult prisoners with mild intellectual disabilities to control their deviant sexual arousal. The mean age of the men was 27.3 years (range 23–34) and all three had been prosecuted for serious sexual offences against children. Singh et al. taught the three participants to use two mindfulness strategies (*Meditation on the Soles of the Feet* and *Mindful Observation of Thoughts*) when they were provided with printed stimulus materials. Subsequent changes to the baseline condition demonstrated that the two mindfulness strategies were more effective than the participants' own self-control strategies.

Despite the enthusiasm for the use of psychological treatments with sexual offending behavior amongst researchers and treatment providers, the evidence for the continued use of group-based treatments for some 'hard-to-treat' behaviors is not convincing. A key component of group treatment is reported to be the participants interacting and providing each other with support and challenge under the guidance of the therapists (e.g., Lindsay, 2009). However, the poor verbal comprehension skills of some sexual offenders with low IQ may mean that they are not always able to contribute effectively (Willner, 2005).

The main weaknesses of the reports discussed above are that they are small, uncontrolled, and have short follow-up times (for reviews, see Cohen & Harvey, 2015; Jones & Chaplin, 2017; Morratto, 2015). It is also possible that adapted-CBT programs used with sexual offenders with IDND, like the mainstream-CBT program Core-SOTP that has now been withdrawn, are actually increasing offending. One way to evaluate the effectiveness of adapted CBT-based treatment programs would be via a randomized controlled trial (RCT) but there are major ethical and practical issues that would have to be overcome first, not least of which is that some individuals who had sexually offended would not receive any treatment or support (see Patterson, 2018, for a discussion).

Single-Subject Treatment and Case Studies

A weakness of treatment models based on psychological treatments is that the outcome measures are usually the person's verbal or written responses to questions on, for example, their arousal level, victim empathy, cognitive distortions, and attitudes to offending. The outcome measures of behavioral treatments are the person's behaviors, which require direct observation of the behavior, a basic tenet of

ABA. Notably, ABA assessment and treatments have been used successfully to treat inappropriate sexual behavior maintained by attention, escape, and access to preferred activities as described in reviews by Davis et al. (2016) and Clay, Bloom, and Lambert (2018).

Yet, direct observation of sexual offending behavior is problematic because most sexual offending behavior takes place in private making direct observation difficult (for a discussion, see Vollmer, Reyes, & Walker, 2012). Accordingly, there are only a small number of single-subject treatment and case studies that report the outcome of behavioral treatments to reduce sexual offending behavior (e.g., Early, Erickson, Wink, McDougle, & Scott, 2012; Dozier, Iwata, & Worsdell, 2011; Pritchard et al., 2011, 2016; Reyes et al., 2006; Reyes, Vollmer, & Hall, 2011; Walker, Joslyn, Vollmer, & Hall, 2014).

Early et al. (2012) describe the treatment of a 16-year-old male diagnosed with ASD who had a preoccupation with his female peers' feet. He would ask to massage the feet of his female classmates, something that was becoming problematic and was likely to lead to his exclusion from school and to his possible isolation. Exposure therapy, relationship and sex education, and social skills training over 17 months was successful in eliminating the behavior. Similarly, Dozier et al. (2011) describe the effective treatment of a foot-shoe fetish presented by a 36-year-old male with ASD. The man engaged in sexual behavior when in the presence of women wearing sandals. A response interruption and time-out procedure quickly eliminated the sexual behavior across multiple settings.

Reyes et al. (2006) used penile plethysmography with 10 men living in a residential program for sexual offenders with IDND. Some of the men became aroused when they viewed deviant stimuli, some men showed arousal to nondeviant stimuli, and some men showed arousal to both deviant and nondeviant stimuli. Reyes et al. (2011) later evaluated the arousal of two males with IDND to deviant and nondeviant stimuli via using the same technology. One participant showed suppressed arousal to both types of stimuli, whereas the other showed suppressed arousal to nondeviant stimuli but not deviant stimuli (an image of a 6 to 7-year-old female). Although this method of assessing arousal perhaps provides empirical evidence of likely risk as opposed to clinical judgment, caution should be given to these results due to the sample size. It has also been reported that some sexual offenders are able to control their arousal response to child-related visual stimuli (Laws & Rubin, 1969). For example, Walker et al. (2014) taught a simple arousal suppression technique (i.e., counting, out loud, backwards from 100) to two adult sex offenders with IDND. Both participants could suppress their arousal to deviant stimuli and one participant was able to do this and successfully maintain arousal to nondeviant stimuli. Walker et al. suggested that suppression instructions be incorporated into treatment programs for sex offenders with intellectual disabilities, but further research is needed.

Multicomponent Behavioral Treatment

Our two case studies (Pritchard et al., 2011, 2016) describe extended multicomponent behavioral treatment in a residential program in the UK for adolescents with IDND. Although uncontrolled, both studies illustrate that two adolescents who had previously been required to live extremely restricted lives could be supported to attend education, to stay safe, and to participate in a wide range of community-based activities.

The participant in the Pritchard et al. (2011) case report was a 16-year-old male (*Iwan*) diagnosed with a mild ID (IQ = 55) and attention-deficit hyperactivity disorder (ADHD). Iwan was admitted to our program for treatment of his severe problem behavior that consisted of harmful sexual behavior, aggression, property damage, and elopement. Shortly prior to admission, he had been charged with a serious sexual offense against a young boy and required to live in a secure setting while his placement in our program was arranged.

On admission, Iwan was enrolled in the normal residential program but there were frequent episodes of harmful sexual behavior, including following young girls during a community visit on two separate occasions. A functional behavioral assessment (FBA) via direct observation using an antecedent-behavior-consequence (ABC) format, analysis of critical incident reports, and interviews were conducted with staff to generate hypotheses about the function of his sexually harmful behavior (Watson & Steege, 2003). The program's incident report format is structured to obtain specific information about possible motivating and reinforcing events and is a record of direct observation of these episodes. The results of the FBA suggested that the Iwan's harmful sexual behavior was maintained by attention from adolescent and adult females that he found attractive and automatically reinforced via stimuli he accessed from the Internet and adult-oriented chat lines.

After Iwan had attended the program for 48 weeks, the multicomponent behavioral treatment (MCBT) was introduced. The MCBT was comprised of the *ACHIEVE!* program (The *ACHIEVE!* Program; Pritchard, Penney, & Mace, 2017), adapted-CBT, visual schedules, and a differential reinforcement of other behavior (DRO) schedule (i.e., *review status*) that made his access to the community contingent on safe behavior. A key component of the *ACHIEVE!* program was a points system, a variation of a token economy. During the 5-h academic day, skill points were awarded every 30 min contingent on Iwan presenting five key pro-social and pro-academic skills, specifically being on time, completing the task, using safe words, and speaking respectfully.

The adapted-CBT component consisted of individualized weekly sessions during which key messages were reiterated, for example, keeping hands to self, staying with staff, and following staff instructions. Iwan also received weekly relationship and sex education lessons which focused on key issues such as consent, relationships, and public and private behavior. Iwan struggled to read, so visual schedules were used to help him develop the necessary skills to behave appropriately in the community. The schedules also ensured that Iwan knew where he was going, what he would be doing, and what was expected of him when he returned to the center. Immediately after the MCBT was implemented there were reductions in problem behaviors, which were maintained for the following 30 weeks.

Review status was implemented if Iwan presented sexual behavior. The consequence for noncontact sexual behavior (e.g., sexual comments) was him being restricted from going off-site for 2 days. Contact sexual behavior (e.g., sexual touching) required Iwan being restricted from going off-site for 3 days. Restrictions of this nature are not uncommon and formed part of the program's risk management process (e.g., Rea, Dixon, & Zettle, 2014). Although not reported in the original case report, Iwan was later supported by program staff to buy adult-oriented magazines which he kept in his own room. The only problem behaviors that occurred were when he used center telephones to ring adult chat lines without permission.

In the second case report from our program (Pritchard et al., 2016) we described how the MCBT was associated with the reduction in harmful sexual behavior in a 17-year-old male (*Osian*) with ASD. Prior to his admission to the program, Osian had been convicted on eight occasions for a variety of serious offences, including sexual touching, assault and burglary, and had been detained in mainstream secure accommodation on four separate occasions.

In addition to the points system described above, a level system had been integrated into the *ACHIEVE!* program. The primary purpose of the level system was to motivate Osian to work toward long-term goals, but the levels also provided staff with an assessment of the level of risk presented by him because level progression was correlated with extended periods of safe behavior. In week 29, he reached Level 2 of the program which had earned him the privilege of him spending more supervised time in the community and having access to the Internet (Pritchard et al., 2017). However, in week 46, his problem behavior relapsed and there were a number of problem behaviors in the following 20 weeks.

Direct observation and analysis of the incident reports written by staff indicated that the problem behavior was associated with Osian's increased time on his tablet computer and his reluctance to move on to his next scheduled activity. The information from the analysis of the incident reports and the frequency of problem behavior chart was shared with Osian, his family and his funding agency and in week 66, a behavior contingency contract (BCC) was implemented (Heward, 2007). The BCC specified a contingency between his safe behavior, his supervised access to his tablet computer during his leisure periods, and his supervised time in the community (Fig. 1). The BCC was written and signed by Osian, his mother, program staff, and colleagues from his funding agency. Implementation of the BCC was associated with an immediate reduction in problem behavior. The BCC was withdrawn when Osian reached Level 2+ of the program in week 87 when there had been 8 weeks without any problem behavior. Osian went on to attend, with staff support, local further education college and two work experience placements in local cafés. He was supported by program staff to engage in a relationship with an age-appropriate male that he had met during his community visits (Griffiths, Thomson, Frijters, Hoath, & Wilson, 2018).

BEHAVIOR CONTINGENCY CONTRACT

'OSIAN JONES'

SAFE USE OF HIS TABLET COMPUTER

- From 18 February, Osian can take his tablet computer to the internet café once a week.
- The timing and duration of the visit will be stated on his weekly person-centered plan.
- He will be supervised by two staff until he reaches Level 2+.
- On his other community visits during out-of-school hours, the tablet computer must be locked away in his room (Osian has a cash box for this purpose and a spare key is kept in the main office).
- Osian must demonstrate socially appropriate use of his tablet computer (i.e., he must not take photographs, videos, or record conversations of his peers, staff, or members of the public).
- Osian can take his tablet computer to class so that he can use the internet to download music during his two daily reward periods (12pm-12.30pm and 3pm-3.30pm).

OSIAN HAS FULL RESPONSIBILITY FOR THE SAFE USE OF HIS TABLET COMPUTER. INAPPROPRIATE USE MAY RESULT IN THE TEMPORARY OR PERMANENT LOSS OF THIS PRIVILEGE AND, IF NECESSARY, HIS BEHAVIOR WILL BE REPORTED TO THE POLICE.

THIS CONTRACT WILL BE REVIEWED AT OSIAN'S CORE GROUP MEETING ON 27 MARCH AND WILL BE WITHDRAWN WHEN OSIAN REACHES LEVEL 2+.

Parties to this contract:

Osian Jones: _____ Date: _____

Mrs Jones (Mother): _____ Date: _____

Key Worker: _____ Date: _____

Social Worker: _____ Date: _____

Class Teacher: _____ Date: _____

Classroom Assistant: _____ Date: _____

Program Staff: _____ Date: _____

Program Staff: _____ Date: _____

Program Therapist: _____ Date: _____

Program Coordinator: _____ Date: _____

Fig. 1 Behavior Contingency Contract: Use of Tablet Computer

A key feature of the program described in the two case studies and in the subsequent report on the *ACHIEVE!* program (Pritchard et al., 2017) was the direct observation of each individual throughout their waking day and the explicit teaching of independent living and socio-sexual skills with an emphasis on community safety. Progress was tracked via data that was collected on each young person and reviewed each day, along with any incident reports, by senior supervisory staff. Depending on the level of risk, each young person was provided with frequent opportunities each week to spend time in community-based settings (e.g., shops, cafes, library, college, leisure centers) so that the skills learned would generalize and maintain over time (See Table 1).

Each adolescent had an individualized risk assessment and management plan (RAMP). The RAMP specified the level of supervision each young person was to receive across settings. For example, young people who had previously presented sexual offending behavior, even if they had not been prosecuted because of their age or degree of ID, were initially provided with at least 2:1 staff support when they were out in the community. There were restrictions on where they could go at certain times (e.g., they were not allowed to access settings similar to where they had previously presented sexual behavior), how far they could travel, and which staff were permitted to supervised them off-site until they had demonstrated safe behavior for specified periods of time and progressed through the levels.

The adapted-CBT took place during weekly one-to-one sessions because of concerns that the young people would not be able to respect the usual confidentiality rules of group-based sessions. One-to-one therapy sessions also reduce the possibility of any of the young people being exposed to details of deviant behavior that any

Table 1 ACHIEVE! Program community-based activities and staff ratios

Level	Staff ratio	School trips	Leisure trips
1	2:1	Supermarket Leisure center Café	Castles Beach Local walks Local bike rides
1+	2:1	Gym	Play pool in a pub Fast food lunch
2	1:1	Work experience College	Cinema Ice skating Bowling Museums
2+	1:1[a]	Work experience College Public transport	Zoo Fishing Golf Football match
3	N/A[b]	Work experience College Public transport	High-ropes course Go-karting Adventure/leisure park Music concert

[a]Staff not providing direct 'eyes-on' supervision but nearby to support if required
[b]Dependent on individualized risk assessment

of the adolescents had presented prior to their admission to the program (Blasingame, Boer, Guidry, & Wilson, 2014). The weekly one-to-one sessions enabled the program therapist and each participant to establish rapport and for the therapist to challenge the participant on any behavioral issues or concerns that been observed by staff in the previous week (e.g., Lindsay et al., 1999; Rea et al., 2014).

At the core of the MCBT were the principles of contingency management. Contingent on the consistent presentation of appropriate behavior, the participants gained access to a prescribed set of privileges such as preferred activities, being able to travel further away from the center to participate in preferred activities, and spend increasing amounts of time in the community. At Level 3, the participants could visit the community spontaneously if staff were available to support them. Of the nine participants described in Pritchard et al. (2017), six had been referred to the program for treatment of their harmful sexual behavior. Two of the six had been convicted for sexual offenses prior to their admission to the program; the other four had been diverted from prosecution by the degree of their ID. The severity of these behaviors should not be conflated with problematic sexual behavior that has attention, tangible or escape functions. It is our experience that these behaviors can be effectively treated by consistent use of an appropriate function-based treatment (Davis et al., 2016). Similarly, sexual behaviors that are automatically reinforced can effectively be treated with response interruption and redirection and/or response interruption (e.g., Cividini-Motta, Moore, Fish, Priehs, & Ahearn, 2019).

Despite the level of support and supervision that the adolescents enrolled in the program received, two of the six had convictions during their time in the program for downloading illegal pornography. These episodes occurred when they were on supported community visits, one in an Internet café and the other in the local further education college during recess. These 'inadvertent probes' illustrate the serious consequences for some young people with IDND being allowed unsupervised access to the Internet, even for brief periods. The lessons learnt from these 'inadvertent probes' were subsequently integrated into the staff training program. These episodes and other 'near misses' were recorded on a chronology that was kept on each young person's file and read by all staff working with the young people. The chronologies include relevant information on each episode such as date, time, location, staff ratio, age and gender of potential victim, which agencies were notified, and resulting consequences.

Although the series of case studies described in our report lack internal validity, as an example of outcome research they point to the potential of contingency management as a treatment for sexual offending behavior (Clay et al., 2018). Also, replication of the MCBT across the nine participants and heterogeneity of the sample in terms of their age, multiple diagnoses (ASD, ADHD, conduct disorder), topography of problem behavior, and length of time in the program suggests that the treatment has some generality although the results are only correlational (Kazdin, 1982).

Sadly, despite the hard work of Osian, his family, and the staff that supported him throughout his time in the program, his problem behavior relapsed within days of his discharge from our program. Against the advice of the program staff who knew him far better than colleagues working for his funding agency, he was discharged to a community-based hostel where the support he received was woefully inadequate. He was subsequently convicted of abducting a 13-year-old boy whom he had met via social media and was sentenced to 26-months imprisonment although no sexual behavior had occurred. He served his sentence in a mainstream jail, despite his diagnosis of ASD and ID. He was released after 1 year, reoffended within days (a noncontact Internet-related sexual offense), and was returned to the same jail to serve the remainder of his sentence.

Sexual Offenders with Autism Spectrum Disorder: A Special Case?

The three participants in the SOTSEC-ID sample who relapsed post-treatment were reported to have ASD, as did the participant in the Early et al. (2012) case study and the participant in our second case study. A number of researchers have recently reviewed and evaluated the literature on sex offenders who have been diagnosed with ASD, namely Allely and Creaby-Attwood (2016), Creaby-Attwood and Allely (2017), and Mongavero (2016). Allely and Creaby-Attwood argue that more research is urgently needed to identify effective treatments that can prevent the risk of reoffending by males with ASD. Mogavero notes the association between ASD and deviant sexual behavior and propose that sex offending behavior can sometimes be explained by ASD, that is, the deviant behaviors are characteristic of the person's ASD symptomology and lack any malicious intent. However, sex offending behavior is seldom seen as a function of ASD symptomology by the criminal justice system notwithstanding that 21 California Superior Court Justices reported they would take into account the accused person's diagnosis of autism and that treatment and other sentencing options would be considered during sentencing (Berryessa, 2016).

Murrie, Warren, Kristiansson, and Dietz (2002) reviewed six cases of individuals who had been diagnosed with ASD, four of whom had been convicted of sexual offenses, including voyeurism, sexual assault against children, assaults against two women, and an assault against a teenage male. Murrie et al., observed that the four men all had deficits in empathy, lacked remorse, and seemed 'genuinely unaware of the harm they caused their victims' (p. 66). Restricted interests and repetitive patterns of behavior are diagnostic features of ASD and Murrie et al. note that a preoccupation with sex was common in all four cases. If we accept that a preoccupation with sexual behavior is an example of a restricted interest, then behavior analysts providing treatment for sexual offending behavior need to be aware that their clients who have ASD may present a different treatment challenge to those offenders without ASD.

Relationship and Sex Education

A key component of most sex offending treatment programs is relationship and sex education, especially for children and adolescents. Baarsma et al. (2016) reported that a cohort of 44 boys had less sexual knowledge and demonstrated negative atti-

Table 2 Relationship and sex education

Age	Topic	Content
11–13	Relationships	Friendships Family relationships Dating Bullying Peer pressure and influence Values Communication Healthy vs. unhealthy relationships Self-esteem Loyalty Trust Honesty Respect
	Puberty	Body changes (male and female)
13–15	Relationships and sex	Puberty Peer pressure and influence Bullying Assertiveness Self-confidence Masturbation Public and private Different types of relationships Consent Dating Staying safe (face-to-face and online) Intimate relationships Contraception Accessing appropriate advice and support
15+	Relationships and sex	Pornography Online safety Social media
	Sexually transmitted infections (STIs)	Signs and symptoms Routes of transmission Short- and long-term effects Prevention Testing Treatment Prevention Myths
	Alcohol and substance misuse	Impact of alcohol and substance misuse on sexual relationships

tudes toward pornography. However, and perhaps counter-intuitively, sex offenders have been reported to have greater sexual knowledge than non-offending controls (Lunsky, Frijters, Griffiths, Watson, & Williston, 2007). Nevertheless, treatment providers have a duty to ensure that their clients are able to develop an understanding of important concepts such as staying healthy, consent, contraception, and public and private contexts especially those with ASD who may have particular difficulties in this area stemming from their symptomology (Mongavero, 2016). In our center, we have developed an integrated relationship and sex education curriculum that is taught to the young people on an individual basis as part of their school program by a qualified teacher and the program therapist (See Table 2). The young people also gain nationally recognized qualifications in personal and social education as they work through the curriculum.

There is a need for sexual offenders with IDND to be taught to use the Internet safely, especially those that use social media and dating apps (Tullis & Zangrillo, 2013). The dangers of sexting (i.e., the use of messaging media to send and receive inappropriate images) needs to be understood by sex offenders with IDND, as does the need for them to adhere to any restrictions on Internet and social media use made on them by their treatment providers or the courts. In our program, we teach the young people the dangers of inappropriate Internet and social media use as part of their personal and social education program (see Table 3) as well has having several layers of online security in the center.

Table 3 Online safety

Age	Topic	Content
11–13	Staying safe online	Using a computer What is online personal information Online security settings and passwords
13–15		Social media Sharing images—What is safe and what is not Understanding that once a picture is shared you have lost control of it Knowing people aren't always who they say they are online Reliability of what is on the internet Online gaming Cyberbullying
15+		Pornography Social media Sharing images—What is safe/unsafe Understanding that once a picture is shared, you have lost control of it People are not always who they say they are online Reliability of what is on the internet—Not always as it seems

Legal Issues

The tensions inherent in balancing the right of the person to live in the community and participate in everyday activities with the need to keep everyone safe are familiar to behavior analysts working in this complex field. For example, in residential programs that are also schools and colleges, it is acceptable in most jurisdictions to keep external doors locked, thus keeping the both the clients and the local community safe. However, this is not generally acceptable in residential programs that provide care, support, and treatment to adults with IDND. Instead, adults living in a residential home or supported living arrangement in the UK are sometimes made subject to legal restrictions such as Deprivation of Liberty Safeguards (DoLS; Royal College of Psychiatrists, 2015). Persons in the UK who have sexually offended are usually subject to restrictions under the Multi-Agency Public Protection Arrangements (MAPPA; Ministry of Justice, 2012). Under MAPPA, sexual offenders are managed by multiple agencies including social services, mental health teams, and probation departments. The restrictions usually include being required to stay away from environments frequented by vulnerable people. Sexual Offences Prevention Orders (SOPO) were introduced in the UK by the Sexual Offences Act (2003) and are issued by the courts if there is deemed to be a risk of severe sexual harm to the public. There is no requirement that the person be found guilty of any offense; a SOPO can be handed down on the basis of alleged behavior and breach of a SOPO can result in a fine or a prison sentence of up to 5 years.

Research Findings and Implications

Behavior analysts seeking to treat sexually offending behavior can find themselves trying to eliminate severe behaviors that are occurring frequently and across many settings. They can also find themselves in disagreement with parole, probation, treatment, and residential service providers over what constitutes the best form of treatment (Newstrom, Miner, Hoefer, Hanson, & Robinson, 2018). As discussed above, if the sexual offending behavior is presented by a person with ASD, it can be especially prone to relapse during treatment, post-treatment, or when the person moves to a setting where supervision is less robust.

Treatment Relapse

The failure of treatment gains to generalize and maintain in post-treatment settings can perhaps be conceptualized by the renewal relapse paradigm. Renewal has been evaluated in basic, translational, and applied research (for review, see Podlesnik, Kelley, Jimenez-Gomez, & Bouton, 2017). In one of the first reports on the renewal of problem behavior, Lalli, Casey, and Kates (1997) observed that disruptive behavior presented by three children successfully treated in a clinic relapsed in two of the participants when they returned to their homes and schools, despite their parents and teachers implementing the treatment with integrity.

In terms of sexual offending behavior, ABA renewal refers to the relapse of sexual offending behavior when the person moves from Context B, the treatment context (e.g., a clinic, hospital, residential program, etc.) back to Context A, the context in which the sexual offending behavior initially occurred. In ABC renewal, Context A refers to the setting in which the sexual offending behavior occurred, Context B is the treatment setting and Context C is a novel setting that the person is discharged to post-treatment. Recent research on the renewal paradigm has demonstrated that problem behavior may relapse simply with a change of context (for a discussion, see Bouton, 2014). To avoid renewal entirely, behavior analysts should treat the sexually offending behavior in the context in which it first occurs but, of course, this is not possible when the offender is required to leave the context or when there is any risk to potential victims.

Translational researchers have demonstrated that treatment relapse can be mitigated by extended time in the treatment context (Wacker et al., 2011). The more durable treatment effects of extended time in treatment have also been reported in the sex offending literature relevant to individuals with IDND (Courtney & Rose, 2004; Lindsay & Smith, 1998). Renewal may also be mitigated by treating the behavior in multiple contexts such as clinic, community, hostel, and public transport settings. Basic research findings also suggest that ensuring that the treatment and post-treatment contexts are dissimilar to the context in which the offending behavior occurred may also mitigate renewal (Todd, Winterbauer, & Bouton, 2012).

Strategies for mitigating renewal of sexual offending behavior are all empirical questions that can be investigated via translational research using the ABA and ABC renewal paradigms. The reinstatement relapse paradigm should also be mentioned at this point (Bouton, 2014). In basic research with non-human animals, reinstatement of responding following extinction occurs when the animal is exposed to the stimuli that previously maintained responding, either contingently or non-contingently. In the context of sexual offending, unconditioned stimuli can lead to the person becoming aroused when he is exposed to these stimuli, for example, likely victims or images on social media. Sexual offenders with IDND need to consistently demonstrate that they will avoid environments where these stimuli are likely to occur, or if they cannot be avoided and the stimuli elicit arousal, they should be able to reliably absent themselves before any sexual behavior escalates.

These relapse-prevention skills need to be taught as part of any treatment program, an area of work that is fraught with difficulty because these skills need to be tested in the community (Stevenson, Lynn, Miller, & Hingsburger, 2011). Nevin and Wacker (2013) recommend that the generalization and maintenance of treatment is tested under suboptimal conditions; in the case of sexual offending behavior this means that supervision needs to be deliberately reduced in environments where stimuli likely to elicit arousal and evoke sexual behavior may occur. Rea et al. (2014) used a multi-element design to assess the generalization of 11 relapse-prevention behaviors of 10 sexual offenders with IDND aged 18–28 years ($M = 23.8$) across treatment staff, non-treatment staff who worked at the agency but not with the participants, and community adults who had not worked with the participants. Rea et al. reported that the highest rates of compliance were observed in the treatment staff/participant dyads and speculated that this outcome occurred because treatment staff had a history with the participants of providing corrective feedback and reliably reporting episodes of non-compliance to supervisors. Rea et al. also reported that the lowest levels of generalization were demonstrated by older participants who had previously displayed a range of deviant behaviors. The relapse-prevention behaviors of staying with staff and not talking to or touching potential victims were those that would have led to serious consequences for the participants had they not been observed.

Sadly, some persons are discharged from treatment providers with inadequate support. The persistence of sexual offending behavior points toward the need for appropriate treatment and levels of supervision to be in place long after persons with IDND are discharged from the clinic or hospital or released from prison. However, communities are unlikely to accept that people with IDND who have sexually offended will still be receiving treatment when they are discharged from a hospital or clinic and living in relatively unrestricted settings. It will require changes in public opinion and policy before this synthesis of treatment and supervision can be evaluated (Mace & Critchfield, 2010; Podlesnik & Kelley, 2017). In the case of young people leaving programs such as ours in the UK, the problems are exacerbated by the handover of the case from children's to adult services; in our experience adult services do not always take enough care in sourcing appropriate placements for these vulnerable young people.

Ethical Issues

Board Certified Behavior Analysts (BCBAs) are required to adhere to the Professional and Ethical Compliance Code of the Behavior Analyst Certification Board (BACB, 2019). The code was written to ensure that certified behavior analysts practice in a manner that ensures the needs of each individual client and the society at large are met. Behavior analysts delivering treatment to sexual offenders with IDND need to be mindful of four areas of their ethical code when considering whether or not to take on these cases. Firstly, the code stipulates that clients have a right to effective treatment that is evidence-based and validated as having short- and long-term benefits to both the client and society. As discussed above, relapse during or following treatment is common so treatment cannot currently be regarded as effective. Secondly, the code stipulates interventions delivered by behavior analysts should be adapted to the individual being treated. Given that most adapted-CBT interventions are group-based and not specifically designed to meet the needs of the individual, this requirement could put BCBAs in breach of their ethical code. Thirdly, behavior analysts should only practice in areas that they are already competent. If not competent, they should ensure that they receive supervision from an appropriately qualified and experienced behavior analyst. Fourthly, behavior analysts should only take on clients whose needs they are able to meet. Given the serious consequences if a client reoffends during or post-treatment, this is an area of work that should not be entered into by behavior analysts without a careful assessment of each case and an honest appraisal of their service's ability to meet the needs of the client and community members.

Risk Assessment

Behavior analysts are not yet able to refer to a body of evidence that can help them identify effective and individualized treatments for sexual offending behavior presented by persons with IDND (Blasingame et al., 2014; Jones & Chaplin, 2017). However, they are somewhat better served by recent research on risk assessment and the likelihood of the behavior relapsing following treatment (Lindsay et al., 2018; Lofthouse et al., 2013; Stephens, Newman, Cantor, & Seto, 2018).

Actuarial assessments are used to assess the level of risk based on an evaluation of static and dynamic risks. Static risks refer to those risks that do not change over time or with circumstances, for example, the offense, age of the offender when the offense occurred, and degree of the offender's intellectual disability. Dynamic risk assessments refer to factors that change over time, sometimes rapidly, as with emotional state, level of staff supervision, and support staff changes. The Static-99R is an actuarial risk assessment that has been shown to predict reoffending with sex offenders with intellectual disabilities (Stephens et al., 2018). The Static-99R is comprised of 10 items, including the age of the offender, any convictions for violence, and type of victim (i.e., unrelated victims, stranger victims, and male victims). Stephens et al. reviewed the data on a large sample of 454 male sex offenders, 83% of whom had committed contact and noncontact offenses against children under the age of 15. A strength of the study was that the follow-up period was 10 years. Despite the encouraging results, Stephens et al. recommend that practitioners be cautious when using the Static-99R with sex offenders whose ID is at either end of the IQ distribution. They also recommend that behavior analysts use a dynamic risk assessment alongside the STATIC-99R.

Two dynamic risk variables are the individual sex offender himself (e.g., any substance abuse, emotional state) and environmental variables (e.g., staff knowledge of the sex offender, level of supervision, changes in living accommodation). The *Assessment of Risk Manageability for Individuals with Developmental and Intellectual Limitations who Offend-Sexually* (ARMIDILO-S; Boer, Tough, & Haaven, 2004; Boer et al., 2013) is a dynamic risk assessment that provides a measure of individual-specific and environmental variables. Lofthouse et al. (2013) completed the STATIC-99 and the ARMIDILO-S with a sample of 64 adult males with intellectual disabilities, all of whom had a history of sexual offending behavior, and found that the ARMIDILO-S predicted the risk of sexual reoffending more accurately than the STATIC-99.

Risk assessments for sexually offending behavior presented by adolescents with IDND are not yet routinely used (for review, see Blasingame, 2018). In the UK the dominant assessment tool used with adolescents with IDND is the adapted-AIM2 (O'Callaghan, 2002; Print et al., 2007). Using a retrospective review of case files, Griffin and Vettor (2012) compared the mainstream AIM2 assessment with the adapted-AIM2 assessment and found that both assessment tools predicted similar risk ratings. However, further research by independent investigators is needed as the research used an extremely small sample size (i.e., reoffenders, $n = 9$, non-reoffenders, $n = 18$; cf. Miccio-Fonseca & Rasmussen, 2013, where $n = 224$). The AIM2 has recently been replaced by the AIM3 (Leonard & Hackett, 2019) which assesses the level of concern under five 'domains': sexual behavior, non-sexual behavior, developmental; environmental/family; and, self-regulation. Scores range from 0–20, with scores above 14 indicating significant need. This instrument differs from the previous AIM models, which categorized the young person as being at low, medium, and high risk of reoffending. Although the ARMIDILO-S was designed for use with adults, Blasingame, Creeden, and Rich (2015) suggest that the measures incorporated into the ARMIDILO-S are also relevant to adolescents with ID. For example, environmental factors such as staff knowledge of the individual's risk profile, specified and actual supervision levels, and the manageability of the individual within the setting, are all factors that apply to adolescents with IDND when assessing their risk of reoffending. Further research is needed, and behavior analysts working with adolescents who present sexually offending behavior are well placed to evaluate the validity of both the ARMIDILO-S and AIM3.

Practice Recommendations

The relapse of sexual offending behavior presented by some males with IDND points toward the need for some of these hard-to-treat behaviors to require more effective treatment. Some persons will require robust and long-term supervision long after their treatment has ended and they have been discharged from their program. Every episode of harmful sexual behavior should be thoroughly investigated by the service provider and funding agency, with the aim being to improve all services and keep people safe, and not simply to apportion blame. The findings should then be used to train staff to ensure they remain vigilant at all times. Regulatory agencies will need to monitor these services to ensure that quality is maintained but at the same time acknowledge that treatment relapse is sometimes inevitable, and work with the service provider and funding agency to evaluate what went wrong.

As well as improved treatment and supervision, sexual offenders with IDND also need to experience a service delivery model that enables them to develop their independent living skills. The Good Lives Model (GLM; Willis, Yates, Gannon, & Ward, 2013) focuses on the development of pro-social behavior, age-appropriate activities, and community participation skills and is similar to other service delivery models that have been used successfully with persons with IDND for many years (Lindsay, Taylor, & Murphy, 2018).

In our program, we utilize person-centered planning which is facilitated, in part, by weekly house meetings, which all the young people and staff have to attend (DoH, 2001). These meetings enable honest discussions between the staff and each young person and ensure that all staff are aware of any behavioral issues, either current or emerging. Staff are able to provide an appropriate level of support and challenge to the young people, including reminders of the serious consequences of any reoffending (cf. Lindsay et al., 1999). When supporting the young people to help write their weekly activity support plans, the staff direct them toward activities and environments where there are fewer risks (e.g., cycling, fishing, gardening) and away from environments with known risks (e.g., swimming pools, amusement arcades, beaches).

Keller (2016) refers to this collaboration as being a 'fourth generation' approach. It requires all stakeholders and the offender to develop an individualized program that treats the sexual offending behavior, provides an appropriate level of supervision, and provides multiple opportunities for the person to develop a comprehensive range of independent living and safety skills. This level of treatment, supervision, and skill teaching is expensive and is sometimes resisted by funding agencies because of the costs involved and by some of the persons who will assert their right to live more independently. Agencies have to balance the right of the person to live independently with the risk the person presents to the community (Griffiths et al., 2018). Although intrusive, measures such as legal restrictions, covert monitoring, frequent probes, and GPS tracking (Vollmer et al., 2012) may be necessary before some sexual offenders with IDND can live independently in the community. Whatever the supervision level, it is important that the person is enabled to participate in everyday activities and develop the skills necessary so that they are able to live more independently at some time in the future.

Conclusion and Research Directions

Most of the research published in the UK is by a small number of researchers in a few settings, with adapted-CBT treatments currently dominant. These treatments have been shown to not always be effective and the faith of both the treatment providers and funding agencies in them may be misplaced, especially among offenders with ASD. The need for a large-scale, RCT of existing treatments is clear, however, given the complexities inherent in carrying out a RCT, it may be that single-case experimental designs can be utilized to good effect. For example, contingency management treatment could be evaluated using a multiple-baseline design, perhaps across a number of participants or across a number of settings. An alternating-treatments design could be used to compare the efficacy of two different treatments within individual participants. In typical alternating treatment designs, the two treatments are alternated rapidly and their effect on the dependent variable is measured. Given that the treatment for sexual offending behavior needs to be delivered over 1 or 2 years, or even longer in those cases where the behavior is hard-to-treat and relapsing during treatment, it may be necessary to counter-balance the treatments across participants and over extended time periods.

The renewal relapse paradigm suggests that where the person will be living post-treatment should affect treatment length and that post-treatment support be sufficiently robust, especially given the risk posed by access to the Internet and social media. Behavior analysts treating sexual offending behavior should consider conducting research based on the ABA and ABC renewal and reinstatement relapse paradigms. In the meantime, treatment relapse suggests that service providers should build relapse-prevention strategies into their treatment and transition plans and that placing agencies need to properly fund and monitor these plans rigorously. Until such time as behavior analysts working in this complex field develop more effective treatment programs and are better at identifying and minimizing the risk factors most strongly associated with reoffending, some hard-to-treat behaviors will make it necessary for some sexual offenders with IDND to be in intensive and long-term supervision programs that optimize intervention integrity, program evaluation, and community safety.

References

Allely, C. S., & Creaby-Attwood, A. (2016). Sexual offending and autism spectrum disorder. *Journal of Intellectual Disabilities and Offending Behaviour, 7*, 35–51. https://doi.org/10.1108/jidob-09-2015-0029

Baarsma, E. M., Boonmann, C., 't Hart-Kerkhoffs, L. A., de Graaf, H., Doreleijers, T. A. H., Vermeiren, R. R. J. M., et al. (2016). Sexuality and autistic-like symptoms in juvenile sex offender: A follow-up after 8 years. *Journal of Autism and Developmental Disorders, 46*, 2679–2691. https://doi.org/10.1007/s10803-016-2805-6

Behavior Analyst Certification Board. (2019). *Professional and ethical compliance code for behavior analysts*. Retrieved from http://www.bacb.com/wp-content/uploads/170706-compliance-code-english.pdf

Berryessa, C. M. (2016). Brief Report: Judicial attitudes regarding the sentencing of offenders with high functioning autism. *Journal of Autism and Developmental Disorders, 46*, 2770–2773. https://doi.org/10.1007/s10803-016-2798-1

Blasingame, G. D. (2018). Risk assessment of adolescents with intellectual disabilities who exhibit sexual behavior problems or sexual offending behavior. *Journal of Child Sexual Abuse, 27*, 955–971. https://doi.org/10.1080/10538712.2018.1452324

Blasingame, G. D., Boer, D. P., Guidry, L., & Wilson, R. J. (2014). *Assessment, treatment, and supervision of individuals with intellectual disabilities and problematic sexual behaviors*. Beaverton, OR: Association for the Treatment of Sexual Abusers. Retrieved from www.atsa.com

Blasingame, G., Creeden, K., & Rich, P. (2015). *Assessment and treatment of adolescents with intellectual disabilities who exhibit sexual problems or offending behaviors*. Beaverton, OR: Association for the Treatment of Sexual Abusers. Retrieved from www.atsa.com

Boer, D. P., Haaven, J., Lambrick, F., Lindsay, B., McVilly, K., Sakdalan, J., & Frize, M. (2013). *ARMIDILO: The assessment of risk and manageability of individuals with developmental and intellectual limitations who offend.* Retrieved from www.armidilo.net

Boer, D. P., Tough, S., & Haaven, J. (2004). Assessment of risk manageability of intellectually disabled sex offenders. *Journal of Applied Research in Intellectual Disabilities, 17*, 275–283. https://doi.org/10.1111/j.1468-3148.2004.00214.x

Bouton, M. E. (2014). Why behavior change is difficult to sustain. *Preventive Medicine, 68*, 29–36. https://doi.org/10.1016/j.ypmed.2014.06.010

Cividini-Motta, C., Moore, K., Fish, L. M., Priehs, J. C., & Ahearn, W. A. (2019). Reducing public masturbation in individuals with ASD: An assessment of response interruption procedures. *Behavior Modification, 44*(3), 429–448. https://doi.org/10.1177/0145445518824277

Clay, C. C., Bloom, S. E., & Lambert, J. M. (2018). Behavioral interventions for inappropriate sexual behavior with developmental disabilities and acquired brain injury: A review. *American Journal on Intellectual and Developmental Disabilities, 123*, 254–282. https://doi.org/10.1352/1944-7558-123.3254

Cohen, G., & Harvey, J. (2015). The use of psychological interventions for adult male sex offenders with a learning disability: A systematic review. *Journal of Sexual Aggression, 22*, 202–223. https://doi.org/10.1080/13552600.2015.1077279

Courtney, J., & Rose, J. (2004). The effectiveness of treatment for male sex offenders with learning disabilities: A review of the literature. *Journal of Sexual Aggression, 10*, 215–236.

Craig, L. A., Stringer, I., & Sanders, C. E. (2012). Treating sexual offenders with intellectual limitations in the community. *The British Journal of Forensic Practice, 14*, 5–20. https://doi.org/10.1108/14636641211204423

Creaby-Attwood, A., & Allely, C. S. (2017). A psycho-legal perspective on sexual offending in individuals with autism spectrum disorder. *International Journal of Law and Psychiatry, 55*, 72–80. https://doi.org/10.1016/j.ijlp.2017.10.009

Davis, T. N., Machalicek, W., Scalzo, R., Kobylecky, A., Campbell, V., Pinkelman, S., et al. (2016). A review and treatment selection model for individuals with intellectual and developmental disabilities who engage in inappropriate sexual behavior. *Behavior Analysis in Practice, 9*, 389–402.

Department of Health. (2001). *Valuing people: A new strategy of learning disability for the 21st century.* London: DoH.

Dozier, C., Iwata, B., & Worsdell, A. (2011). Assessment and treatment of foot-shoe fetishism displayed by a man with autism. *Journal of Applied Behavior Analysis, 44*, 133–137. https://doi.org/10.1901/jaba.2011.44-133

Early, M. C., Erickson, C. A., Wink, L. K., McDougle, C. J., & Scott, E. L. (2012). Case report: 16-year-old male with autistic disorder with preoccupation with female feet. *Journal of Autism and Developmental Disorders, 42*, 1133–1137. https://doi.org/10.1007/s10803-011-1340-8

Griffin, H. L., & Vettor, S. (2012). Predicting sexual re-offending in a UK sample of adolescents with intellectual disabilities. *Journal of Sexual Aggression, 18*, 64–80. https://doi.org/10.1080/13552600.2011.617013

Griffiths, D. M., Thomson, K., Frijters, J., Ioannou, S., Hoath, J., & Wilson, R. J. (2018). Teaching alternative or coping skills for sex offending behavior. In Griffiths, D. M., Thomson, K., Ioannou, S., Hoath, J., & Wilson, R. J. (Eds). *Sex offending behavior of persons with an intellectual disability: A multi-component applied behavior analytic approach.* Kingston, NY: NADD Press.

Griffiths, D. M., Thomson, K., Frijters, J., Ioannou, S., Hoath, J., & Wilson, R. J. (2018). Ethical dilemmas in treating persons with intellectual disabilities who have sexually offended. In D. M. Griffiths, K. Thomson, S. Ioannou, J. Hoath, & R. J. Wilson (Eds.), *Sex offending behavior of persons with an intellectual disability: A multi-component applied behavior analytic approach.* Kingston, NY: NADD Press.

Heaton, K. M., & Murphy, G. H. (2013). Men with intellectual disabilities who attended sex offender treatment groups: A follow up. *Journal of Applied Research in Intellectual Disabilities, 26*, 489–500. https://doi.org/10.1111/jar.12038

Heward, W. L. (2007). Contingency contracting. In J. O. Cooper, T. E. Heron, & W. L. Heward (Eds.), *Applied behavior analysis*. Upper Saddle River, NJ: Merrill Prentice Hall.

Jones, E., & Chaplin, E. (2017). A systematic review of the effectiveness of psychological approaches in the treatment of sex offenders with intellectual disabilities. *Journal of Applied Research in Intellectual Disabilities, 33*, 79–100. https://doi.org/10.1111/jar.12345

Kazdin, A. E. (1982). *Single-case research designs: Methods for clinical and applied settings*. New York: Oxford University Press.

Keller, J. (2016). Improving practices of risk assessment and intervention planning for persons with intellectual disabilities who sexually offend. *Journal of Policy and Practice in Intellectual Disabilities, 13*, 75–85. https://doi.org/10.1111/jppi.12149

Lalli, J. S., Casey, S. D., & Kates, K. (1997). Noncontingent reinforcement as treatment for severe problem behavior: Some procedural variations. *Journal of Applied Behavior Analysis, 30*, 127–137. https://doi.org/10.1901/jaba.1997.30-127

Laws, D. R., & Rubin, H. B. (1969). Instructional control of an autonomic sexual response. *Journal of Applied Behavior Analysis, 2*, 93–99.

Leonard, M., & Hackett, S. (2019). *The AIM3 assessment model: Assessment of adolescents and harmful sexual behaviour*. Stockport: The AIM Project.

Lindsay, W. R. (2009). *The treatment of sex offenders with developmental disabilities: A practice workbook*. Hoboken, NJ: Wiley.

Lindsay, W. R., Michie, A. M., Steptoe, L., Moore, F., & Haut, F. (2011). Comparing offenders against women and offenders against children on treatment outcome for offenders with intellectual disability. *Journal of Applied Research in Intellectual Disabilities, 24*, 361–369.

Lindsay, W. R., Olley, S., Baillie, N., & Smith, A. H. W. (1999). Treatment of adolescent sex offenders with intellectual disabilities. *Mental Retardation, 37*, 201–211.

Lindsay, W. R., & Smith, A. H. W. (1998). Responses to treatment for sex offenders with a learning disability: A comparison of men with 1- and 2-year probation sentences. *Journal of Intellectual Disability Research, 42*, 346–353.

Lindsay, W. R., Steptoe, L. R., Haut, F., Miller, S., Macer, J., & McVicker, R. (2018). The protective scale of the Armidilo-S: The importance of forensic and clinical outcomes. *Journal of Applied Research in Intellectual Disabilities, 33*, 654–661. https://doi.org/10.1111/jar.12456

Lindsay, W. R., Taylor, J. L., & Murphy, G. H. (2018). The treatment and management of sex offenders. In W. R. Lindsay & J. L. Taylor (Eds.), *The Wiley handbook on offenders with intellectual and developmental disabilities: Research, training, and practice* (pp. 229–247). Hoboken, NJ: Wiley.

Lofthouse, R. E., Lindsay, W. R., Totsika, V., Hastings, R. P., Boer, D. P., & Haaven, J. L. (2013). Prospective dynamic assessment of risk of sexual reoffending in individuals with an intellectual disability and a history of sexual offending behaviour. *Journal of Applied Research of Intellectual Disabilities, 26*, 394–403. https://doi.org/10.1111/jar.12029

Lunsky, Y., Frijters, J., Griffiths, D. M., Watson, S. L., & Williston, S. (2007). Sexual knowledge and attitudes of men with intellectual disability who sexually offend. *Journal of Intellectual and Developmental Disability, 32*, 74–81. https://doi.org/10.1080/13668250701408004

Mace, F. C., & Critchfield, T. S. (2010). Translational research in behavior analysis: Historical traditions and imperative for the future. *Journal of the Experimental Analysis of Behavior, 93*, 293–312. https://doi.org/10.1901/jeab.2010.93-293

Mews, A., Di Bella, L., & Purver, M. (2017). *Impact evaluation of the prison-based core sex offender treatment programme*. London: Ministry of Justice Analytical Services.

Miccio-Fonseca, L. C., & Rasmussen, L. A. (2013). Applicability of MEGA to sexually abusive youth with low intellectual functioning. *Journal of Mental Health Research in Intellectual Disabilities, 6*, 42–59. https://doi.org/10.1080/19315864.2011.650788

Ministry of Justice. (2012). Retrieved March 17, 2019, from https://mappa.justice.gov.uk/connect.ti/MAPPA/groupHome

Mongavero, M. C. (2016). Autism, sexual offending, and the criminal justice system. *Journal of Intellectual Disabilities and Offending Behaviour, 7*, 116–126. https://doi.org/10.1108/jidob-02-2016-0004

Morratto, P. L. (2015). A systematic review of behavioral health interventions for sex offenders with intellectual disabilities. *Sexual Abuse: A Journal of Research and Treatment, 29*, 148–185. https://doi.org/10.1177/1079063215569546

Murrie, D. C., Warren, J. I., Kristiansson, M., & Dietz, P. E. (2002). Asperger's syndrome in forensic settings. *International Journal of Forensic Mental Health, 1*, 59–70.

Nevin, J. A., & Wacker, D. P. (2013). Response strength and persistence. In G. J. Madden, W. V. Dube, T. D. Hackenberg, G. P. Hanley, & K. A. Lattal (Eds.), *APA handbook of behavior analysis, Vol. 2: Translating principles into practice* (pp. 109–128). Washington, DC: American Psychological Association. https://doi.org/10.1037/13938-005

Newstrom, N. P., Miner, M., Hoefer, C., Hanson, R. K., & Robinson, B. E. (2018). Sex offender supervision: Communication, training, and mutual respect are necessary for effective collaboration between probation officers and therapists. *Sexual Abuse, 31*(5), 607–631. https://doi.org/10.1177/1079063218775970

O'Callaghan, D. (2002). *A framework for undertaking initial assessments of young people with intellectual disabilities present problematic/harmful sexual behaviours*. Manchester: The AIM Project.

Patterson, C. (2018). Does the adapted sex offender treatment programme reduce cognitive distortions? A meta-analysis. *Journal of Intellectual Disabilities and Offending Behaviour, 9*(4). https://doi.org/10.1108/JIDOB-08-2017-0018

Podlesnik, C. A., & Kelley, M. E. (2017). Beyond intervention: Shaping policy for addressing persistence and relapse of severe problem behavior. *Policy Insights From the Behavioral and Brain Sciences, 4*, 17–24. https://doi.org/10.1177/2372732216683403

Podlesnik, C. A., Kelley, M. E., Jimenez-Gomez, C., & Bouton, M. E. (2017). Renewed behavior produced by context change and its implications for treatment maintenance: A review. *Journal of Applied Behavior Analysis, 50*, 675–697. https://doi.org/10.1002/jaba.400

Print, B., Griffin, H., Beech, A. R., Quayle, J., Bradshaw, H., Henniker, J., et al. (2007). *AIM2: An initial assessment model for young people who display sexually harmful behaviour*. Manchester: The AIM Project.

Pritchard, D., Graham, N., Ikin, A., Penney, H., Kovacs, L., Mercer, D., et al. (2011). Managing sexually harmful behavior in a residential special school. *British Journal of Learning Disabilities, 40*, 302–309. https://doi.org/10.1111/j.1468-3156.2011.00712.x

Pritchard, D., Graham, N., Penney, H., Owen, G., Peters, S., & Mace, F. C. (2016). Multi-component behavioral intervention reduces harmful sexual behavior in a 17-year-old male with autism spectrum disorder: A case study. *Journal of Sexual Aggression, 22*, 368–378. https://doi.org/10.1080/13552600.2015.1130269

Pritchard, D., Penney, H., & Mace, F. C. (2017). The *ACHIEVE!* program: A point and level system for reducing severe problem behavior. *Behavioral Interventions, 31*, 41–55. https://doi.org/10.1002/bin.1506

Rea, J. A., Dixon, M. R., & Zettle, R. D. (2014). Assessing the generalization of relapse-prevention behaviors of sexual offenders diagnosed with an intellectual disability. *Behavior Modification, 38*, 25–44. https://doi.org/10.1177/0145445513505109

Reyes, J. R., Vollmer, T. R., & Hall, A. (2011). The influence of presession factors in the assessment of deviant arousal. *Journal of Applied Behavior Analysis, 44*, 707–717. https://doi.org/10.1901/jaba.2011.44-707

Reyes, J. R., Vollmer, T. R., Sloman, K. N., Hall, A., Reed, R., Jansen, G., et al. (2006). Assessment of deviant arousal in adult male sex offenders with developmental disabilities. *Journal of Applied Behavior Analysis, 39*, 173–188. https://doi.org/10.1901/jaba.2006.46-05

Rose, J., Rose, D., Hawkins, C., & Anderson, C. (2012). A sex offender treatment group for men with intellectual disabilities in a community setting. *The British Journal of Forensic Practice, 14*, 21–28. https://doi.org/10.1108/14636641211204432

Royal College of Psychiatrists. (2015). Retrieved March 17, 2019, from https://Www.Rcpsych.Ac.Uk/Mental-Health/Treatments-And-Wellbeing/Deprivation-Of-Liberty-Safeguards

Sex Offender Treatment Services Collaborative – Intellectual Disabilities (SOTSEC-ID). (2010). Effectiveness of group cognitive behavioural treatment for men with intellectual disabilities at risk of sexual offending. *Journal of Applied Research in Intellectual Disabilities, 23*, 537–551. https://doi.org/10.1111/j.1468-3148.2010.00560.x

Singh, N. N., Lancioni, G. E., Winton, A. W., Singh, A. N., Adkins, A. D., & Singh, J. (2011). Can adult offenders with intellectual disabilities use mindfulness-based procedures to control their deviant sexual arousal? *Psychology, Crime & Law, 17*, 165–179. https://doi.org/10.1080/10683160903392731

Stephens, S., Newman, J. E., Cantor, J. M., & Seto, M. C. (2018). The Static-99R predicts sexual and violent recidivism for individuals with low intellectual functioning. *Journal of Sexual Aggression, 24*, 1–11. https://doi.org/10.1080/13552600.2017.1372936

Stevenson, B., Lynn, L., Miller, K., & Hingsburger, D. (2011). The way back: A reasoned and data based approach to increasing community access during and post-treatment. *Journal of Learning Disabilities and Offending Behaviour, 2*, 63–71. https://doi.org/10.1108/20420921111152478

Todd, T. P., Winterbauer, N. E., & Bouton, M. E. (2012). Effects of the amount of acquisition and contextual generalization on the renewal of instrumental behavior after extinction. *Learning & Behavior, 40*, 145–157. https://doi.org/10.3758/s13420-011-0051-5

Tullis, C. A., & Zangrillo, A. N. (2013). Sexuality education for adolescents and adults with autism spectrum disorders. *Psychology in the Schools, 50*, 866–875. https://doi.org/10.1002/pits.21713

Vollmer, T. R., Reyes, J., & Walker, S. F. (2012). Behavioral assessment and intervention for sex offenders with intellectual and developmental disabilities. In J. K. Luiselli (Ed.), *The handbook of high-risk challenging behaviors: Assessment and intervention* (pp. 121–144). Baltimore, MD: Paul H. Brookes.

Wacker, D. P., Harding, J. W., Berg, W. K., Lee, J. F., Schieltz, K. M., Padilla, Y. C., et al. (2011). An evaluation of persistence of treatment effects during long-term treatment of destructive behavior. *Journal of the Experimental Analysis of Behavior, 96*, 261–282. https://doi.org/10.1901/jeab.2011.96-261

Walker, S. F., Joslyn, P. R., Vollmer, T. R., & Hall, A. (2014). Differential suppression of arousal by sex offenders with intellectual disabilities. *Journal of Applied Behavior Analysis, 47*, 639–644. https://doi.org/10.1002/jaba.142

Watson, T. S., & Steege, M. W. (2003). *Conducting school-based functional behavioral assessments: A practitioner's guide*. New York: The Guildford Press.

Willis, G. M., Yates, P. M., Gannon, T. A., & Ward, T. (2013). How to integrate the Good Lives Model into treatment programs for sexual offending: An introduction and overview. *Sex Abuse: A Journal of Research and Treatment, 25*, 123–142.

Willner, P. (2005). The effectiveness of psychotherapeutic interventions for people with learning disabilities: A critical overview. *Journal of Intellectual Disability Research, 49*, 73–85.

Inpatient and Residential Treatment of Violence Aggression

Nicole L. Hausman, Michael P. Kranak, Molly K. Bednar, and Louis P. Hagopian

Abstract Individuals with intellectual and developmental disabilities often display problem behaviors, including aggression. Sometimes, aggression, or other problem behaviors, can become so severe that more intensive supports and treatment are necessary. In such cases, individuals may undergo assessment and treatment of aggression in inpatient and residential settings. In this chapter, we describe a general assessment and treatment process for aggressive behaviors that may be well suited for inpatient and residential settings. Recommendations for improving client outcomes through assessment modifications, staff and caregiver training, and treatment generalization are also discussed.

Keywords Aggression · Severe problem behavior · Functional assessment · Behavioral treatment · Staff training

Engaging in aggression creates barriers to involvement in community activities and is a leading cause of placement in non-community settings such as residential facilities or inpatient units among individuals diagnosed with intellectual and developmental disabilities (IDD; Rojahn, Matson, Esbensen, & Smalls, 2001; Tenneij &

N. L. Hausman (✉) · L. P. Hagopian
Kennedy Krieger Institute, Baltimore, MD, USA

The Johns Hopkins University School of Medicine, Baltimore, MD, USA
e-mail: drhausmanbcbad@fullspectrumaba.com

M. P. Kranak
Oakland University, Rochester, MI, USA

M. K. Bednar
Kennedy Krieger Institute, Baltimore, MD, USA

© Springer Nature Switzerland AG 2021
J. K. Luiselli (ed.), *Applied Behavior Analysis Treatment of Violence and Aggression in Persons with Neurodevelopmental Disabilities*, Advances in Preventing and Treating Violence and Aggression,
https://doi.org/10.1007/978-3-030-68549-2_8

Koot, 2008). Aggression is more likely to be displayed by males, individuals with more severe intellectual disability, and comorbid psychopathology (Crocker et al., 2006; Linaker, 1994; Sigafoos, Elkins, Kerr, & Attwood, 1994). Aggressive behavior also results in the use of medications such as sedatives or antipsychotics and restrictive, reactive procedures such as restraint and seclusion (Allen, 2000; Crocker et al., 2006; Robertson et al., 2000). In a study examining correlates of restraint and seclusion for 81 adults diagnosed with IDD, over 60% of participants had experienced restraint and/or seclusion following aggressive behavior, with seclusion occurring most often and mechanical restraint occurring the least often (Merineau-Cote & Morin, 2014). Individuals displaying more severe forms of aggressive behavior were more likely to experience seclusion than restraint.

Additionally, aggression is associated with increased treatment costs relative to other, less severe problem behaviors such as noncompliance or inappropriate vocalizations, perhaps because individuals who engage in this topography of problem behavior are more likely to be placed outside of the home into inpatient or residential treatment settings (Gardner & Moffatt, 1990; Merineau-Cote & Morin, 2014; Tenneij & Koot, 2008; Wehman & McLaughlin, 1979). These increased treatment costs may place a financial burden on families and public and private funding sources.

Safety Considerations in Inpatient and Residential Settings

Aggressive behavior has been shown to negatively impact staff working with individuals who have neurodevelopmental disabilities (Edwards & Miltenberger, 1991; Hunter & Carmel, 1992; Merineau-Cote & Morin, 2014). Aggression has been linked to staff stress and burnout, which may, in turn lead to deterioration of the therapeutic environment (Edwards & Miltenberger, 1991). Burnout can impact direct care and supervisory staff, but supervisory staff can experience higher levels of burnout due to their added responsibilities (Edwards & Miltenberger, 1991). Additionally, aggression can result in injuries to staff, some of which can be severe. To illustrate some of these examples, consider the case of Matt, an adolescent male diagnosed with autism spectrum disorder and severe intellectual disability, who was referred to a specialized hospital unit for the assessment and treatment of severe problem behavior including aggression, property destruction, and self-injurious behavior. Matt had a history of previous hospitalizations due to the intensity of his problem behavior, and had spent 6 months in the emergency department of a local medical center prior to his transfer to the specialized facility for treatment.

To mitigate some of the negative effects of aggressive behavior on staff, it is critical that adequate staffing levels be maintained to allow staff to safely and appropriately manage aggressive behavior. For individuals who engage in episodic, severe outbursts of aggressive behavior, it may be necessary to have extra staffing available to help manage outbursts when and if they occur. For inpatient and residential settings specializing in the treatment and support of individuals who engage in aggressive behavior, these extra staffing requirements should be included in behavior plans, and subsequently included in budgets to ensure funding is available for these higher staffing ratios. Upon admission to the specialized inpatient unit, two staff members were assigned to work with Matt during all waking hours, and additional staff were available to assist during behavioral outbursts. During baseline, Matt often required 4–5 staff members to manage his problem behavior safely during behavioral outbursts.

Furthermore, environmental modifications are critical to provide a safe environment for the management of aggressive behavior in inpatient and residential settings. These modifications may improve safety for both clients and staff members. For example, creating large, open areas with furniture that can be removed quickly in the event of aggressive outbursts may assist with staff management of these behaviors. Protective equipment for staff, such as arm guards, padded gloves, helmets, shin guards, and chest protectors, may further protect staff from injuries. This equipment should be made readily available in common areas of the inpatient and residential setting, and staff should be encouraged to wear this equipment at their discretion. For patients with more severe aggressive behavior with a history of causing staff injuries, forms of protective equipment that protect the targeted areas of the body can be mandated, such as helmets for staff, when working with individuals with a history of head butting and arm guards for working with individuals who have a history of biting. Matt typically spent waking hours in a large common area with his assigned staff members, and furniture was quickly removed from this area during behavioral outbursts for safety reasons. Matt's staff also wore helmets, arm, chest, and shin guards, as well as padded gloves at all times to prevent injury.

Staff should be appropriately trained in approved physical management procedures for aggressive behavior before working with aggressive individuals, and competency in using the procedures should be reassessed frequently (Aljadeff-Abergel, Peterson, Wiskirchen, Hagen, & Cole, 2017). Reassessment of behavior management training should be conducted at least annually, through direct observations of staff during management of aggressive behavior, or during didactic instruction. Approved behavior management procedures may vary from state to state, or across organizations, but several behavior management curricula are commercially available for organizations to consult with (e.g., Crisis Prevention Institute [CPI]). This not only enables staff to use approved and safe physical management procedures when aggressive behaviors occur, but also may help to reduce staff and client injuries.

Considerations for Functional Behavior Assessment in Inpatient and Residential Settings

Conducting a thorough functional behavior assessment (FBA) or functional analysis (FA) of aggressive behavior is integral to developing an appropriate, function-based intervention. Although previous chapters in this text have described FBA and FA procedures generally, conducting these assessments in inpatient settings or residential facilities may warrant additional considerations, which are discussed in greater detail, below. These modifications may be more or less appropriate depending on the specific topographies of aggressive behavior the individual engages in, the training and experience of staff conducting the FBA, and the availability of staff and client safety equipment (e.g., padded mats, helmets, arm guards, rooms devoid of furniture, padded treatment rooms, etc.). Longer-term placement in inpatient hospital or residential settings may be beneficial in that observations can be conducted over longer time periods, and treatment can be evaluated across gradually increasing durations of time.

Placement in more restrictive inpatient or residential treatment settings has both advantages and disadvantages for both functional assessment and treatment processes. However, with the exception of these specific considerations, it is still important for staff working in these settings to conduct a functional assessment to determine the specific variables maintaining an individual's aggressive behavior, and to develop evidence- and function-based treatments.

Safety Considerations

Although FAs of problem behavior have been demonstrated to be safe when conducted in inpatient settings with trained therapists (Kahng et al., 2015), it is important to consider how best to prevent injuries to both the client and staff when reinforcing aggressive behavior within these sessions. As mentioned above, protective equipment for staff and clients can be essential for providing services in inpatient or residential settings. Protective equipment such as helmets and arm guards is also commonly used in FAs of severe problem behavior (Borrero, Vollmer, Wright, Lerman, & Kelley, 2002; Fisher, Rodriguez, Luczysnki, & Kelley, 2013; Oropeza, Fritz, Nissen, Terrell, & Phillips, 2018). Before proceeding with a FA, it is necessary to determine if protective equipment is necessary and available. When considering how much protective equipment to use, it should be the least amount necessary, ensure both staff and client safety, and not be associated of reallocation of aggressive responses toward unprotected parts of the body (Lin, Luiselli, Gilligan, & Dacosta, 2012; Parenteau, Luiselli, & Keeley, 2013; Urban, Luiselli, Child, & Parenteau, 2011).

Descriptive Analysis

Descriptive analysis (DA) may be appropriate to identify antecedents and consequences in a residential setting. DA has several advantages, including allowing for extended observations of clients and caregivers within the natural environment. Given that they are conducted in the natural environment DAs can also be easier to complete. Moreover, they do not require as many safety precautions as an FA and there is usually less training and supervision needed. Data collected from a DA may

(1) provide information to help clinicians formulate hypotheses regarding the antecedents and consequences for problem behavior, (2) help to inform the design of test and control conditions in a subsequent FA of aggression, and (3) inform assessment and treatment decisions. Furthermore, DAs may enable clinicians to collect data on the antecedents and consequences of aggression more efficiently for large samples of individuals in the same location during the observation period. For example, Thompson and Iwata (2001) conducted a DA of problem behavior, including aggression, for a sample of 27 adults in a residential facility. Results from the DA suggested that staff most commonly delivered attention following occurrences of problem behavior, and aggression was the most likely topography of problem behavior to receive social consequences from staff. Although not as thorough as an FA, DAs can serve as a starting point for the assessment of aggressive behaviors in inpatient and residential settings.

Modifications to Traditional FA Methodology

Previous literature suggests that aggressive behavior is most commonly maintained by social negative reinforcement in the form of escape from demands or social interaction and social positive reinforcement in the form of attention or access to items or food (Beavers, Iwata, & Lerman, 2013; Embregts, Didden, Schreuder, Huitnik, & van Nieuwenhuijzen, 2009). Beavers and colleagues evaluated results from 158 studies that included a FA of problem behavior and found that aggression was assessed in almost half of these studies and maintained by social positive and/or negative reinforcers in 97.8% of FAs; automatic reinforcement was only reported in one case (2.2%). Given that it is unlikely for aggression to be maintained by automatic reinforcers, it is usually not necessary to include ignore conditions in functional analyses of aggression, unless patterns of responding in the FA suggest that aggression persists in the absence of social contingencies. It is also hard to ignore aggression, rendering ignore conditions impractical.

The most common measure of aggression in FAs is frequency of occurrence and the differences across test and control conditions (Iwata, Dorsey, Slifer, Baumen, & Richman, 1982/1994). While this measure can provide invaluable information about behavior function,, it can also allow individuals being assessed with multiple opportunities to engage in harmful behavior to themselves or others. In addition to following safety protocols and using protective equipment, modifying FA procedures can also potentially mitigate injuries to staff and clients. Table 1 depicts a brief summary of these modifications to standard FA methodology (e.g., Iwata et al., 1982/1994).

Latency FA Latency FAs measure the time between the onset of a condition and the first emission of the target behavior (Thomason-Sassi, Iwata, Neidert, & Roscoe, 2011). Typically, the condition is terminated following one instance of the target behavior, thus reducing opportunities for injury to either staff or clients. The shorter the latency, the greater the likelihood that session's motivating opera-

Table 1 Modifications to standard functional analysis

Type of modification	Primary deviations from Standard FA Methodology
Latency FA	• Latency between onset of condition and occurrence of target behavior as response measure • Visual inspection—Lower data paths indicative of function
Precursor FA	• Target behavior for FA is a less severe behavior than targeted aggression
Brief FA	• Condition lengths are 2 min, 5 min max • Conditions repeated only once or twice
Extended FA	• Only one condition assessed per day/session • Durations are longer

tion is controlling the behavior. Latency FAs involve using latency to the first response as the measure, and relative latency across test and control conditions to isolate the probable function. When visually interpreting latency FA results, it is *essential* to recall that the data paths and points with lower latencies are those that are the likely function. This is opposite of other FA graphs, where the higher data paths depicting rate data indicate possible functions. Returning to our clinical case example, many FAs completed with Matt in the specialized inpatient unit were latency-based because he engaged in very severe aggression directed toward the head and face of staff members and had caused serious injuries to multiple, trained staff members when attempting to manage his aggressive outbursts. Therefore, a clinical decision was made by his case supervisor to terminate sessions immediately following the first occurrence of aggression for staff safety.

Precursor FA Aggression is sometimes preceded by less severe behaviors such as crying, whining, or protesting, to name a few. Those behaviors that occur before aggression are called precursors. Aggression is more likely to occur after a precursor relative to times that the precursor does *not* occur. Moreover, most of the time the precursor occurs, aggression follows. Precursors are commonly in the same response class as aggression, that is, they serve the same function. If a precursor is in the same response class rather than part of a chain, using those precursors as the target behavior(s) for FAs can alleviate evoking aggression altogether (Herscovitch, Roscoe, Libby, Bourret, & Ahearn, 2009; Najdowski, Wallace, Ellsworth, MacAleese, & Cleveland, 2008). In situations where a precursor is part of a behavior chain (i.e., *must* occur before aggression can occur), aggression could occur if the chain is blocked. Therefore, caution still must be taken when using precursors as target behaviors during FAs.

Brief FA Another way to limit potential opportunities for injuries is to reduce the number of sessions and duration of sessions during an FA. Brief FAs involve conditions that last, typically, only 2 min to 5 min. Each condition is implemented only once or twice. Although this arrangement may result in sequencing effects or less reliable results, it certainly provides a means of analysis with a limited potential of injury. However, brief FA may not be appropriate for individuals who do not engage in high-frequency aggression (Derby et al., 1992). Thus, this modification may be better suited as a probe for potential reinforcers.

Extended FA Aggressive behavior sometimes occurs in a cyclical pattern, or occurs in the context of low frequency, high intensity outbursts. This pattern of aggression may co-occur with underlying mood disorders (Lewis, Silva, & Gray-Silva, 1995). If a more traditional, briefer session FA does not evoke behavior, the establishing operation (EO) should be increased. If the increased EO does not evoke behavior *and* the observed behavior is episodic, a larger sample is needed. This pattern may be well suited for assessment in longer-term inpatient or residential settings where observation can be conducted over longer time periods (i.e., 30 min, 60 min, then longer if necessary). In these cases, extended FA durations may be necessary to capture naturally occurring variability in rates of problem behavior across days. For example, Kahng, Abt, and Schonbachler (2001) evaluated extended FA sessions on an inpatient hospital unit. Only one FA condition, similar to those described by Iwata et al. (1982/1994), was assessed each day during the hours of 9:00 a.m.–4:00 p.m. These procedures were replicated and extended by Davis, Kahng, Schmidt, Bowman, and Boelter (2012) to include a tangible condition, also in an inpatient hospital unit.

An Alternative to FAs

Despite the aforementioned modifications to FAs, there are conditions that could still preclude an FA from occurring. These conditions include: (a) safety concerns, (b) feasibility, (c) staff shortages, and (d) limited resources. In light of these restraints, a potential alternative may be a concurrent operants assessment (COA; Hood, Rodriguez, Luczynski, & Fisher, 2019) that involves arranging two concurrent schedules of reinforcement (i.e., a test and control condition) for the target behavior. The contingencies are typically arranged in the same room within proximity to the individual. The test schedule/area provides the hypothesized reinforcer (e.g., attention) for the problem behavior. The control schedule/area does not provide reinforcement (i.e., extinction is in place). Therapists then measure to which area and associated contingency the client allocates his or her time/responding. If the individual allocates more responding to the test condition, then that would be indicative of the function of the problem behavior.

Treatment of Aggression in Inpatient and Residential Settings

Related to the discussion of FBA and FA methodology, treatment of aggressive behavior may proceed similarly in inpatient hospital and residential settings, with a few notable differences. Similar to behavioral treatment for aggression in outpatient settings, treatment in inpatient or residential treatment settings should be based on the function of the aggressive behavior, as identified through an FBA, when possible. Typically, individuals referred to inpatient and residential treatment settings for aggressive behavior remain in these settings for longer time periods. In some settings, this situation enables the assessment and treatment process to continue over longer periods of the day compared to treatment that occurs on an outpatient basis (which might be limited to the session visit). In inpatient settings, if there are sufficient resources to create a highly controlled environment, it may be possible to control access to functional reinforcers to support therapeutic goals (e.g., limiting reinforcement for inappropriate behavior) while reinforcing appropriate behavior. That is, if aggressive behavior is maintained by staff attention, staff may be better able to withhold attention outside of behavioral intervention sessions where the client is able to request attention using a picture card exchange or sign. Increased staffing ratios in inpatient and residential settings may also enable staff to implement extinction procedures with integrity, which may also improve outcomes for individuals referred for treatment of aggression.

Results of functional analyses for Matt suggested that his aggression was maintained by social negative reinforcement in the form of escape from work and social interaction. A treatment package to address these functions was then evaluated with trained behavioral staff members, and later generalized to novel staff, caregivers, and into the community. Treatment components included a structured daily schedule of preferred and non-preferred activities, teaching appropriate requests for staff to move away from Matt or leave the room (dependent upon activity), reinforcing compliance during academic periods, and planned ignoring. Additionally, extensive rapport building including engagement in preferred activities, proximity fading, and noncontingent reinforcement was conducted with all staff members assigned to work with Matt, given the dangerous nature of his aggressive behavior.

Care Coordination

Inpatient and residential treatment may also improve access to integrated, multidisciplinary care, which may be necessary for complex cases that have not responded to outpatient interventions. For example, placement in an inpatient hospital or structured residential treatment setting may enable and individual to experience behavioral assessment and intervention with psychopharmacological treatment that is collaborative and data-driven (Hagopian & Caruso-Anderson, 2010; McGuire et al., 2016). Resources in these settings may include access to integrated behavior-analytic and psychiatric services under the direction of a behavior analyst and medical professional, who are trained to review data and intervene systematically to ensure behavioral and psychiatric interventions are producing the desired reductions in aggressive behavior. Furthermore, multidisciplinary treatment teams may include social workers, speech and language pathologists (SLPs), and special educators, who work together to develop appropriate treatment goals for each client and help to ensure discharge planning meets the individual's needs.

Data Collection

Data on each individual's aggressive behavior plays a crucial role during and after treatment. These data can be used to visually inspect patterns of aggressive behavior over time, provide a baseline to compare treatment effects to, and to monitor treatment effects over time. Reviewing data on a daily weekly basis enables clinical staff to monitor ongoing interventions, and respond appropriately to any increases in aggressive behavior.

Staff and Caregiver Training

Effective and efficient training for staff and other caregivers (e.g., parents) is one of the most critical components of service provision for individuals who engage in aggression. All staff should receive general training on common behavioral interventions as well as individualized training on specific behavior support plans to ensure implementation integrity in inpatient and residential treatment settings. Effective training can pay dividends for the individuals receiving treatment, direct care staff, and caregivers (Shapiro & Kazemi, 2017). First, training staff and caregivers to implement behavioral interventions with high fidelity can result in positive outcomes (i.e., a reduction in aggressive behaviors) for individuals receiving services (St. Peter Pipkin, Vollmer, & Sloman, 2010). Second, proper training can result in proactive behavior management and alleviate situations wherein direct care staff and caregivers may be injured. Although inpatient and residential settings may have their own variation of training, the methods should be evidence-based, as described and illustrated below.

Behavioral Skills Training (BST) BST is an empirically supported training strategy that consists of (a) providing a rationale and description of the target skill, (b) modeling of the skill, (c) guided practice and role play, and (d) supportive or corrective feedback (Parsons, Rollyson, & Reid, 2012). BST has been associated with the highest, most consistent improvement of treatment fidelity in the special education literature (Brock et al., 2017). Moreover, BST has been used to teach skills to practitioners who work with aggressive individuals such as designing and conducting functional analyses (Ward-Horner & Sturmey, 2012), implementing behavioral interventions (Sawyer et al., 2017), and graphical creation and interpretation (Kranak, Shapiro, Sawyer, Deochand, & Neef, 2018; Maffei-Almodovar, Feliciano, Fineup, & Sturmey, 2017). BST also has high marks of consumer satisfaction (Shapiro & Kazemi, 2017).

Considerations for Using BST in Inpatient and Residential Settings Although BST is effective in a variety of settings, each setting comes with its own unique challenges to staff and caregiver training. Inpatient and residential settings are not immune to such challenges. These settings can be stressful, high-stakes environments. Therefore, it is imperative to be cognizant of barriers to effective training in order to avoid deleterious effects on both clients and staff alike (Carrol, Kodak, & Fisher, 2013; St. Peter, Byrd, Pence, & Foreman, 2016).

Trainer Availability A trainer who is proficient in the skill to be taught is an essential component to BST (Parsons et al., 2012). However, inpatient and residential settings often require expert staff (i.e., potential trainers) to be working with and providing services to clients due to low staff-to-patient/client ratios (e.g., Coleman & Gordon, 2001). One way to alleviate this issue is to equip other staff members with the skillset necessary to train others on interventions, rather than rely on a few expert trainers, through pyramidal training, (Neef, 1995). Pyramidal training involves an expert practitioner training a single individual or small group on a skill to mastery (Tier 1), as well as *how* to train *others* on the targeted skill. Then, the individual(s) that received training from the expert train others (Tier 2), making this approach is a viable option to increase trainer availability in a given setting (Andzik & Cannella-Malone, 2017).

Time Constraints One common issue with BST is that it is resource and time intensive. Indeed, one argument for devoting a substantial amount of time and resources to using BST is its effectiveness. However, time that may be devoted to staff and procedural training may need to be reallocated to service provision, crisis management, or other various demands. In order to avoid time barriers, staff training sessions could be kept at less than, ideally, 1 h (e.g., 15–30 min; Nigro-Bruzzi & Sturmey, 2010). Although this may not seem like a sufficient amount of time to train effectively, shorter training periods can result in the same positive outcomes as longer training periods (Nigro-Bruzzi & Sturmey, 2010; Shapiro & Kazemi, 2017).

Alternatives to BST Given that BST is not always a viable option for staff training in residential settings, it may be important to consider antecedent- or computer-based training procedures, which can be used in isolation, or in combination, as a form of self-instructional package. A self-instructional package involves the trainee working through the instructional steps in a self-paced fashion. There are various forms of self-instructional packages such as written instructions (i.e., task analyses; Thiessen et al., 2009), video or picture models and/or prompts (Rosales, Gongola, & Homilitas, 2015), and computer-based instruction (CBI). The distinct advantage

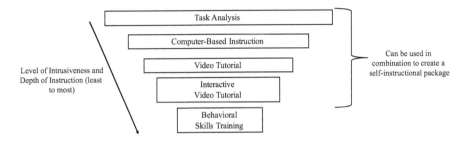

Fig. 1 Hierarchy of potential, evidence-based staff training procedures

of these alternatives over BST is twofold. First, employees can work through the protocols at designated times and at their own pace. Second, it allows more senior, likely trainer, staff to attend other duties such as supervision or direct care provision. Shapiro and Kazemi (2017) highlight additional advantages, as well as disadvantages relative to technological barriers and computer access.

Self-instructional packages can also be used as a first step in a training protocol. They are not as intrusive, and may not be needed for staff that can acquire skills with more parsimonious trainings than BST. Figure 1 depicts a potential model for staff training ranging from least-to-most intrusive training protocols. Additionally, another alternative to BST is group training (cf. Hardesty, McIvor, Wagner, Hagopian, & Bowman, 2014). Group trainings should include opportunities for trainees to respond, whether it be through choral responding or response boards (Hardesty et al.), to maximize learning opportunities and increase effectiveness.

Treatment Generalization

Following successful assessment of aggressive behavior, function-based treatment evaluations should be conducted to obtain a clinically significant reduction in aggression relative to baseline. If treatment was applied across all contexts within the residential facility, it should be possible to generalize treatment to community settings post-discharge and with multiple caregivers. If treatment was applied under limited conditions, the general process for treatment generalization should be: (1) to other conditions, (2) with other staff and caregivers, and (3) over longer periods of time. Then, generalize it to the community or discharge settings. For Matt, treatment generalization occurred over a period of months until Matt was able to participate in community outings while maintaining low rates of aggressive behavior. Upon discharge from this specialized facility, Matt returned to his home state and was placed in a group home with experience providing services to individuals with severe behavior disorders and attended a specialized school. Matt continued to engage in low rates of problem behavior during his transition home, and treatment gains have been maintained.

Summary

Aggression is one of the leading causes of placement in more restrictive inpatient and residential settings (Rojahn et al., 2001; Tenneij & Koot, 2008). Inpatient and residential settings offer several distinct benefits. First, higher staffing ratios of experienced and well-trained staff are generally found in inpatient and residential treatment settings. The amount of staff is beneficial, in part, because it allows for continuous observation of client behavior. Clinicians are then able to carefully monitor response-to-treatment and promptly make any necessary changes to behavior treatment plans and protocols. Similarly, the amount of staff also enables greater, precise control over the environment. That is, higher levels of procedural integrity can be expected, potentially leading to quicker treatment gains than would be expected in less controlled settings. Lastly, inpatient and residential settings typically have access to the best-available safety equipment and precautions (e.g., protective equipment, staff trained in behavior management procedures). Given the intensity with which aggression can occur, it is essential for safety to be a top priority in treatment settings.

There are also some drawbacks to inpatient and residential service provision. First, inpatient hospitalization or residential treatment settings can be more costly than treatment in outpatient settings. The costs may be more justifiable in situations where a client has not responded to treatment in less-intensive settings, or in situations where the aggressive behavior is too dangerous to assess and treat in an outpatient setting. Additionally, the highly controlled and unnatural setting of an inpatient facility, in particular, may pose issues with treatment generalization. All other settings, ranging from clients' homes to less-intensive group homes, will likely not have sufficient staff, environmental control, or resources compared to inpatient or residential settings, possibly impacting the success of treatment following discharge. Accordingly, a thorough discharge plan should be in place in place, which includes extensive generalization to other caregivers and across multiple settings. Discharge planning also includes ongoing discussion with providers at the next lower level of care (e.g., a less-intensive group home, the parents, etc.) to ensure necessary resources are available to support the individual during the transition from the more to less restrictive setting.

In sum, we have described a general assessment and treatment process for aggressive behaviors in inpatient and residential settings. The chapter also provided recommendations for improving client outcomes through assessment modifications, staff and caregiver training, and treatment generalization. These settings provide an opportunity for individuals with aggressive behaviors to undergo thorough functional assessments; and receive function-based treatment evaluation, generalization, and ongoing caregiver training and data monitoring.

References

Aljadeff-Abergel, E., Peterson, S. M., Wiskirchen, R. R., Hagen, K. K., & Cole, M. L. (2017). Evaluating the temporal location of feedback: Providing feedback following performance vs. prior to performance. *Journal of Organizational Behavior Management, 37*, 171–195.

Allen, J. J. (2000). Seclusion and restraint of children: A literature review. *Journal of Child and Adolescent Psychiatric Nursing, 13*, 159–167.

Andzik, N. R., & Cannella-Malone, H. I. (2017). A review of the pyramidal training approach for practitioners working with individuals with disabilities. *Behavior Modification, 41*, 558–580.

Beavers, G. A., Iwata, B. A., & Lerman, D. C. (2013). Thirty years of research on the functional analysis of problem behavior. *Journal of Applied Behavior Analysis, 46*, 1–21.

Borrero, J. C., Vollmer, T. R., Wright, C. S., Lerman, D. C., & Kelley, M. E. (2002). Further evaluation of the role of protective equipment in the function analysis of self-injurious behavior. *Journal of Applied Behavior Analysis, 35*, 69–72.

Brock, M. E., Cannella-Malone, H. I., Seaman, R. L., Andzik, N. R., Schaefer, J. M., Page, E. J., et al. (2017). Findings across practitioner training studies in special education: A comprehensive review and meta-analysis. *Exceptional Children, 84*, 7–26.

Carrol, R. A., Kodak, T., & Fisher, W. W. (2013). An evaluation of programmed treatment-integrity errors during discrete-trial instruction. *Journal of Applied Behavior Analysis, 46*, 379–394.

Coleman, J. C., & Gordon, P. L. (2001). Relationship between staffing ratios and the effectiveness of inpatient psychiatric units. *Psychiatric Services, 52*, 1374–1379.

Crocker, A. G., Mercier, C., Lachapelle, Y., Brunet, A., Morin, D., & Roy, M. E. (2006). Prevalence and types of aggressive behavior among adults with intellectual disabilities. *Journal of Intellectual Disability Research, 50*, 652–662.

Davis, B. J., Kahng, S., Schmidt, J., Bowman, L. G., & Boelter, E. W. (2012). Alterations to functional analysis methodology to clarify the functions of low rate, high intensity problem behavior. *Behavior Analysis in Practice, 5*, 27–39.

Derby, K. M., Wacker, D. P., Sasso, G., Steege, M., Northup, J., Cigrand, K., et al. (1992). Brief functional assessment techniques to evaluate aberrant behavior in an outpatient setting: A summary of 79 cases. *Journal of Applied Behavior Analysis, 25*, 713–721.

Edwards, P., & Miltenberger, R. (1991). Burnout among staff members at community residential facilities for persons with mental retardation. *Mental Retardation, 29*, 125–128.

Embregts, P. J., Didden, R., Schreuder, N., Huitnik, C., & van Nieuwenhuijzen, M. (2009). Aggressive behavior in individuals with moderate to borderline intellectual disabilities who live in a residential facility: An evaluation of functional variables. *Research in Developmental Disabilities, 30*, 682–688.

Fisher, W. W., Rodriguez, N. M., Luczysnki, K. C., & Kelley, M. E. (2013). The use of protective equipment in the management of severe behavior disorders. In D. Reed, F. DiGennaro Reed, & J. K. Luiselli (Eds.), *Handbook of crisis intervention and developmental disabilities* (pp. 87–105). New York: Springer-Verlag.

Gardner, W. I., & Moffatt, C. W. (1990). Aggressive behaviour: Definition, assessment, and treatment. *International Review of Psychiatry, 2*, 91–100.

Hagopian, L. P., & Caruso-Anderson, M. E. (2010). Integrating behavioral and pharmacological interventions for severe problem behavior displayed by children with neurogenetic and developmental disorders. In *Neurogenetic syndromes: Behavioral issues and their treatment* (pp. 217–239).

Hardesty, S. L., McIvor, M. M., Wagner, L. L., Hagopian, L. P., & Bowman, L. G. (2014). A further evaluation of response cards: Teaching direct care staff basic behavioral principles. *Journal of Organizational Behavior Management, 34*, 156–164.

Herscovitch, B., Roscoe, E. M., Libby, M. E., Bourret, J. C., & Ahearn, W. H. (2009). A procedure for identifying precursors to problem behavior. *Journal of Applied Behavior Analysis, 42*, 697–702.

Hood, S. A., Rodriguez, N. M., Luczynski, K. C., & Fisher, W. W. (2019). Evaluating the effects of physical reactions on aggression via concurrent-operant analyses. *Journal of Applied Behavior Analysis, 52*, 642–651.

Hunter, M., & Carmel, H. (1992). The cost of staff injuries from patient violence. *Hospital & Community Psychiatry, 43*, 586–588.

Iwata, B. A., Dorsey, M. F., Slifer, K. J., Baumen, K. E., & Richman, G. S. (1982/1994). Toward a functional analysis of self-injury. *Journal of Applied Behavior Analysis, 27*, 197–209.

Kahng, S. W., Abt, K. A., & Schonbachler, H. E. (2001). Assessment and treatment of low-rate high-intensity problem behavior. *Journal of Applied Behavior Analysis, 34*, 225–228.

Kahng, S., Hausman, N. L., Fisher, A. B., Donaldson, J. M., Cox, J. R., Lugo, M., et al. (2015). The safety of functional analyses of self-injurious behavior. *Journal of Applied Behavior Analysis, 48*, 107–114.

Kranak, M. P., Shapiro, M. N., Sawyer, M. R., Deochand, N., & Neef, N. A. (2018). Using behavioral skills training to improve graduate students' graphing skills. *Behavior Analysis: Research and Practice, 19*, 247–260.

Lewis, M. H., Silva, J. R., & Gray-Silva, S. (1995). Cyclicity of aggression and self-injurious behavior in individuals with mental retardation. *American Journal on Mental Retardation, 99*, 436–444.

Lin, T., Luiselli, J. K., Gilligan, K., & Dacosta, S. (2012). Preventing injury from child aggression: Single-case evaluation of staff-worn protective equipment. *Developmental Neurorehabilitation, 15*, 298–303.

Linaker, O. M. (1994). Assaultiveness among institutionalised adults with mental retardation. *British Journal of Psychiatry, 164*, 62–68.

Maffei-Almodovar, L., Feliciano, G., Fineup, D. M., & Sturmey, P. (2017). The use of behavioral skills training to teach graph analysis to community based teachers. *Behavior Analysis in Practice, 10*, 355–362.

McGuire, K., Fung, L. K., Hagopian, L., Vasa, R. A., Mahajan, R., Bernal, P., et al. (2016). Irritability and problem behavior in autism speectrum disorder: A practice pathway for pediatric primary care. *Pediatrics, 137*(Supplement 2), S136–S148.

Merineau-Cote, J., & Morin, D. (2014). Restraint and seclusion: The perspective of service users and staff members. *Journal of Applied Research in Intellectual Disabilities, 27*, 447–457.

Najdowski, A. C., Wallace, M. D., Ellsworth, C. L., MacAleese, A. N., & Cleveland, J. M. (2008). Functional analyses and treatment of precursor behavior. *Journal of Applied Behavior Analysis, 41*, 97–105.

Neef, N. A. (1995). Pyramidal parent training by peers. *Journal of Applied Behavior Analysis, 28*, 333–337.

Nigro-Bruzzi, D., & Sturmey, P. (2010). The effects of behavioral skills training on mand training by staff and unprompted vocal mands by children. *Journal of Applied Behavior Analysis, 43*, 757–761.

Oropeza, M. E., Fritz, J. N., Nissen, M. A., Terrell, A. S., & Phillips, L. A. (2018). Effects of therapist-worn protective equipment during functional analysis of aggression. *Journal of Applied Behavior Analysis, 51*, 681–686.

Parenteau, R., Luiselli, J. K., & Keeley, M. (2013). Direct and collateral effects of staff-worn protective equipment on injury prevention from child aggression. *Developmental Neurorehabilitation, 16*, 73–77.

Parsons, M. B., Rollyson, J. H., & Reid, D. H. (2012). Evidence-based staff training: A guide for practitioners. *Behavior Analysis in Practice, 5*, 2–11.

Robertson, J., Emerson, E., Gregory, N., Hatto, C., Turner, S., Kessissoglou, S., et al. (2000). Lifestyle related risk factors for poor health in residential settings for people with intellectual disabilities. *Research in Developmental Disabilities, 21*, 469–486.

Rojahn, J., Matson, J. L., Esbensen, A. J., & Smalls, Y. (2001). The behavior problems inventory: An instrument for the assessment of self-injury, stereotyped behavior, and aggression/destruction in individuals with developmental disabilities. *Journal of Autism and Developmental Disorders, 31*, 577–588.

Rosales, R., Gongola, L., & Homilitas, C. (2015). An evaluation of video modeling with embedded instructions to teach implementation of stimulus preference assessments. *Journal of Applied Behavior Analysis, 48*, 209–214.

Sawyer, M. R., Andzik, N. A., Kranak, M. P., Willke, C. P., Curiel, E. S. L., Hensley, L. E., et al. (2017). Improving pre-service teachers' performance skills through behavioral skills training. *Behavior Analysis in Practice, 10*, 296–300.

Shapiro, M., & Kazemi, E. (2017). A review of training strategies to teach individuals implementation of behavioral interventions. *Journal of Organizational Behavior Management, 37*, 32–62.

Sigafoos, J., Elkins, J., Kerr, M., & Attwood, T. (1994). A survey of aggressive behaviour among a population of persons with intellectual disability in Queensland. *Journal of Intellectual Disability Research, 38*, 369–381.

St. Peter, C. C., Byrd, J. D., Pence, S. T., & Foreman, A. P. (2016). Effects of treatment-integrity failures on a response-cost procedure. *Journal of Applied Behavior Analysis, 49*, 308–328.

St. Peter Pipkin, C. C., Vollmer, T. R., & Sloman, K. N. (2010). Effects of treatment integrity failures during differential reinforcement of alternative behavior: A translational model. *Journal of Applied Behavior Analysis, 43*, 47–70.

Tenneij, N. H., & Koot, H. M. (2008). Incidence, types and characteristics of aggressive behaviour in treatment facilities for adults with mild intellectual disability and severe challenging behavior. *Journal of Intellectual Disability Research, 52*, 114–124.

Thiessen, C., Fazzio, D., Arnal, L., Martin, G. L., Yu, C. T., & Keilback, L. (2009). Evaluation of a self-instructional manual for conducting discrete-trials teaching with children with autism. *Behavior Modification, 33*, 360–373.

Thomason-Sassi, J. L., Iwata, B. A., Neidert, P. L., & Roscoe, E. (2011). Response latency as an index of response strength during functional analyses of problem behavior. *Journal of Applied Behavior Analysis, 44*, 51–67.

Thompson, R. H., & Iwata, B. A. (2001). A descriptive analysis of consequences following problem behavior. *Journal of Applied Behavior Analysis, 34*, 169–178.

Urban, K. D., Luiselli, J. K., Child, S. N., & Parenteau, R. (2011). Effects of protective equipment on frequency and intensity of aggression-provoked staff injury. *Journal of Developmental and Physical Disabilities, 23*, 555–562.

Ward-Horner, J., & Sturmey, P. (2012). Component analysis of behavior skills training in functional analysis. *Behavioral Interventions, 27*, 75–92.

Wehman, P., & McLaughlin, P. J. (1979). How to evaluate your LD program. *Academic Therapy, 15*, 145–156.

Training and Performance Management of Care Providers

Raymond G. Miltenberger, Jennifer L. Cook, and Marissa Novotny

Abstract This chapter discusses behavioral approaches to staff training and performance management. The first section covers staff training procedures consisting of behavioral skills training, pyramidal training, and the use of video and technology in training. The section reviews the steps involved in best practices for staff training. The second section discusses performance management procedures designed to maintain the correct use of job skills by staff. After a brief review of antecedent and consequent approaches to managing staff performance, the second section discusses resources available to supervisors and managers to assess, promote, and maintain staff performance of their staff. The chapter includes a table listing resources available to organizations seeking to improve staff training and management.

Keywords Staff training · Performance management · Behavioral skills training · Pyramidal training · Video · Technology · Aggression · Violence · Intellectual disabilities · Autism

Staff training and performance management within educational and treatment settings are essential for ensuring that staff members to do their jobs effectively. Staff training procedures impart the skills staff need to carry out their job responsibilities and performance management arranges the conditions that increase the likelihood that staff will continue to carry out their responsibilities as trained. Training and performance management are particularly important for supervisors, clinicians, and care providers who develop treatment plans and intervene directly

R. G. Miltenberger (✉) · J. L. Cook · M. Novotny
University of South Florida, Tampa, FL, USA
e-mail: miltenbe@usf.edu

© Springer Nature Switzerland AG 2021
J. K. Luiselli (ed.), *Applied Behavior Analysis Treatment of Violence and Aggression in Persons with Neurodevelopmental Disabilities*, Advances in Preventing and Treating Violence and Aggression,
https://doi.org/10.1007/978-3-030-68549-2_9

with persons who have neurodevelopmental disabilities, are violent, and demonstrate aggression. This chapter will first discuss staff training and then performance management, focusing on procedures and practices that have good evidence support and can be recommended to a broad base of service practitioners.

Staff Training

Review of Pertinent Research Literature

According to a recent review by Gravina et al. (2018) staff training is a growing area of research within both applied behavior analysis (ABA) and organizational behavior management (OBM). A number of procedures are used to train staff, including behavioral skills training, pyramidal training, and video and automatic trainings.

Behavioral Skills Training Behavioral skills training (BST) consisting of instructions, modeling, rehearsal, and feedback (Kirkpatrick, Akers, & Rivera, 2019) is one form of staff training that is used in a variety of settings. According to DiGennaro Reed, Blackman, Erath, Brand, and Novak (2018), during the instruction component of BST, the trainer provides a description of the procedure care providers are expected to perform. The trainer then models the correct implementation of the procedures in a role-play simulating an interaction with a client that requires the use of the skills being taught. Next, the trainer requires each of the care providers to practice the procedures in a role-play and provides positive feedback consisting of descriptive praise for correct performance and corrective feedback consisting of further instruction for incorrect aspects of the performance. The role-play is structured to simulate the discriminative stimuli that should evoke the skills the staff is learning. DiGennaro Reed et al. state that the care providers should practice the procedures until they meet a mastery criterion of 90% for two or three consecutive practice opportunities.

Substantial research shows BST is effective in teaching skills to staff members in a variety of settings (e.g., Hogan, Knez, & Kahng, 2015; Madzharova, Sturmey, & Jones, 2012; Madzharova, Sturmey, & Yoo, 2018; Palmen, Didden, & Korzilius, 2010; Phillips & Mudford, 2008). For example, Phillips and Mudford (2008) used BST to teach four residential caregivers to conduct functional analyses. The experimenter first provided the caregivers with verbal and written instructions. Next, the caregivers watched an individual model each component of a functional analysis and then practiced each of the components in role-plays. Caregivers continued to rehearse the skills in role-play scenarios until they reached a mastery criterion of 95% correct steps implemented. Three caregivers increased to 100% correct after receiving BST and one participant required enhanced training, which included within-session prompting.

Hogan et al. (2015) used BST to teach four school staff to implement behavior intervention plans (BIPs) that included extinction, noncontingent reinforcement, and differential reinforcement. During training, the experimenter provided the participants with copies of the BIP, had them implement the procedures, and delivered feedback on performance. If the participants engaged in 90% or greater correct implementation of the BIP after instructions alone, no further intervention was provided for that component of the BIP. However, if staff did not reach this mastery criterion, they received the modeling, rehearsal, and feedback component of BST. Training continued until participants reached the mastery criteria of 90% correct implementation. All four participants required instructions, modeling, rehearsal, and feedback to reach mastery criteria for all components of the BIP. This study suggests instructions alone are not likely to be a successful training strategy and points to the importance of the rehearsal and feedback components of BST for teaching skills to staff.

Madzharova et al. (2018) used a modified form of BST to teach classroom staff how to implement a BIP with a 10-year-old boy diagnosed with Autism Spectrum Disorder. Participants first received feedback on their previous implementation of the BIP followed by the trainer modeling the implementation of the BIP with the student. The staff then conducted the BIP with the student and received feedback and modeling until they completed three consecutive trials with 90% accuracy or better. All three of the participants reached the mastery criterion, and two of the three continued to engage in all of the steps of the BIP during post-training and maintenance phases. These results indicate that the modeling, rehearsal, and feedback components of BST were effective for training staff. Although instructions were not initially provided, the corrective feedback component of BST consists of instruction for improved performance so all components of BST were eventually present.

Pyramidal Training One concern with the use of BST for staff training is the amount of time it takes. This concern is especially important if multiple staff require training (Parsons, Rollyson, & Reid, 2012). One way to address this concern is through pyramidal training, which consists of training a small group of staff, usually supervisors, who then train other staff to conduct the intervention (Parsons, Rollyson, & Reid, 2013). Not only can pyramidal training be more efficient, but it can also help with maintenance of staff performance, due to the staff trainers being a part of the organization. Having staff trainers allows new staff to be trained immediately, instead of having to wait for a behavior analyst to conduct a training (Parsons et al., 2013).

Parsons et al. (2013) used BST to train 10 staff members at an adult education program to conduct BST. The participants then used BST with other staff members to train them on different job-related activities. In two 1-h BST sessions, the participants learned how to provide instructions, modeling, rehearsal opportunities, and feedback, and how to collect data during the observations. Training occurred until all participants demonstrated correct implementation of all BST steps during role-play scenarios and on-the-job assessments. One limitation is that Parsons et al. did not collect data on the correct implementation of skills by the staff members trained by the participants.

Haberlin, Beauchamp, Agnew, and O'Brien (2012) compared pyramidal training to consultant-led training with 44 direct care staff in two community-based day programs. Experimenters collected data on knowledge of ABA principles and the percentage of correct teaching procedures performed by the participants. In the consultant-led training groups and pyramidal training groups, participants were provided with lectures, instructed to discuss the materials as related to their jobs and consumers, and completed worksheets and role-play scenarios. For the consultant-led group, an experimenter conducted the training, and for the pyramidal group, a supervisor conducted the training. Before conducting training, the experimenters trained the supervisors using the same materials. Both groups had similar results for the knowledge-based tests with mean increases of around 20% following training. Both groups also showed an increase in performance after training. However, the group that received pyramidal training had a 10% larger increase than the consultant-led group in correct teaching procedures. Additionally, for the pyramidal training group, increases maintained during a 3-month follow-up while the scores of the consultant-led group decreased to baseline levels.

Results of Haberlin et al. (2012) indicate that pyramidal training may be more effective then consultant-led training, possibly because during pyramidal training, the participants were able to discuss how they would implement the skills with their specific consumers. The experimenters did not facilitate similar discussions during the consultant-led training. Additionally, Haberline et al. discuss how participants who received pyramidal training were more likely to receive ABA focused feedback while on the job; however, they did not collect data on the provision of feedback.

Video and Automated Trainings Another way to increase the efficiency of staff training is to use video or automated training. These training formats could decrease the time and cost of training (Macurik, O'Kane, Malanga, & Reid, 2008) and provide greater consistency across each iteration of training (Lambert, Lloyd, Staubitz, Weaver, & Jennings, 2014).

Macurik et al. (2008) compared live training to video-based training with 38 direct care staff at two homes within a residential center for adults with severe disabilities. Experimenters trained three groups of staff to implement a behavior plan for a specific individual in their care. Within each group, participants were randomly assigned to a live trainer or video training. Experimenters collected data on the percentage of quiz questions answered correctly, the percentage of on-the-job components completed correctly, and the training time required per staff member. During live training, the behavior analyst described the treatment plan to the participants and answered questions. For video training, participants watched a video of the behavior analyst describing each of the components with intermittent bullet points on the monitor. Video training was more effective and efficient than live training. Participants who received video training scored higher than participants who received live training during the on-the-job assessments. Additionally, less experimenter time was required for video training then for live training. These results indicate that video training might be as or more effective than live training while being more efficient.

Research on computer-based training is still relatively new, with most research concentrating on training undergraduate or master students to work with children with disabilities. Although these studies do not focus on care providers of individuals who demonstrate violence and aggression, the findings may be relevant to such care providers.

Pollard, Higbee, Akers, and Brodhead (2014) used an interactive computer training to teach four undergraduate students how to conduct discrete trial training (DTT) with children with autism. The training had four modules that discussed collecting data, prompting strategies, and managing antecedents and consequences. The computer-based training included PowerPoint presentations with embedded videos demonstrating how to complete DTT correctly and open-ended questions to check comprehension. At the end of each module, participants completed a quiz, and if they did not get 80% on the quiz, they reviewed the correct answers and took a new quiz. Before training, all participants implemented DTT with below 40% accuracy both while role-playing with an adult and working with a child diagnosed with autism. After completing the four modules, correct implementation increased to 90% for all participants when role-playing with an adult while one of the participants required additional feedback to reach 90% when working with a child.

Lambert et al. (2014) conducted similar research to train graduate students to conduct a trial-based functional analysis (FA). Lambert et al. provided participants with a PowerPoint training that included embedded video clips and evaluative slides to test participants' knowledge. Experimenters collected data on participants' treatment fidelity of each condition of a FA. All participants showed an increase in correct implementation for at least one of the FA conditions after training, but none of the participants reached the mastery criterion of 90% correct implementation for all conditions. These finding suggest PowerPoint instructions and modeling alone may not be effective but may be a beneficial component of a training package.

Schnell, Sidener, DeBar, Vladescu, and Kahng (2018) provided 20 graduate students with a computer-based training to teach them how to arrange a functional analysis (FA), analyze the FA data, and implement procedural modifications. The training was broken up into four modules and, to progress through the modules, participants had to score 100% correct on the module quiz. Experimenters collected data on correct responding during a pre-test and post-test along with probes in which students analyzed a novel case and a corresponding FA graph. The students answered questions regarding what the hypothesized function was along with what the next steps in the FA process should be. After training, there was an increase in scores for 19 of the 20 participants from the pre-test to the post-test and novel case probes. These results indicate that computer-based training might be effective to teach individuals how to analyze FA graphs. This study is limited in scope because the target behavior consisted on analyzing figures but did not involve staff behavior required to carry out procedures with clients.

Practice Recommendations

Staff training should be an active process consisting of antecedent strategies to evoke correct responses in the correct circumstances (instructions and modeling) and the opportunity to rehearse the skills with feedback until staff demonstrate competence. Reid (2019) recommends seven steps when conducting staff training. These steps incorporate each of the BST components.

Step 1. Explain the rationale for the skills the staff is being trained to carry out.
Steps 2 and 3. Provide a description of the skills verbally and then in writing.
Step 4. Demonstrate the skills either in person or by the use of a video.
Step 5. Have the staff members rehearse the skills on-the-job or through role-play scenarios. If staff are unable to engage in on-the-job rehearsal of the skills during the initial training, such rehearsal should occur soon after. Providing staff with on-the-job rehearsal with the consumers increases the likelihood that skills will generalize outside of the training setting (Parsons et al., 2012).
Step 6. Provide the staff members with feedback on their performance in role-plays and on-the-job rehearsals, including praise for what they did correctly and corrective feedback (further instruction) for improvement.
Step 7. Have the staff members rehearse the skills and receive feedback until they demonstrate mastery.

Synthesis of Research Findings and Future Research

Overall, research has shown that BST and pyramidal training are effective and that video-based training shows promise for teaching caregivers a variety of skills. These skills range from implementation of behavioral acquisition programming to implementing behavior plans to decrease problem behaviors. Most studies evaluating caregiver training have included some if not all components of BST. However, the format in which each of the components is delivered differs (Reid, 2019). Using technology is a promising cost-saving approach for delivering certain components of training (Shapiro & Kazemi, 2017). Training videos (Weldy, Rapp, & Capocasa, 2014) or interactive computer training (Higbee et al., 2016) are most useful for the instructions and modeling components of training. A live trainer may then more efficiently dedicate time to rehearsal and feedback components, as well as post-training observations (DiGennaro Reed & Henley, 2015). As technology advances, research needs to continue to look at the effectiveness of such formats because they have been shown to decrease the time and cost of training (Reid, 2019).

Research is still limited on computer-based training, but so far, research has indicated that it might be a useful tool to train caregivers. These training formats might be especially practical for those with an undergraduate or master's degree (Pollard et al., 2014). More research is needed to evaluate whether computer-based training is effective for caregivers who only have a high school diploma, the minimum education required to become a registered behavior technician (RBT). This research is important as RBTs are increasingly likely to be the ones carrying our behavioral interventions.

Additionally, research demonstrates that pyramidal training might be more effective then consultant-based training (Haberlin et al., 2012). However, more research is needed to establish the robustness of this finding. Furthermore, it is important to investigate what components of pyramidal training are likely to increase its effectiveness over consultant training (e.g., additional feedback, consumer-focused training). Lastly, regarding pyramidal training, researchers have suggested that pyramidal training may result in the maintenance of skills (Parsons et al., 2013). However, to date no research has looked at long term maintenance and whether pyramidal training decreases the need for behavior analysts to conduct follow-up training of staff trainers or caregivers.

Performance Management

Procedural fidelity, defined as staff members' continued correct use of job skills with clients, is a product of initial training and performance management (e.g., Brady, Padden, & McGill, 2019; Diener, McGee, & Miguel, 2009). Once a staff member acquires a new skill following staff training, supervisors use performance management procedures to promote continued use of the skill. Performance management is important to promote quality implementation of support plans designed to decrease aggressive or other challenging behavior, and lack of performance management procedures puts both client and staff well-being at risk (Shapiro & Kazemi, 2017). Further, performance management is a necessary activity for behavior analysts to meet their basic ethical obligations for the delivery of quality behavior services (e.g., Brodhead & Higbee, 2012; DiGennaro Reed & Henley, 2015; Turner, Fisher, & Luiselli, 2016).

Review of Pertinent Research Literature

Producing and maintaining behavioral change for clients requires systematic contingencies designed to maintain the behaviors of (a) direct care staff implementing behavioral treatments *and* (b) the supervisors implementing performance management procedures (Reid, O'Kane, & Macurik, 2011). The literature has long described work performance failures to be a direct result of having ineffective or nonexistent performance management procedures in place to ensure staff correctly implement the skills they were trained to use (Liberman, 1983; Reid & Parsons, 2000).

Performance management consists of arranging antecedents and/or consequences for staff performance. A number of antecedent and consequent strategies are utilized in performance management; antecedent strategies are used to evoke the correct performance and consequence strategies are used to reinforce correct performance and decrease performance problems (for reviews see Brady et al., 2019 and Gravina et al., 2018).

Antecedent strategies to evoke correct performance include (a) goal setting (e.g., Gil & Carter, 2016; Miller, Carlson, & Sigurdsson, 2014; Squires & Wilder, 2010), (b) video modeling (DiGennaro-Reed, Codding, Catania, & Maguire, 2010), (c) self-monitoring (e.g., Mowery, Miltenberger, & Weil, 2010; Petscher & Bailey, 2006; Plavnick, Ferreri, & Maupin, 2010), and (d) prompts and other cueing strategies (e.g., Casella et al., 2010; May, Austin, & Dymond, 2011; Petscher & Bailey, 2006). Examples of these antecedent strategies include the use of tactile prompts and self-monitoring to increase correct implementation of a token economy by teaching assistants (Petscher & Bailey, 2006), the addition of cue cards to help therapist implement teaching procedures more accurately (May et al., 2011), and video modeling to increase the correct implementation of behavior plans by teachers (DiGennaro-Reed et al., 2010). Consequence strategies are also combined frequently with antecedent approaches to promote staff performance of their job responsibilities.

Praise and feedback are the most common consequence strategies to maintain staff performance (e.g., Arco, 2008; Green, Rollyson, Passante, & Reid, 2002; Hall, Grundon, Pope, & Romero, 2010; Mangiapanello & Hemmes, 2015; Parsons et al., 2012; Parsons & Reid, 1995; van Vonderen, Didden, & Beeking, 2012). Feedback, delivered after a supervisor observes staff job performance, is designed to tell staff what aspects of the job they performed correctly and provide instructions for improvement when needed. Other consequence strategies include rewards (monetary and non-monetary) for correct performance (e.g., Cook & Dixon, 2006; Huberman & O'Brien, 1999; Miller et al., 2014), and punishment or negative reinforcement for incorrect performance (e.g., DiGennaro, Martens, & Kleinmann, 2007; Nabeyama & Sturmey, 2010). To use feedback and other consequence strategies effectively, a monitoring system must be in place to observe and record staff performance so supervisors can base the delivery of feedback or other consequences on staff behavior observed in the workplace. Examples of consequence strategies include goal setting and performance feedback to increase correct implementation of a behavioral intervention for inappropriate behavior (DiGennaro et al., 2007), video feedback to increase the accurate implementation of teaching procedures by staff with individuals with disabilities (van Vonderen et al., 2012), and a lottery system in which staff could earn a chance to receive a bonus for completing a number of required forms correctly (Cook & Dixon, 2005).

Many managers and supervisors in human service organizations underutilize the approaches found to be effective in staff training and performance management research (DiGennaro Reed & Henley, 2015; Reid & Parsons, 2000) perhaps because the breadth of the literature overwhelms them. Busy managers require concise and efficient information that is easily accessible, such as assessment and measurement tools, guidelines and recommendations, and at-a-glance lists of references and other resources. Reviews by Gravina et al. (2018) and Brady et al. (2019) are useful in this regard. This section of the chapter highlights available tools, curricula, and guidelines as potential resources for performance management, with a focus on recent advancements.

Synthesis of Research Findings and Implications

Performance Analysis Both desirable and undesirable behavior are acquired and maintained by reinforcing consequences as the behavior occurs in the presence of specific antecedent stimuli or events that function as discriminative stimuli and establishing operations (e.g., Miltenberger, Bloom, Sanchez, & Valbuena, 2016). In the same way, poor performance or competent performance by staff is maintained by reinforcement contingencies. To determine what contingencies (antecedents and consequences) are maintaining a given problem behavior for a client, a functional assessment is conducted (Miltenberger et al., 2016). Similarly, functional performance analysis tools, such as the Performance Diagnostic Checklist (PDC; Austin, 2000), have been developed to assess staff performance in the private business sector. The PDC has substantial research support within the organizational behavior management literature (e.g., Austin, Weatherly, & Gravina, 2005; Rodriguez et al., 2005). The Performance Diagnostic Checklist – Human Services (PDC-HS; Carr, Wilder, Majdalany, Mathisen, & Strain, 2013), has been adapted specifically for performance management in human services settings. The PDC-HS is an assessment designed to identify variables maintaining problematic staff behavior, which can then inform a function-based solution. For example, the results may indicate that a particular solution requires the redesign of ineffective program tools, rather than defaulting to retraining a staff member who may be otherwise competent in treatment implementation (Carr et al., 2013). There are 20 questions in the PDC-HS across four domains: (a) training, (b) task clarification and prompting, (c) resources and materials, and (d) performance consequences, effort, and competition. Some responses are provided via indirect assessment (i.e., self-report), and others require direct observations. (Carr & Wilder, 2016). The PDC-HS also includes information on potential function-based interventions that match the assessment results.

Carr et al. (2013) assessed the predictive validity of the PDC-HS in a comparison study. Specifically, they evaluated the ability of PDC-HS to identify factors related to employee's deficiencies in keeping treatment rooms clean in a center that provided autism interventions. They used the results of the assessment to compare two interventions: (a) a function-based treatment (matched to the function identified in the assessment) consisting of training and graphed feedback, and (b) an arbitrary treatment comprised of task clarification and increased materials. They found that the function-based intervention was effective while the arbitrary intervention was not. Since Carr et al. first introduced the PDC-HS, several studies have conducted evaluations extending its predictive validity (e.g., Bowe & Sellers, 2018; Ditzian, Wilder, King, & Tanz, 2015; Wilder, Lipschultz, & Gehrman, 2018), or otherwise successfully used the PDC-HS to inform effective treatments (e.g., Goings, Carr,

Maguire, Harper, & Luiselli, 2019; Sellers, Clay, Hoffman, & Collins, 2019; Smith & Wilder, 2018). Furthermore, the PDC-HS has become a commonly recommended assessment tool for performance management within human service settings (DiGennaro Reed & Henley, 2015; Gravina et al., 2018; Kazemi, Shapiro, & Kavner, 2015; Lerman, LeBlanc, & Valentino, 2015; Sellers, LeBlanc, & Valentino, 2016; Sellers, Valentino, Landon, & Aiello, 2019; Wilder, Lipschultz, King, Driscoll, & Sigurdsson, 2018).

Martinez-Onstott, Wilder, and Sigurdsson (2016) created another adaption of the PDC, the PDC-Safety, to assess barriers related to work safety and provide information that can lead to effective interventions. Work safety is of vital importance in human service organizations (Casella et al., 2010; Weatherly, 2019) and requirements by insurance agencies or federal and state policies may begin to emerge with the burgeoning of behavioral services (Grauerholz-Fisher, Vollmer, Peters, Perez, & Berard, 2019). The use of the PDC-Safety and other organizational functional assessments has already gained support by researchers as beneficial for efficient behavioral safety assessments (Cruz et al., 2019; Weatherly, 2019; Wilder, Lipschultz, King, et al., 2018). The PDC-Safety might have particular relevance in a setting where staff must address violent and aggressive behavior of their clients.

Performance Management Systems To implement a performance management system effectively, managers within an organization may consider a standardized curriculum that serves to guide upper-tier supervisors and managers in training lower-tier supervisory staff to train and maintain staff behavior. Reid, Parsons, and Green (2011) developed an accessible supervisor training curriculum, which utilizes evidenced-based supervisory practices, and has been highly recommended in the literature on performance management (e.g., Lerman et al., 2015). The curriculum is comprised of 11 training modules, includes presentation slides, instructions, activities, quizzes, and visual aids. Trumpet Behavioral Health is a national organization that used this curriculum (with some customization) to train staff in all of their divisions across more than 10 states. The organization's two lead trainers were able to adapt a pyramidal training model using the curriculum, resulting in all of their 800 team members becoming trained within 9 months of its initial implementation (Lerman et al., 2015). Alternatively, the Supervisor's Guidebook (Reid, Parsons, & Green, 2012) describes best practices for implementing competency-based training and performance management. This reader-friendly guide provides a seven-step protocol for evidence-based supervision, while detailing critical supervisory skills and solutions for common performance problems.

Curriculum options specializing in supervision within certain professions are also available, such as those designed for board certified behavior analysts and those seeking certification. One such example, developed by Courtney, Hartley, LaMarca, Rosswurm, and Reid (2017), provides an evidenced-based training curriculum targeting board certified behavior analysts who are training supervisees to train and supervise frontline staff in the implementation of behavior programs. This curriculum includes a manual for the trainer and trainee, recommended readings, and competency form templates. It has nine modules, with each module consisting of a module summary page, presentation content, trainee worksheets, trainee mastery checks, and presentation slides (Celiberti & Treadaway, 2019).

Another resource, authored by Kazemi, Rice, and Adzhyan (2018), targets supervisees of the same profession. This handbook provides forms and checklists, and guides potential behavior professionals throughout the stages of their experience, providing information on preparing for academic fieldwork and selecting a supervisor, using effective supervisee behaviors, becoming competent in evidenced-based supervision strategies, writing the board exam, and creating a portfolio. Although these guides are specialized to fit a specific profession's criteria, they focus on supervisory relationships involving mentorship and accompanying best practices that most any profession in the human services could adopt successfully.

Similarly, Sellers, Valentino, and LeBlanc (2016) described a set of practice guidelines for supervisors to provide a successful mentorship experience. Guideline 1 describes establishing an effective supervisor-supervisee relationship by using supervision contracts, setting clear expectations, preparing the process for receiving and accepting feedback, and creating a committed and positive relationship. Guideline 2 suggests planning for structured content and competency assessments. Guideline 3 emphasizes the importance of evaluating the effects of supervision by soliciting feedback from the supervisor being mentored or other relevant professionals, and directly collecting data on outcomes related to professional, administrative, or clinical goals. Guideline 4 describes integrating ethics and professional development throughout the experience. The final guideline suggests continuing the professional relationship beyond the mentorship contract, to provide ongoing support.

In a complementary article, Sellers, LeBlanc, and Valentino (2016) provided guidelines for supervisors to identify potential indicators of three common issues related to mentoring individual supervisees and the supervisory relationship. The persistent supervision issues addressed are (a) disorganization and poor time management, (b) poor interpersonal skills, and (c) difficulty accepting and applying feedback. They also provide recommendations and specific resources to assess and solve these issues. Importantly, the authors emphasize that supervisors should also always assess their own behavior related to the target issue and the supervisory relationship, and consider some possible modifications of their behavior as a supervisor to affect positive change.

In a follow-up study on supervisory practices, Sellers, Clay, et al. (2019) conducted a survey within the United States, elucidating some current supervisory practices by 284 board certificated behavior analysts across all 50 states. The survey identified the top five areas of strength in supervisory practices, including; (a) using a contract, (b) evaluating caseload capacity (also see Dixon et al., 2016, for caseload recommendations), (c) setting expectations, (d) using a range of evaluations, and (e) incorporating ethics and literature. Additionally, the survey identified five top barriers to effective supervision, consisting of: a) not setting clear expectations for receiving feedback, (b) not providing ongoing evaluation of the supervisory relationship, (c) not using competency-based evaluations and tracking outcomes, (d) not assessing and teaching professionalism, and (e) not obtaining feedback on supervisory practices. To address these barriers, the authors provided some guidelines for improvement across these five domains, and included a corresponding Supervisor "To-Do" Checklist. As before, although these supervisory recommendations and resulting checklist were based on a survey a board certified behavior analysts, these evidenced-based supervisory practices would be useful for any individual providing mentorship or individualized supervision in human services.

Some Specific Practices Within Performance Management Other researchers have developed several tools (e.g., checklists, guidelines) that may be useful for promoting good supervisory practices.

Interpersonal and Professional Skills Valentino, LeBlanc, and Sellers (2016) outlined the potential benefits and provided detailed recommendations for conducting group supervision. Besides efficiency for the supervisor, group supervision benefits the supervisees in that they can develop a more well-rounded professional repertoire. For example, participants will have direct experiences in networking, engaging in productive discussion, observational learning, rehearsal of skills, and peer feedback. The authors present recommendations for the group supervisor to structure and conduct group sessions successfully.

Relatedly, managers and supervisors in human service settings will spend a great deal of time in meetings, with clients, colleagues, or supervisees. Meetings often are viewed as unproductive and unpleasant; however, when they are conducted systematically, meetings can be a highly productive venues for problem solving and decision making. LeBlanc and Nosik (2019) reviewed the function of meetings in the workplace and prescribed a set of detailed guidelines for effective meetings, including a problem-solving diagram, a checklist for planning and leading, a meeting agenda template, and a list of meeting rules.

Ecological Factors One understudied area in performance management is how to improve the ecology of organizational settings. This area may be important for preserving the health and safety of clients and staff, reducing practical barriers or competing contingencies in the workplace, enhancing efficiency of tasks through an organized environment, creating a quality and meaningful environment for staff and clients, and maintaining pleasing esthetics for an organization to display for potential consumers and other business stakeholders. Some authors have created tools that may assist with measurement of permanent products related to the organizational ecology. Schmidt, Urban, Luiselli, White, and Harrington (2013) developed a Classroom Ecology Checklist (CEC), which evaluated the general classroom arrangement, classroom appearance, and safety hazards in an educational setting for students diagnosed with autism or another intellectual disability. They used the CEC to evaluate four classrooms identified by administrators as the most disorganized and hazardous. The investigators used the CEC to score permanent products during 5-min observations once per day, one to two times per week. In another study, Goings et al. (2019) utilized the CEC at a human services educational facility for children and youth with intellectual disabilities. This study is notable because it combined the use of the PDC-HS with the CEC, resulting in an efficient and effective intervention.

Quality Client Services In many human services setting, there are critical service standards that are directly related to the quality of the service delivery. For example, Joslyn, Vollmer, Dickens, and Walker (2018) developed a checklist for use in a secure residential facility for offenders with intellectual disabilities. The checklist consisted of four domains considering both permanent products and behaviors of staff and residents: (a) environment, (b) resident condition, (c) resident activity, and (d) staff activity. Each criterion for each category had detailed definitions, referred to as "scoring rules" for use in time-sample data collection.

Grauerholz-Fisher et al. (2019) utilized a similar form in an applied behavior analysis treatment center. The form had three broad categories consisting of staff behavior (i.e., positive and negative interactions), client behavior, and environment (i.e., clutter and safety). The authors of these studies described this tool as a useful and efficient method to "pinpoint client outcomes," while using direct observations rather than the commonly used indirect assessments for measuring quality of care and staff-resident interactions.

Practice Recommendations

As this chapter illustrates, several training methods and management systems have been incorporated into empirical practice tools (e.g., Carr et al., 2013), evidence-based systems (e.g., Reid, Parsons, & Green, 2011), and practice guidelines (e.g., LeBlanc & Luiselli, 2016). Thus, our recommendations for supervisors and managers to implement best practices is to use this chapter as a resource for the most recently established evidence-based tools, curricula, and guidelines (see Table 1), with a description of each in the synthesis of the research above.

Research Direction

The social significance of effective behavioral-based training and performance management methods is limited if the findings are not accessible or utilized (Reid, Parsons, & Green, 2011). Dissemination of effective practices needs to reach clinical professionals, but also managers and administrators in organizations who are responsible for the larger systems and resources. When agencies have employees who are not sufficiently supported and who may have unsatisfactory relationships with their supervisors, they are more prone to high turnover rates (DiGennaro Reed & Henley, 2015; Strouse, Carroll-Hernandez, Sherman, & Sheldon, 2003). There are no financial savings from foregoing quality training and performance manage-

Table 1 Tools, curricula, and guidelines for best practices of performance management

Performance analysis	Reference
Performance Diagnostic Checklist—Human Services (PDC-HS)	Carr et al. (2013)
Performance Diagnostic Checklist—Safety (PDC-Safety)	Martinez-Onstott et al. (2016)
Performance management systems and systematic supervisory practices	
Supervisor Training Curriculum	Reid, Parsons, and Green (2011)
The Supervisor's Guidebook	Reid et al. (2012)
The Training Curriculum for Supervisors of ABA Technicians in Autism Programs	Courtney et al. (2017)
Fieldwork and Supervision for Behavior Analysts: A Handbook	Kazemi et al. (2018)
Guidelines: Practices for Individual Supervision	Sellers, Valentino, and LeBlanc (2016)
Guidelines: Barriers to Successful Supervision	Sellers, Valentino, and LeBlanc (2016)
Supervisor "To-Do" Checklist for Individual Supervision	Sellers, Clay, et al. (2019); see appendix
Interpersonal and professional skills	
Guidelines: Group Supervision	Valentino et al. (2016)
Effective Professional Meetings: Guidelines, Diagram, Checklist, Agenda Template, and Meeting Rules	LeBlanc and Nosik (2019)
Ecological factors	
Classroom Ecology Checklist (CEC)	Schmidt et al. (2013)
Quality Client Services	
Assessment of Quality Care in Secure Residential Facilities: Data Form and Operational Definitions	Joslyn et al. (2018)
Assessment of Quality of Care in ABA Center: Data Form and Operational Definitions	Grauerholz-Fisher et al. (2019)
Procedural Integrity Checklist for DTT	Lerman et al. (2015)
Evidenced-Based Practice Classroom Observation Measure (EBP-COM)	Paff, Trump, Wunderlich, Harrison, and Ayres (2019)

ment when turnover creates substantial financial costs in the recruiting and hiring process and the initial training for each new employee (DiGennaro Reed & Henley, 2015). Future research should consider how to make best practices known and accessible. Emphasizing synthesized information in tools and recommendations may be attractive to administrators, managers, and supervisors who do not have the time, or possibly the skill, to sift through academic literature.

Research should also consider cost effective methods for putting systems in place. One way to promote the use of performance management systems is to have upper-tier managers and behavioral consultants implement a collaborative approach that involves managers and administrators in the initial training program. This approach may have been a major contributing factor to the 30-year maintenance of successful training systems described by Reid, Parsons, and Jensen (2017).

Using empirically supported practices for ongoing training and performance management of staff at all levels of human service agencies is critical for quality of care for consumers and desired outcomes for both consumers and staff (Digennaro Reed & Henley, 2015; Reid, 2019). With a focus on bolstering supervision in the human service setting (LeBlanc & Luiselli, 2016; Sellers, LeBlanc, & Valentino, 2016), several review and practice recommendation articles are a welcome supplement to the research literature in supervision and performance management. The latter part of this chapter has consolidated some of these recommendations, along with recent advancements in the applied literature, providing an overview and a resource for practitioners and organizations to consider within their supervisory practices.

Finally, the training and performance management practices reviewed in the chapter should be considered the "gold standard" within service settings for persons who have neurodevelopmental disabilities and require treatment for violence-aggression. We have several considerations specifically for agencies working with this population.

Initial thorough staff training is particularly important to prepare staff to manage violent and aggressive behavior effectively and prevent harm to clients or staff. Training to mastery should occur in realistic role-plays so staff get it right the first time when using procedures with violent and aggressive clients. Furthermore, frequent and consistent monitoring should occur to inform supervisors if retraining is needed.

With violent and aggressive clients, performance management should be implemented initially with high intensity. We recommend initial discussions with staff emphasizing the importance of procedural fidelity to promote success and safety with difficult clients; antecedent procedures to evoke successful performance and structure the environment for safety; frequent monitoring so it is clear supervisors are present in the environment and supportive; and immediate and frequent feedback to reinforce successful performance. We believe these strategies send a message to staff that supervisors care and management has their back.

Supervisors need to assess ecological factors that can affect the safety of staff and clients and design preventative strategies. Ecological factors influencing safety may include such issues such as glass (windows, mirrors), unstable furniture, electrical outlets, clutter, writing utensils, scissors, hot drinks, jewelry, loose or unstable shoes, loose clothing, long hair, and eye glasses to name a few.

Agencies working with clients with violent or aggressive behavior should arrange crisis management training for all staff upon initial employment. Supervisors must ensure staff are proficient in their use of crisis management techniques and have ongoing opportunities to practice them outside of a real crisis scenario. Supervisors should also be trained in these techniques and practice regularly for additional crisis support for staff as required.

References

Arco, L. (2008). Feedback for improving staff training and performance in behavioral treatment programs. *Behavioral Interventions, 23*, 39–64.

Austin, J. (2000). Performance analysis and performance diagnostics. In J. Austin & J. E. Carr (Eds.), *Handbook of applied behavior analysis* (pp. 321–349). Reno: Context Press.

Austin, J., Weatherly, N. L., & Gravina, N. E. (2005). Using task clarification, graphic feedback, and verbal feedback to increase closing-task completion in a privately owned restaurant. *Journal of Applied Behavior Analysis, 38*, 117–120. https://doi.org/10.1901/jaba.2005.159-03

Bowe, M., & Sellers, T. P. (2018). Evaluating the performance diagnostic checklist-human services to assess incorrect error-correction procedures by preschool paraprofessionals. *Journal of Applied Behavior Analysis, 51*, 166–176. https://doi.org/10.1002/jaba.428

Brady, L., Padden, C., & McGill, P. (2019). Improving procedural fidelity of behavioural interventions for people with intellectual and developmental disabilities: A systematic review. *Journal of Applied Research in Intellectual Disabilities, 32*, 762–778. https://doi.org/10.1111/jar.12585

Brodhead, M. T., & Higbee, T. S. (2012). Teaching and maintaining ethical behavior in a professional organization. *Behavior Analysis in Practice, 5*, 82–88.

Carr, J. E., & Wilder, D. A. (2016). The performance diagnostic checklist—Human services: A correction. *Behavior Analysis in Practice, 9*, 63. https://doi.org/10.1007/s4061-015-0099-3

Carr, J. E., Wilder, D. A., Majdalany, L., Mathisen, D., & Strain, L. A. (2013). An assessment based solution to a human-service employee performance problem: An initial evaluation of the performance diagnostic checklist—Human services. *Behavior Analysis in Practice, 6*, 16–32.

Casella, S. E., Wilder, D. A., Neidert, P., Rey, C., Compton, M., & Chong, I. (2010). The effects of response effort on safe performance by therapists at an autism treatment facility. *Journal of Applied Behavior Analysis, 43*, 729–734. https://doi.org/10.1901/jaba.2010.43-729

Celiberti, D., & Treadaway, S. (2019). Review of "the training curriculum for supervisors of ABA technicians in autism programs." *Science in Autism Treatment, 16*(1). Retrieved from https://asatonline.org/research-treatment/book-reviews/book-review-training-curriculum-aba/

Cook, T., & Dixon, M. R. (2006). Performance feedback and probabilistic bonus contingencies among employees in a human service organization. *Journal of Organizational Behavior Management, 25*, 45–63. https://doi.org/10.1300/J075v25n03_04

Courtney, W. T., Hartley, B. K., LaMarca, V. J., Rosswurm, M., & Reid, D. H. (2017). *The training curriculum for supervisors of ABA technicians in autism programs*. Cornwall on Hudson, NY: Sloan Publishing.

Cruz, N. J., Wilder, D. A., Phillabaum, C., Thomas, R., Cusick, M., & Gravina, N. (2019). Further evaluation of the performance diagnostic checklist-safety (PDC-safety). *Journal of Organizational Behavior Management, 39*, 266. Advance Online Publication. https://doi.org/10.1080/01608061.2019.1666777

Diener, L. H., McGee, H. M., & Miguel, C. F. (2009). An integrated approach for conducting a behavioral systems analysis. *Journal of Organizational Behavior Management, 29*, 108–135. https://doi.org/10.1002/jaba.171

DiGennaro, F. D., Martens, B. K., & Kleinmann, A. E. (2007). A comparison of performance feedback procedures on teachers' treatment implementation integrity and students' inappropriate behavior in special education classrooms. *Journal of Applied Behavior Analysis, 40*, 447–461. https://doi.org/10.1901/jaba.2007.40-447

DiGennaro Reed, F. D., Blackman, A. L., Erath, T. G., Brand, D., & Novak, M. D. (2018). Guidelines for using behavioral skills training to provide teacher support. *Teaching Exceptional Children, 50*, 373–380.

DiGennaro Reed, F. D., & Henley, A. J. (2015). A survey of staff training and performance management practices: The good, the bad, and the ugly. *Behavior Analysis in Practice, 8*, 16–26. https://doi.org/10.1007/s40617-015-0044-5

DiGennaro-Reed, F. D., Codding, R., Catania, C. N., & Maguire, H. (2010). Effects of video modeling on treatment integrity of behavioral interventions. *Journal of Applied Behavior Analysis, 43*, 291–295. https://doi.org/10.1901/jaba.2010.43-291

Ditzian, K., Wilder, D. A., King, A., & Tanz, J. (2015). An evaluation of the performance diagnostic checklist–human services to assess an employee performance problem in a center-based autism treatment facility. *Journal of Applied Behavior Analysis, 48*, 199–203. https://doi.org/10.1007/s40617-016-0132-1

Dixon, R. D., Linstead, E., Granpeesheh, D., Novack, M. N., Frenach, R., Stevens, E., et al. (2016). An evaluation of the impact of supervision intensity, supervisor qualifications, and caseload on outcomes in the treatment of autism spectrum disorder. *Behavior Analysis in Practice, 9*, 339–348.

Gil, P. J., & Carter, S. L. (2016). Graphic feedback, performance feedback, and goal setting increased staff compliance with a data collection task at a large residential facility. *Journal of Organizational Behavior Management, 36*, 56–70. https://doi.org/10.1080/01608061.2016.1152207

Goings, K., Carr, L., Maguire, H., Harper, J. M., & Luiselli, J. K. (2019). Improving classroom appearance and organization through a supervisory performance improvement intervention. *Behavior Analysis in Practice, 12*, 430–434. https://doi.org/10.1007/s40617-018-00304-7

Grauerholz-Fisher, E., Vollmer, T. R., Peters, K. P., Perez, B. C., & Berard, A. M. (2019). Direct assessment of quality of care in an applied behavior analysis center. *Behavioral Interventions, 34*, 1–15. https://doi.org/10.1002/bin.1680

Gravina, N., Villacorta, J., Albert, K., Clark, R., Curry, S., & Wilder, D. (2018). A literature review of organizational behavior management interventions in human service settings from 1990 to 2016. *Journal of Organizational Behavior Management, 38*, 191–224. https://doi.org/10.1080/01608061.2018.1454872

Green, C. W., Rollyson, J. H., Passante, S. C., & Reid, D. H. (2002). Maintaining proficient supervisor performance with direct support personnel: An analysis of two management approaches. *Journal of Applied Behavior Analysis, 35*, 205–208.

Haberlin, A. T., Beauchamp, K., Agnew, J., & O'Brien, F. (2012). A comparison of pyramidal staff training and direct staff training in community-based day programs. *Journal of Organizational Behavior Management, 32*, 65–74.

Hall, L. J., Grundon, G. S., Pope, C., & Romero, A. B. (2010). Training paraprofessionals to use behavioral strategies when educating learners with autism spectrum disorders across environments. *Behavioral Interventions, 25*, 37–51. https://doi.org/10.1002/bin.294

Higbee, T. S., Aporta, A. P., Resende, A., Nogueira, M., Goyos, C., & Pollard, J. S. (2016). Interactive computer training to teach discrete-trial instruction to undergraduates and special educators in Brazil: A replication and extension. *Journal of Applied Behavior Analysis, 49*, 780–793. https://doi.org/10.1002/jaba.329

Hogan, A., Knez, N., & Kahng, S. (2015). Evaluating the use of behavioral skills training to improve school staffs' implementation of behavior intervention plans. *Journal of Behavioral Education, 24*, 242–254.

Huberman, W. L., & O'Brien, R. M. (1999). Improving therapist and patient performance in chronic psychiatric group homes through goal-setting, feedback, and positive reinforcement. *Journal of Organizational Behavior Management, 19*, 13–36. https://doi.org/10.1300/J075v19n01_04

Joslyn, P. R., Vollmer, T. R., Dickens, E. N., & Walker, S. F. (2018). Direct assessment of quality of care in secure residential treatment facilities for criminal offenders with intellectual disabilities. *Behavioral Interventions, 33*, 13–25. https://doi.org/10.1002/bin.1501

Kazemi, E., Rice, B., & Adzhyan, P. (2018). *Fieldwork and supervision for behavior analysts: A handbook*. New York: Springer.

Kazemi, E., Shapiro, M., & Kavner, A. (2015). Predictors of intention to turnover in behavior technicians working with individuals with autism spectrum disorder. *Research in Autism Spectrum Disorders, 17*, 106–115. https://doi.org/10.1016/j.rasd.2015.06.012

Kirkpatrick, M., Akers, J., & Rivera, G. (2019). Use of behavioral skills training with teachers: A systematic review. *Journal of Behavioral Education, 28*, 344–361.

Lambert, J. M., Lloyd, B. P., Staubitz, J. L., Weaver, E. S., & Jennings, C. M. (2014). Effect of an automated training presentation on pre-service behavior analysts' implementation of trial-based functional analysis. *Journal of Behavioral Education, 23*, 44–367.

LeBlanc, L. A., & Luiselli, J. K. (2016). Refining supervisory practices in the field of behavior analysis: Introduction to the special section of supervision. *Behavior Analysis in Practice, 9*, 271–271. https://doi.org/10.1007/s40617-016-0156-6

LeBlanc, L. A., & Nosik, M. R. (2019). Planning and leading effective meetings. *Behavior Analysis in Practice, 12*, 696–708. https://doi.org/10.1007/s40617-019-00330-z

Lerman, D. C., LeBlanc, L. A., & Valentino, A. L. (2015). Evidence-based application of staff and care-provider training procedures. In H. S. Roane, J. E. Ringdahl, & T. S. Falcomata (Eds.), *Clinical and organizational applications of applied behavior analysis*. New York: Elsevier.

Liberman, R. P. (1983). Guest editor's preface. *Analysis and Intervention in Developmental Disabilities, 3*, iii–iv.

Macurik, K. M., O'Kane, N. P., Malanga, P., & Reid, D. H. (2008). Video training of support staff in intervention plans for challenging behavior: Comparison with live training. *Behavioral Interventions, 23*, 143–163.

Madzharova, M. S., Sturmey, P., & Jones, E. A. (2012). Training staff to increase manding in students with autism: two preliminary case studies. *Behavioral Interventions, 27*, 224–235. https://doi.org/10.1002/bin.1349

Madzharova, M. S., Sturmey, P., & Yoo, J. H. (2018). Using in-vivo modeling and feedback to teach classroom staff to implement a complex behavior intervention plan. *Journal of Developmental and Physical Disabilities, 30*, 329–337.

Mangiapanello, K. A., & Hemmes, N. S. (2015). An analysis of feedback from a behavior analytic perspective. *The Behavior Analyst, 38*, 51–75. https://doi.org/10.1007/s40614-014-0026-x

Martinez-Onstott, B., Wilder, D., & Sigurdsson, S. (2016). Identifying the variables contributing to at-risk performance: Initial evaluation of the performance diagnostic checklist–safety (PDC-safety). *Journal of Organizational Behavior Management, 36*, 80–93. https://doi.org/10.1080/01608061.2016.1152209

May, R. J., Austin, J. L., & Dymond, S. (2011). Effects of stimulus prompt display on therapists' accuracy, rate, and variation of trial type delivery during discrete trial teaching. *Research in Autism Spectrum Disorders, 5*, 305–316. https://doi.org/10.1016/j.rasd.2010.04.013

Miller, M. V., Carlson, J., & Sigurdsson, S. O. (2014). Improving treatment integrity in a human service setting using lottery-based incentives. *Journal of Organizational Behavior Management, 34*, 29–38. https://doi.org/10.1080/01608061.2013.873381

Miltenberger, R. G., Bloom, S. E., Sanchez, S., & Valbuena, D. A. (2016). Functional assessment. In N. N. Singh (Ed.), *Clinical handbook of evidence-based practices for individuals with intellectual and developmental disabilities* (pp. 69–97). New York: Springer. https://doi.org/10.1007/978-3-319-26583-4_4

Mowery, J. D., Miltenberger, R. G., & Weil, T. M. (2010). Evaluating the effects of reactivity to supervisor presence on staff response to tactile prompts and self-monitoring in a group home setting. *Behavioral Interventions, 25*, 21–35. https://doi.org/10.1002/bin.296

Nabeyama, B., & Sturmey, P. (2010). Using behavioral skills training to promote safe and correct staff guarding and ambulation distance of students with multiple physical disabilities. *Journal of Applied Behavior Analysis, 43*, 341–345. https://doi.org/10.1901/jaba.2010.43-341

Paff, M. L., Trump, C. E., Wunderlich, K. L., Harrison, A. J., & Ayres, K. M. (2019). Development and evaluation of the evidenced-based practice classroom observation measure (EBP-COM). *Behavior Analysis in Practice, 34*, 163–180. https://doi.org/10.1002/bin.1662

Palmen, A., Didden, R., & Korzilius, H. (2010). Effectiveness of behavioral skills training on staff performance in a job training setting for high-functioning adolescents with autism spectrum disorders. *Research in Autism Spectrum Disorders, 4*, 731–740. https://doi.org/10.1016/j.rasd.2010.01.012

Parsons, M. B., & Reid, D. H. (1995). Training residential supervisors to provide feedback for maintaining staff teaching skills with people who have severe disabilities. *Journal of Applied Behavior Analysis, 28*, 317–322. https://doi.org/10.1901/jaba.1995.28-317

Parsons, M. B., Rollyson, J. H., & Reid, D. H. (2012). Evidenced-based staff training: A guide for practitioners. *Behavior Analysis in Practice, 5*, 2–11.

Parsons, M. B., Rollyson, J. H., & Reid, D. H. (2013). Teaching practitioners to conduct behavioral skills training: A pyramidal approach for training multiple human service staff. *Behavior Analysis in Practice, 6*, 4–16.

Petscher, E. S., & Bailey, J. S. (2006). Effects of training, prompting, and self-monitoring on staff behavior in a classroom for students with disabilities. *Journal of Applied Behavior Analysis, 39*, 215–226. https://doi.org/10.1901/jaba.2006.02-05

Phillips, K. J., & Mudford, O. C. (2008). Functional analysis skills training for residential caregivers. *Behavioral Interventions, 23*, 1–12.

Plavnick, J. B., Ferreri, S. J., & Maupin, A. N. (2010). The effects of self-monitoring on the procedural integrity of a behavioral intervention for young children with developmental disabilities. *Journal of Applied Behavior Analysis, 43*, 315–320. https://doi.org/10.1901/jaba.2010.43-315

Pollard, J. S., Higbee, T. S., Akers, J. S., & Brodhead, M. T. (2014). An evaluation of interactive computer training to teach instructions to implement discrete trials with children with autism. *Journal of Applied Behavior Analysis, 47*, 765–776.

Reid, D. H. (2019). Training staff to provide quality support for adults with autism spectrum disorder: Recommended practices and target skills. *Advances in Neurodevelopmental Disorders, 3*, 457–467. https://doi.org/10.1007/s41252-019-00107-z

Reid, D. H., O'Kane, N. P., & Macurik, K. M. (2011). Staff training and management. In W. W. Fisher, C. C. Piazza, & H. S. Roane (Eds.), *Handbook of applied behavior analysis* (pp. 281–294). New York: Guilford Press.

Reid, D. H., & Parsons, M. B. (2000). Organizational behavior management in human services. In J. Austin & J. E. Carr (Eds.), *Handbook of applied behavior analysis* (pp. 275–294). Reno: Context Press.

Reid, D. H., Parsons, M. B., & Green, C. W. (2011). *The supervisor training curriculum: Evidence-based ways to promote work quality and enjoyment among support staff*. Washington, DC: American Association on Intellectual and Developmental Disabilities.

Reid, D. H., Parsons, M. B., & Green, C. W. (2012). *The supervisor's guidebook: Evidence-based strategies for promoting work quality and enjoyment among human service staff*. Morganton, NC: Habilitative Management Consultants.

Reid, D. H., Parsons, M. B., & Jensen, J. M. (2017). Maintaining staff performance following a training intervention: Suggestions from a 30-year case example. *Behavior Analysis in Practice, 10*, 12–21. https://doi.org/10.1007/s40617-015-0101-0

Rodriguez, M., Wilder, D. A., Therrien, K., Wine, B., Miranti, R., Daratany, K., et al. (2005). Use of the performance diagnostic checklist to select an intervention designed to increase the offering of promotional stamps at two sites of a restaurant franchise. *Journal of Organizational Behavior Management, 25*, 17–35.

Schmidt, J. D., Urban, K. D., Luiselli, J. K., White, C., & Harrington, C. (2013). Improving appearance, organization, and safety of special education classrooms: Effects of staff training in a human services setting. *Education and Treatment of Children, 36*, 1–13.

Schnell, L. K., Sidener, T. M., DeBar, R. M., Vladescu, J. C., & Kahng, S. (2018). Effects of computer-based training on procedural modifications to standard functional analyses. *Journal of Applied Behavior Analysis, 51*, 87–98.

Sellers, T. P., Clay, C. J., Hoffman, A. N., & Collins, S. D. (2019). Evaluation of a performance management intervention to increase use of trial-based functional analyses by clinicians in a residential setting for adults with intellectual disabilities. *Behavior Analysis in Practice, 12*, 412–417. https://doi.org/10.1007/s40617-018-00276-8

Sellers, T. P., LeBlanc, L. A., & Valentino, A. L. (2016). Recommendations for detecting and addressing barriers to successful supervision. *Behavior Analysis in Practice, 9*, 309–319. https://doi.org/10.1007/s40617-016-0142-z

Sellers, T. P., Valentino, A. L., Landon, T. J., & Aiello, S. (2019). Board certified behavior analysts' supervisory practices of trainees: Survey results and recommendations. *Behavior Analysis in Practice, 12*, 536–546. https://doi.org/10.1007/s40617-019-00367-0

Sellers, T. P., Valentino, A. L., & LeBlanc, L. A. (2016). Recommended practices for individual supervision of aspiring behavior analysts. *Behavior Analysis in Practice, 9*, 274–286. https://doi.org/10.1007/s40617-016-0110-7

Shapiro, M., & Kazemi, E. (2017). A review of training strategies to teach individuals implementation of behavioral interventions. *Journal of Organizational Behavior Management, 37*, 32–62. https://doi.org/10.1080/01608061.2016.1267066

Smith, M., & Wilder, D. A. (2018). The use of the performance diagnostic checklist-human services to assess and improve the job performance of individuals with intellectual disabilities. *Behavior Analysis in Practice, 11*, 148–153. https://doi.org/10.1007/s40617-018-0213-4

Squires, A., & Wilder, D. A. (2010). A preliminary investigation of the effect of rules on employee performance. *Journal of Organizational Behavior Management, 30*, 57–69. https://doi.org/10.1080/01608060903529756

Strouse, M. C., Carroll-Hernandez, T. A., Sherman, J. A., & Sheldon, J. B. (2003). Turning over turnover: The evaluation of a staff scheduling system in a community-based program for adults with developmental disabilities. *Journal of Organizational Behavior Management, 23*, 45–63.

Turner, L. B., Fisher, A. J., & Luiselli, J. K. (2016). Towards a competency-based, ethical, and socially valid approach to supervision of applied behavior analytic trainees. *Behavior Analysis in Practice, 9*, 287–298. https://doi.org/10.1007/s40617-016-0121-4

Valentino, A. L., LeBlanc, L. A., & Sellers, T. P. (2016). The benefits of group supervision and a recommended structure for implementation. *Behavior Analysis in Practice, 9*, 320–338. https://doi.org/10.1007/s40617-016-0138-8

van Vonderen, A., Didden, R., & Beeking, F. (2012). Effectiveness of instruction and video feedback on staff's trainer behavior during one-to-one training with children with severe intellectual disability. *Research in Developmental Disabilities, 33*, 283–290. https://doi.org/10.1016/j.ridd.2011.07.040

Weatherly, N. L. (2019). A behavioral safety model for clinical settings: Coaching for institutionalization. *Perspectives on Behavior Science, 42*, 973. Advanced Online Publication. https://doi.org/10.1007/s40614-019-00195-1

Weldy, C. R., Rapp, J. T., & Capocasa, K. (2014). Training staff to implement brief stimulus preference assessments. *Journal of Applied Behavior Analysis, 47*, 214–218. https://doi.org/10.1002/jaba.98

Wilder, D. A., Lipschultz, J. L., & Gehrman, C. (2018). An evaluation of the performance diagnostic checklist—Human services (PDC-HS) across domains. *Behavior Analysis in Practice, 11*, 129–138. https://doi.org/10.1007/s40617-018-0243-y

Wilder, D. A., Lipschultz, J. L., King, A., Driscoll, S., & Sigurdsson, S. (2018). An analysis of the commonality and type of preintervention assessment procedures in the journal of organizational behavior management (2000–2015). *Journal of Organizational Behavior Management, 38*, 5–7. https://doi.org/10.1080/01608061.2017.1325822

Mindfulness Care Giving and Support for Anger and Aggression Management

Nirbhay N. Singh, Giulio E. Lancioni, and Yoon-Suk Hwang

Abstract In recent years, mindfulness-based programs and practices have been recognized as effective treatment and training approaches congruent with Applied Behavior Analysis (ABA) principles and applications. In this chapter, we introduce definitions of mindfulness and possible mechanisms of its actions as used in the context of anger and aggression management. We then briefly discuss research on mindfulness-based programs and practices taught to (a) parents and caregivers with the expectation that the effects of their own mindfulness practice will cascade and spillover to those they care for who engage in aggressive behavior, and (b) to individuals with intellectual and developmental disabilities (IDD). Finally, we conclude this chapter with a few thoughts on how behavior analysts may incorporate mindfulness-based programs and practices in their professional operations for the provision of clinical services that are more responsive to the holistic and complex needs of their clients.

Keywords Mindfulness-based programs and practices · Anger · Aggression · Intellectual and developmental disabilities

---

N. N. Singh (✉)
Department of Psychiatry and Health Behavior, Medical College of Georgia, Augusta University, Augusta, GA, USA
e-mail: nisingh@augusta.edu

G. E. Lancioni
University of Bari, Bari, Italy

Y.-S. Hwang
Centre for Disability Studies, University of Sydney, Camperdown, NSW 2050, Australia

© Springer Nature Switzerland AG 2021
J. K. Luiselli (ed.), *Applied Behavior Analysis Treatment of Violence and Aggression in Persons with Neurodevelopmental Disabilities*, Advances in Preventing and Treating Violence and Aggression,
https://doi.org/10.1007/978-3-030-68549-2_10

Anger is a negative emotional state as evidenced by increased physiological arousal, negative thoughts, and predisposition to verbal and physical aggression (Berkowitz & Harmon-Jones, 2004). In terms of emotion regulation, there is the experience of anger (i.e., a person's inner feelings) and the expression of anger (e.g., temper tantrums, irritability, defiant behavior, aggression). Aggression is an overt behavior that may cause mental or physical harm to self and others. As for subtypes, aggression has been described as rooted in angry affect giving rise to impulsive, reactive, hostile behavior, or instrumental, proactive, and planned harmful behavior that is driven by machinations of the mind (Vitiello & Stoff, 1997). Another conceptualization of aggression differentiates between overt (e. g., arguing and fighting) and covert (e.g., lying, stealing, and breaking rules) antisocial behavior (Frick et al., 1993). Depending on the age of onset, different forms of anger and aggression take a different developmental trajectory that may end in violent or nonviolent behavior, and/or mental health problems (Kjelsberg, 2002; Loeber, Green, Kalb, & Lahey, 2000; Nagin & Tremblay, 1999).

Given the diversity in the nature, motivation, and topography of anger and aggression, several treatment options are available, but none of them are effective with all who need intervention. For some children, cognitive behavior therapy provides a range of emotion regulation strategies for effectively coping with anger (Sukhodolsky & Scahill, 2012). Anger and aggression arising from inconsistent parenting practices and family interactions that may lead to and maintain these behaviors have been treated with a number of parent training programs. For example, parent management training (Barkley, 2013) has been reported to be effective in improving parental competence in dealing with their children's challenging behaviors (Michelson, Davenport, Dretzke, Barlow, & Day, 2013), which produces stable behavioral changes in the children that can prevent adult antisocial behavior (Scott, Briskman, & O'Connor, 2014). Other interventions include pharmacotherapy, but there is little evidence that drugs reduce aggression without serious side effects (Lane, Kjome, & Moeller, 2011).

Applied behavior analysis (ABA) provides an evidence-based approach to the treatment of aggression (Luiselli & Ricciardi, 2017). Treatment is based on identifying the function of each topography of the aggressive behavior across settings and then developing a case formulation, which leads to a behavior support plan. The specific procedure used in the behavior support plan is aligned with the specific function or motivation of the aggressive behavior. As an example, for attention-maintained aggressive behavior, a typical behavior support plan may include the withholding of attention contingent of the occurrence of the target behavior through social extinction. This is followed by the delivery of noncontingent attention to the person for the non-occurrence of the target behavior on a differential reinforcement schedule. If the person exhibiting the aggressive behavior has communication problems, such as a child with autism spectrum disorder (ASD) with cognitive and speech limitations, an alternative plan would include functional communication training, which teaches the person socially acceptable communication alternatives to the aggressive behavior (Reichle & Wacker, 2017). While generally effective, the positive results are occasionally difficult to maintain over time and/or implementation of the plan itself is labor intensive, which may lead to caregiver stress and burnout.

According to the General Aggression Model (Anderson & Bushman, 2002) adaptive emotion regulation leads to socially acceptable interpersonal interactions. Maladaptive emotional regulation, including both under-regulation and overregulation, may lead to anger, aggression, and violent behavior (Roberton, Daffern, & Bucks, 2012). Mindfulness-based programs have emerged over the last two decades for dealing with anger, aggression, and violence because they effectively recalibrate one's response to events that give rise to emotional dysregulation (Singh, Lancioni, & Winton, 2017). Mindfulness provides a range of practices by which an individual can self-regulate their emotional experience and expression, thus preempting the rise of anger and aggression. Indeed, recent reviews of research on aggression and violence suggest that mindfulness-based programs may be effective in reducing aggression and violence through emotion regulation practices (Fix & Fix, 2013; Gillions, Cheang, & Duarte, 2019; Morley, Jantz, & Fulton, 2019).

In recent years, mindfulness-based programs and practices have been recognized as effective treatment and training approaches congruent with ABA principles and applications (Felver & Singh, 2020). In this chapter, we introduce definitions of mindfulness and possible mechanisms of its actions as used in the context of anger and aggression management. We then briefly discuss research on mindfulness-based programs and practices taught to (a) parents and caregivers with the expectation that the effects of their own mindfulness practice will cascade and spillover to those they care for who engage in aggressive behavior, and (b) to individuals with intellectual and developmental disabilities (IDD). Finally, we present a few thoughts on how behavior analysts may incorporate mindfulness-based programs and practices in their services.

Mindfulness

The word *mindfulness* has been defined in a number of ways since the Buddha first contextualized it as right mindfulness in the *satipaṭṭhāna sutta*. In the current academic research lexicon, mindfulness has been defined by Kabat-Zinn (1994, p. 4) as "Paying attention in a particular way: on purpose, in the present moment, and nonjudgmentally." The consensus definition by Bishop et al. (2004), which appears to be used less often in research studies is, "[A] kind of non-elaborative, nonjudgmental, present-centered awareness in which each thought, feeling, or sensation that arises in the attentional field is acknowledged and accepted as it is." (p. 232). The cultivation of mindfulness cannot be divorced from its social dimensions because the development and maintenance of mindfulness is best supported within a community of practitioners (Hanh, 1976). When taking the social dimension of mindfulness into account, it has been defined as "A particular type of social practice that leads the practitioner to an ethically minded awareness, intentionally situated in the here and now (Nilsson & Kazemi, 2016, p. 190)".

In terms of daily practice of mindfulness, Munindra instructed "Whatever you are doing, everything should be done mindfully, dynamically, with totality, completeness, thoroughness. Then it becomes meditation, meaningful, purposeful. It is not thinking, but experiencing from moment to moment, living from moment to moment, without clinging, without condemning, without judging, without criticizing—choiceless awareness…It should be integrated into our whole life. It is actually an education in how to see, how to hear, how to smell, how to eat, how to drink, how to walk with full awareness" (Knaster, 2010, p. 1). Furthermore, mindfulness can be defined in terms of its qualities: mechanistic mindfulness, ethically attuned mindfulness, fully informed mindfulness, and holistic mindfulness (see Amaro & Singh, 2021 for an explication of these qualities of mindfulness).

Mechanisms of Mindfulness in Anger and Aggression

According to Buddhist psychology, the root cause of anger and aggression is the mind, and its control can come about by (re)training the mind. For example, the Buddha taught:

> There is no error greater than hatred
> And nothing mightier than patience.
> So I strive in every way to learn patience.

The eighth century Buddhist monk, Shantideva (2002) taught that patience is the key antidote of anger, the destructive emotion that precedes its verbal and physical expression as aggression:

> There is no evil greater than anger
> And no virtue greater than patience
> Therefore, I should strive in various ways
> To become familiar with the practice of patience (p. 69)

The central instruction in Shantideva's teachings on being patient appears to be the need to *pause* before an automatic reaction to destructive emotions as a form of misguided self-preservation. When an automatic reaction is preempted by a pause, what may emerge is a mindful response. The pause enables various mechanisms to emerge that may produce the mindful response. For example, the pause preempts the triggering of an automatic reaction that results in aggression, with successive stages of the practice helping present-moment awareness and enabling the rising of a mindful response to the emotionally disruptive situation.

Another possibility is that mindfulness facilitates the development of decentering (Fresco et al., 2007), re-perceiving (Shapiro & Carlson, 2009), or metacognitive insight (Bishop et al., 2004), which enables one to view thoughts of anger and aggression as not representative of the true nature of reality. Mindfulness practice provides the insight necessary to view anger-producing thoughts and situations as transient events within a broader context of the flow of life events (Feldman, Greeson, & Senville, 2010), diffuses situational sensitivity (Masuda, Hayes, Sackett, & Twohig, 2003), and provides cognitive flexibility to facilitate responding in a nonaggressive manner (Roemer & Orsillo, 2003). Thus, instead of reacting with anger and aggression to emotionally arousing thoughts and situations, a pause enables the rise of a socially acceptable mindful response. For example, in line with the definition of mindfulness, the person may accept that they are angry and nonjudgmentally observe the emotionally arousing situation until it passes without the need to react to it with verbal or physical aggression. As noted by Hölzel et al. (2011) mindfulness meditation "encompasses focusing attention on the experience of thoughts, emotions, and body sensations, simply observing them as they arise and pass away" (p. 538). The essential aspect of this mechanism is that it enables the person to change the nature of their relationship with their thoughts, feelings, and emotions instead of responding to them with anger and aggression.

Rumination, defined as almost uncontrollable repetitive thoughts about negative emotions and experiences, often leads to and exacerbates anger and aggression (Peled & Moretti, 2009). Although rumination itself is in the present, its focus is on past events and probable future outcomes. Rumination is negatively correlated with facets of mindfulness, including nonjudgment, acting with awareness, and non-reactivity (Eisenlohr-Moul, Peters, Pond Jr, & DeWall, 2016). This suggests that enhancing mindfulness through mindfulness-based programs and practices should decrease rumination because of the present-centered nature of mindfulness. Essentially, responding with nonjudgment, acting with awareness, and non-reactivity to anger-producing thoughts and events in the present moment should result in the reduction and extinction of anger and the resulting aggression. The concept of extinction is based in learning theory which holds that consistently unreinforced anger and aggressive behaviors will initially increase in frequency and then fade and disappear from a person's repertoire. By engaging in nonjudgmental awareness and non-reactivity means that anger is not reinforced and will result in its extinction, thus preempting the occurrence of verbal and physical aggression. Of course, an extinction burst—a temporary increase in the previously reinforced angry rumination—may occur, but the pause enables the individual to remember its transient nature and simply observe its rise and decay without any reaction. Other mechanisms, including the neuroscientific bases of mindfulness that may explain how mindfulness may attenuate anger and aggression, are discussed by Amaro and Singh (2021).

Mindfulness-Based Programs and Practices for Anger and Aggression

Mindfulness is essentially a state of being and a practice that enhances quality of life and may even provide spiritual uplift. While acknowledging the single instance of the Buddha instructing King Pasenadi the need to engage in mindful eating as an antidote to overeating (Anālayo, 2018), it is likely that mindfulness was not intended to be used as an intervention or therapy. Thus, in alignment of its Buddhist roots, in this chapter mindfulness is referred to as a mindfulness-based program (i.e., multicomponent program) or as a mindfulness practice (i.e., a single mindfulness component) instead of mindfulness-based interventions or treatments.

Parents

There is a bidirectional correlation between child psychopathology and parental stress beyond shared genetic and environmental effects, and the correlation is much more robust when the child had IDD, especially ASD (Yorke et al., 2018). A growing number of mindfulness parenting programs have been and are being developed for parents of children with IDD and ASD (see Singh & Hwang, 2021). However, most of these programs have not focused on the effects of mindful parenting on anger and aggression of the children. Some programs have reported the effects of mindful parenting on global measures of child psychopathology (e.g., Bögels, Hellemans, van Deursen, Römer, & van der Meulen, 2014). Although not the main focus of the study, Hwang, Kearney, Klieve, Lang, and Roberts (2015) included data on the effects of mindful parenting on problem behaviors, including aggressive behavior of children with IDD or ASD.

Mindfulness-Based Positive Behavior Support (MBPBS) was developed specifically for parents and other caregivers to use with children and adults with IDD who engage in challenging behaviors (Singh, Lancioni, Chan, Jackman, & McPherson, 2020). It consists of two major components, mindfulness and positive behavior support (PBS), that are both evidence-based interventions. In addition to the principles and practices of PBS, the mindfulness components include standard meditation practices, the five hindrances (i.e., sensory desire, ill will, sloth and torpor, restlessness and remorse, and doubt), the four immeasurables (i.e., lovingkindness, compassion, empathetic joy, and equanimity), the three poisons (i.e., attachment, anger, and ignorance of the true nature of reality), beginner's mind, a series of informal mindfulness practices, and the practice of ethical precepts). MBPBS can be used as a public health prevention program or as an intervention program.

A small series of studies have reported the effects on children and adults with IDD when their parents participated in one of the stepped-care versions of MBPBS (Singh et al., 2006, 2007, 2014, 2019a; Singh, Lancioni, Medvedev, Hwang, & Myers, 2021). For example, in a multiple baseline design study across three parent-child dyads, the 12-week version of the MBPBS program was effective in decreasing aggression, noncompliance, and self-injury in children with autism (Singh, Lancioni, Winton, Fisher, et al., 2006). In a three-arm randomized controlled trial (RCT), the component effects of MBPBS vs. MB vs. PBS was evaluated in terms of mindful parenting by mothers of children with ASD (Singh et al., 2021). The study design included a 10-week pre-intervention control condition, 30 weeks of the three interventions, and a 3-year follow-up period. All three conditions were effective in reducing the children's aggressive and disruptive behaviors, with most to least significant reductions being in the MBPBS, MB, and PBS conditions, respectively. The children's increased responsiveness to their mother's requests followed a similar pattern, with the largest changes in the MBPBS condition, followed by MB, and then PBS. Similar proportional decreases in aggressive and destructive behaviors, and increases in responsiveness to parental requests, were maintained for 3 years post-intervention across the three intervention conditions.

Caregivers

Direct caregivers often provide services to individuals with IDD who engage in severe aggressive behavior that causes serious injury to the caregivers, the individual, and their peers (Knotter et al., 2018). Research shows that teaching mindfulness practices to these caregivers not only enhances their quality of life, but also changes the behaviors of those who receive their services (Singh et al., 2014). For example, group home caregivers participated in an intensive 5-day mindfulness program to develop a personal meditation practice and the effects of their training was measured on the individuals in their care (Singh et al., 2006). Individuals who functioned at severe or profound levels of IDD showed substantial reductions in their aggressive behavior and increases in the number of learning objectives mastered commensurate with caregiver participation in a mindfulness-based program.

A series of studies have reported the effects on individuals with IDD when their caregivers participated in MBPBS (e. g., Singh et al., 2015, Singh, Lancioni, Karazsia, & Myers, 2016, Singh, Lancioni, Karazsia, Chan, & Winton, 2016, Singh et al., 2020). For example, the effects of caregiver participation in MBPBS were compared with training as usual (TAU) in an RCT on the individuals in their care (Singh, Lancioni, Karazsia, Chan, & Winton, 2016). Results showed statistically significant effectiveness of MBPBS when compared to TAU on the individuals' aggressive events, use of physical restraints, emergency psychotropic medication contingent on the individuals' physical aggression, and need for 1 to 1 staffing for the safety of the individuals, caregivers, and peers. In a recent RCT, a component analysis of caregiver training in MBPBS vs. PBS reported both MBPBS and PBS to be effective in changing several variables related to individuals with IDD (Singh, Lancioni, Medvedev, et al., 2020). However, when compared to PBS, significantly greater reductions were evidenced in the MBPBS condition with regard to aggression, injuries to caregivers and peers perpetrated by the individuals, the need for caregivers to use physical restraints for aggressive behaviors of the individuals, the use of emergency medication for the individuals' aggressive behaviors, and 1 to 1 staffing for the safety of the individuals when they were persistently aggressive.

Trained Clinical Caregivers

It is customary for mindfulness meditation instructions to be provided by meditation teachers who have a long-standing personal practice of daily meditation. Most of the research on mindfulness-based programs has reported using experienced meditation teachers. In clinical practice, clinicians provide inpatient and outpatient treatment that may include mindfulness-based practices. As clinical caregivers, they need to have a personal practice in meditation before they can provide mindfulness-based services. We briefly review research that utilized clinical caregivers with demonstrated expertise in meditation who provided instructions directly to people with neurodevelopmental disorders with aggressive behaviors, or indirectly by training their parents and direct caregivers.

Soles of the Feet (SoF) SoF is an informal mindfulness practice that has unique properties when compared to formal mindfulness-based programs. It is portable, easy to use, requires no equipment, does not require continuous instruction from others, and assists with self-management of a wide range of socially undesirable behaviors. At its most basic level, SoF teaches an individual to shift from an automatic reaction to an internal event (e.g., negative thoughts, feelings, or emotions) or an external event (e.g., when someone says something negative that is hurtful) to a mindful or skillful response. This shift enables the person to develop an inhibitory response to emotionally negative arousal situations. The SoF has been replicated many times by the developers of the program and by other independent researchers. The SoF can be taught to new practitioners in either individual or group format, such as an entire classroom (Felver & Singh, 2020).

In a prototypic study, trained clinical caregivers in the community taught individuals who functioned at the mild level of intellectual disability to use SoF as a self-management strategy for their socially maladaptive behaviors (e.g., verbal and physical aggression, destructive behaviors), which threatened their group home placement (Adkins, Singh, Winton, McKeegan, & Singh, 2010). The individuals were able to gradually achieve control of their maladaptive behaviors and maintain their group home placement. Furthermore, the individuals evidenced clinically significant reductions in non-targeted behaviors, including obsessive-compulsive behaviors, depression, state anxiety, property destruction, rectal digging, and urinary incontinence. In a multiple baseline design study, trained clinical caregivers taught mothers to teach their Chinese adolescents with ASD to manage their aggressive and destructive behaviors and maintain their behavioral gains during a 12-month follow-up period (Ahemaitijiang, Hu, Yang, & Han, 2020). Furthermore, the mothers reported that the SoF practice was an effective and socially valid self-management practice for their adolescents. In an RCT, trained clinical caregivers taught parents and direct caregivers to teach individuals with mild disabilities to self-manage their verbal and physical aggression, demonstrating the ability of clinical caregivers, parents, and direct caregivers to successfully teach SoF to large numbers of individuals (Singh et al., 2013).

SOBER Breathing Space This mindfulness practice was developed in the context of substance use but can be used for self-management of aggressive and other behaviors that arise during emotionally arousing situations. SOBER is an acronym for Stop and be aware of what is happening in that moment, Observe the physical sensations and emotional regulation changes in the body, Breathe by deliberately bringing attention to the breath, Expand awareness of the situation and response options, and then Respond mindfully. In a multiple baseline design study, four children with ASD were taught to use this informal mindfulness practice to manage their verbal and physical aggression (Singh et al., 2018). Training was provided at home and the effects of the mindfulness practice were recorded both at home and at school to assess generalization of training effects to another setting. The children's verbal aggression decreased to near-zero levels and maintained at about the same level during the 12-month follow-up at home and at school. Their physical aggression decreased to zero levels at home and was maintained at this level during the 12-month follow-up. Similar results were obtained for three of the four children at school, with the fourth child showing very low levels of aggression. This study hinted at the possibility of using SOBER Breathing Space as an effective self-management practice by young children with ASD.

Surfing the Urge This mindfulness practice was also first used in the context of substance abuse. Given that all phenomena arise, peak, and then fade away, when the urge arises to engage in a harmful or socially unacceptable behavior, repeatedly observing the urge in a nonjudgmental manner with equanimity will reduce its frequency and gradually eliminate it. This is akin to the extinction of a private event because no instance of arising of an urge is reinforced. Given the strength of an urge to engage in an addictive behavior, the individual can use meditation on the breath as a surfboard to ride out the waves of desire to overcome the urge. This informal mindfulness practice can be used as a self-management strategy during virtually any emotionally arousing thought, feeling, or event. Recently, it has been used as a self-management strategy to manage aggressive behavior (Singh et al., 2019b). In this multiple baseline design study, three adolescents were taught by an experienced meditation trainer to use Surfing the Urge for self-management of verbal and physical aggression. The adolescents were able to gradually increase their control of both verbal and physical aggression commensurate with the training in this mindfulness practice and reduce the behaviors to near-zero levels.

Teachers

When compared to other caregivers, there are far fewer studies of teachers using mindfulness-based programs and practices for anger and aggression in school settings and even fewer with students with neurodevelopmental disorders. In a multiple baseline design across classrooms study, three preschool teachers of children with IDD participated in an 8-week (2 h per week) mindfulness-based program that included the following components: basic meditations, developing awareness, beginner's mind, being in the present moment, the four immeasurables (i.e., loving-kindness, compassion, joy, and equanimity), and the three poisons (i.e., attachment, anger, and ignorance of the true nature of reality), but no mindfulness training was provided to the children (Singh, Lancioni, Winton, Karazsia, & Myers, 2013). Results showed that teacher mindfulness cascaded or spilled over to the students in their classrooms. There were statistically significant reductions in the children's aggressive and destructive behaviors and increases in compliance with teacher requests.

In a tele-health multiple baseline design across students study, three teachers were taught basic mindfulness meditation and the SoF mindfulness program (Singh, Chan, Karazsia, McPherson, & Jackman, 2017). When they had developed a personal mindfulness meditation practice and were proficient with the SoF practice, each teacher taught one student with IDD in their classroom the SoF practice for self-management of aggressive behavior. Results showed that tele-health training of teachers in mindfulness was successful, and that the students were able to reduce their verbal and physical aggression to near-zero levels and maintain the behavioral gains during the 12-month follow-up period.

The sparse research with teachers of students with neurodevelopmental disabilities is indicative of the importance of the need to accelerate their training in mindfulness-based programs and programs as is evident with teachers of neuro-typical children (Hwang, Bartlett, Greben, & Hand, 2017). Face-to-face, tele-health, and a task-analyzed instruction manual for individual and group classroom-based instruction in mindfulness (Felver & Singh, 2020) are ways by which this can be achieved.

Implementation of Mindful Caregiving by Behavior Analysts

Behavior analysts are in a perfect position to adopt mindfulness as an adjunctive approach to better serve people with challenging behaviors and their parents and other caregivers. They have solid grounding in analytic methods and an empirical mindset including behavioral assessment, single-subject methodology, methods for assessing fidelity of training and implementation of new interventions, social validity methodology to assess acceptability and importance of an intervention, visual as well as single-subject statistical data analyses, statistical approach to measuring clinical significance of behavior change, methods to assess generalization and maintenance—and on and on. Furthermore, behavior analysts have teachers and colleagues who are already expanding the boundaries of behavior analysis by incorporating other approaches such as dialectical behavior therapy, acceptance and commitment therapy, numerous psychosocial interventions, and mindfulness. The issue is not one of maintaining the purity of behavior analysis but making behavior analysts more responsive to the holistic and complex needs of their clients.

A prerequisite for this to happen is that behavior analysts need to eschew premature cognitive commitment to the old behavioral chestnut that applied behavior analysis has all the answers to the world's problems. Behavior analysts need to have a sense of openness and curiosity to entertain the possibility that other approaches may have answers to issues which have eluded behavior analysis. We need not revisit the old battle of the rise of cognitive behavior therapy in the early days of applied behavior analysis and its eventual acceptance by behavior analysts.

The starting point for incorporating mindfulness into behavior analytic practice is to be practically conversant in basic meditation practices before adopting mindfulness-based programs and practices. Akin to the certification needed to practice behavior analysis, behavior analysts will need to develop a disciplined meditation practice to deliver mindfulness-based services. A meditation practice is simple but not easy to develop, so some concerted effort is needed. A caveat is that behavior analysts should receive training in meditation and mindfulness from authentic teachers who embody mindfulness in their life, services, and teachings. There is much to read in mindfulness, but an ounce of meditation practice is superior to a ton of reading.

References

Adkins, A. D., Singh, A. N., Winton, A. S. W., McKeegan, G. F., & Singh, J. (2010). Using a mindfulness-based procedure in the community: Translating research to practice. *Journal of Child and Family Studies, 19*, 175–183.

Ahemaitijiang, N., Hu, X., Yang, X., & Han, Z. H. (2020). Effects of Meditation on the Soles of the Feet on aggressive and destructive behaviors of Chinese adolescents with autism spectrum disorders. *Mindfulness, 11*, 230–240.

Amaro, A., & Singh, N. N. (2021). Mindfulness: Definitions, attributes, and mechanisms. In N. N. Singh & S. D. Singh Joy (Eds.), *Mindfulness in children and adolescents: Research and practice* (pp. 11–33). London: Routledge.

Anālayo, B. (2018). Overeating and mindfulness in ancient India. *Mindfulness, 9*, 1648–1654.

Anderson, C. A., & Bushman, B. J. (2002). Human aggression. *Annual Review of Psychology, 53*, 27–51.

Barkley, R. A. (2013). *Defiant children: A clinician's manual for assessment and parent training* (3rd ed.). New York: Guilford Press.

Berkowitz, L., & Harmon-Jones, E. (2004). Toward an understanding of the determinants of anger. *Emotion, 4*, 107–130.

Bishop, S. R., Lau, M., Shapiro, S., Carlson, L., Anderson, N. D., Carmody, J., et al. (2004). Mindfulness: A proposed operational definition. *Clinical Psychology: Science and Practice, 11*, 230–241.

Bögels, S. M., Hellemans, J., van Deursen, S., Römer, M., & van der Meulen, R. (2014). Mindful parenting in mental health care: Effects on parental and child psychopathology, parental stress, parenting, co-parenting, and marital functioning. *Mindfulness, 5*, 536–551.

Eisenlohr-Moul, T. A., Peters, J. R., Pond Jr., R. S., & DeWall, C. N. (2016). Both trait and state mindfulness predict lower aggressiveness via anger rumination: A multilevel mediation analysis. *Mindfulness, 7*, 713–726.

Feldman, G., Greeson, J., & Senville, J. (2010). Differential effects of mindful breathing, progressive muscle relaxation, and loving-kindness meditation on decentering and negative reactions to repetitive thoughts. *Behaviour Research and Therapy, 48*, 1002–1011.

Felver, J. C., & Singh, N. N. (2020). *Mindfulness in the classroom: An evidence-based program to reduce disruptive behavior and increase academic engagement*. Oakland, CA: New Harbinger.

Fix, R. L., & Fix, S. T. (2013). The effects of mindfulness-based treatments for aggression: A critical review. *Aggression and Violent Behavior, 18*, 219–227.

Fresco, D. M., Moore, M. T., Van Dulmen, M. H. M., Segal, Z. V., Ma, S. H., Teasdale, J. D., et al. (2007). Initial psychometric properties of the experiences questionnaire: Validation of a self-report measure of decentering. *Behavior Therapy, 38*, 234–246.

Frick, P. J., Lahey, B. B., Loeber, R., Tannenbaum, L., Van Horn, Y., Christ, M. A. G., et al. (1993). Oppositional defiant disorder and conduct disorder: A meta-analytic review of factor analyses and cross-validation in a clinic sample. *Clinical Psychology Review, 13*, 319–340.

Gillions, A., Cheang, R., & Duarte, R. (2019). The effect of mindfulness practice on aggression and violence levels in adults: A systematic review. *Aggression and Violent Behavior, 48*, 104–115.

Hanh, T. N. (1976). *Miracle of mindfulness*. Boston, MA: Beacon.

Hölzel, B. K., Lazar, S. W., Gard, T., Schuman-Olivier, Z., Vago, D. R., & Ott, U. (2011). How does mindfulness meditation work? Proposing mechanisms of action from a conceptual and neural perspective. *Perspectives on Psychological Science, 6*, 537–559.

Hwang, Y.-S., Bartlett, B., Greben, M., & Hand, K. (2017). A systematic review of mindfulness interventions for in-service teachers: A tool to enhance teacher wellbeing and performance. *Teaching and Teacher Education, 64*, 26–42.

Hwang, Y.-S., Kearney, P., Klieve, H., Lang, W., & Roberts, J. (2015). Cultivating mind: Mindfulness intervention for children with autism spectrum disorder and problem behaviors, and their mothers. *Journal of Child and Family Studies, 24*, 3093–3106.

Kabat-Zinn, J. (1994). *Wherever you go, there you are: Mindfulness meditation in everyday life*. New York: Hyperion.

Kjelsberg, E. (2002). Pathways to violent and non-violent criminality in an adolescent psychiatric population. *Child Psychiatry and Human Development, 33*, 29–42.

Knaster, M. (2010). *Living this life fully: Stories and teachings of Munindra*. Boston, MA: Shambhala.

Knotter, M. H., Spruit, A., De Swart, J. J. W., Wissink, I. B., Moonen, X. M. H., Stams, G., et al. (2018). Training direct care staff working with persons with intellectual disabilities and challenging behavior: A meta-analytic review study. *Aggression and Violent Behavior, 40*, 60–72.

Lane, S. D., Kjome, K. L., & Moeller, F. G. (2011). Neuropsychiatry of aggression. *Neurologic Clinics, 29*(1), 49–64.

Loeber, R., Green, S. M., Kalb, L., & Lahey, B. B. (2000). Physical fighting in childhood as a risk factor for later mental health problems. *Journal of the American Academy of Child and Adolescent Psychiatry, 39*, 421–428.

Luiselli, J. K., & Ricciardi, J. N. (2017). Applied behavior analysis and treatment of violence and aggression. In P. Sturmey (Ed.), *The Wiley handbook of violence and aggression*. Hoboken, NJ: Wiley-Blackwell.

Masuda, A., Hayes, S. C., Sackett, C. F., & Twohig, M. P. (2003). Cognitive defusion and self-relevant negative thoughts: Examining the impact of a ninety-year-old technique. *Behaviour Research and Therapy, 42*, 477–485.

Michelson, D., Davenport, C., Dretzke, J., Barlow, J., & Day, C. (2013). Do evidence-based interventions work when tested in the "Real World?" A systematic review and meta-analysis of parent management training for the treatment of child disruptive behavior. *Clinical Child and Family Psychology Review, 16*, 18–34.

Morley, R. H., Jantz, P. B., & Fulton, C. (2019). The intersection of violence, brain networks, and mindfulness practices. *Aggression and Violent Behavior, 46*, 165–173.

Nagin, D., & Tremblay, R. E. (1999). Trajectories of boys' physical aggression, opposition, and hyperactivity on the path to physically violent and nonviolent juvenile delinquency. *Child Development, 70*, 1181–1196.

Nilsson, H., & Kazemi, A. (*2016*). Reconciling and thematizing definitions of mindfulness: The big five of mindfulness. *Review of General Psychology, 20*(2), 183–193.

Peled, M., & Moretti, M. M. (2009). Ruminating on rumination: are rumination on anger and sadness differentially related to aggression and depressed mood? *Journal of Psychopathology and Behavioral Assessment, 32*(1), 108–117.

Reichle, J., & Wacker, D. P. (2017). *Functional communication training for problem behavior.* New York: Guilford.

Roberton, T., Daffern, M., & Bucks, R. S. (2012). Aggression and violent behavior. *Aggression and Violent Behavior, 17,* 72–82.

Roemer, L., & Orsillo, S. M. (2003). Mindfulness: A promising intervention strategy in need of further study. *Clinical Psychology: Science and Practice, 10,* 172–178.

Scott, S., Briskman, J., & O'Connor, T. G. (2014). Early prevention of antisocial personality: Long-term follow-up of two randomized controlled trials comparing indicated and selective approaches. *American Journal of Psychiatry, 171,* 649–657.

Shantideva. (2002). *Guide to the Bodhisattva's way of life.* Ulverston: Tharpa Publications.

Shapiro, S. L., & Carlson, L. E. (2009). *The art and science of mindfulness.* Washington, DC: American Psychological Association.

Singh, N. N., Chan, J., Karazsia, B. T., McPherson, C. L., & Jackman, M. M. (2017). Telehealth training of teachers to teach a mindfulness-based procedure for self-management of aggressive behavior to students with intellectual and developmental disabilities. *International Journal of Developmental Disabilities, 63*(4), 195–203.

Singh, N. N., & Hwang, Y.-S. (2021). Mindfulness in intellectual and developmental disabilities. In N. N. Singh & S. D. Singh Joy (Eds.), *Mindfulness in children and adolescents: Research and practice* (pp. 96–118). London: Routledge.

Singh, N. N., Lancioni, G. E., Chan, J., Jackman, M. M., & McPherson, C. L. (2020). Mindfulness-based positive behavior support. In I. Ivtzan (Ed.), *Handbook of mindfulness-based programmes: Mindfulness interventions from education to health and therapy* (pp. 42–52). London: Routledge.

Singh, N. N., Lancioni, G. E., Karazsia, B. T., Chan, J., & Winton, A. S. W. (2016). Effectiveness of caregiver training in mindfulness-based positive behavior support (MBPBS) vs. training-as-usual (TAU): A randomized controlled trial. *Frontiers in Psychology, 7,* 1549.

Singh, N. N., Lancioni, G. E., Karazsia, B. T., & Myers, R. E. (2016). Caregiver training in mindfulness-based positive behavior supports (MBPBS): Effects on caregivers and adults with intellectual and developmental disabilities. *Frontiers in Psychology, 7,* 98.

Singh, N. N., Lancioni, G. E., Karazsia, B. T., Myers, R. E., Hwang, Y.-S., & Bhikkhu, A. (2019a). Effects of Mindfulness-Based Positive Behavior Support (MBPBS) training are equally beneficial for mothers and their children with autism spectrum disorder or with intellectual disabilities. *Frontiers in Psychology, 10,* 385.

Singh, N. N., Lancioni, G. E., Karazsia, B. T., Myers, R. E., Kim, E., Chan, J., et al. (2019b). Surfing the Urge: An informal mindfulness practice for the self-management of aggression by adolescents with autism spectrum disorder. *Journal of Contextual Behavioral Science, 12,* 170–177.

Singh, N. N., Lancioni, G. E., Karazsia, B. T., Myers, R. E., Winton, A. S. W., Latham, L. L., et al. (2015). Effects of training staff in MBPBS on the use of physical restraints, staff stress and turnover, staff and peer injuries, and cost effectiveness in developmental disabilities. *Mindfulness, 6,* 926–937.

Singh, N. N., Lancioni, G. E., Karazsia, B. T., Winton, A. S. W., Myers, R. E., Singh, A. N. A., et al. (2013). Mindfulness-based treatment of aggression in individuals with intellectual disabilities: A waiting list control study. *Mindfulness, 4,* 158–167.

Singh, N. N., Lancioni, G. E., Medvedev, O. N., Hwang, Y-S., & Myers, R. (2021). A component analysis of the Mindfulness-Based Positive Behavior Support (MBPBS) program for mindful parenting by mothers of children with Autism Spectrum Disorder. *Mindfulness, 12* (2), 463–475.

Singh, N. N., Lancioni, G. E., Medvedev, O. N., Myers, R. E., Chan, J., McPherson, C. L., et al. (2020). Comparative effectiveness of caregiver training in mindfulness-based positive behavior support (MBPBS) and positive behavior support (PBS) in a randomized controlled trial. *Mindfulness, 11*(1), 99–111.

Singh, N. N., Lancioni, G. E., Myers, R. E., Karazsia, B. T., McPherson, C. L., Jackman, M. M., et al. (2018). Effects of SOBER Breathing space on aggression in children with autism spectrum disorder and collateral effects on parental use of physical restraints. *Advances in Neurodevelopmental Disorders, 2*, 362–374.

Singh, N. N., Lancioni, G. E., & Winton, A. S. W. (2017). Mindfulness and the treatment of aggression and violence. In P. Sturmey (Ed.), *The Wiley handbook of violence and aggression*. Hoboken, NJ: Wiley-Blackwell.

Singh, N. N., Lancioni, G. E., Winton, A. S. W., Curtis, W. J., Wahler, R. G., Sabaawi, M., et al. (2006). Mindful staff increase learning and reduce aggression by adults with developmental disabilities. *Research in Developmental Disabilities, 27*, 545–558.

Singh, N. N., Lancioni, G. E., Winton, A. S. W., Fisher, B. C., Wahler, R. G., McAleavey, K., et al. (2006). Mindful parenting decreases aggression, noncompliance and self-injury in children with autism. *Journal of Emotional and Behavioral Disorders, 14*, 169–177.

Singh, N. N., Lancioni, G. E., Winton, A. S. W., Karazsia, B. T., Myers, R. E., Latham, L. L., et al. (2014). Mindfulness-Based Positive Behavior Support (MBPBS) for mothers of adolescents with Autism Spectrum Disorder: Effects on adolescents' behavior and parental stress. *Mindfulness, 5*, 646–657.

Singh, N. N., Lancioni, G. E., Winton, A. S. W., Karazsia, B. T., & Singh, J. (2013). Mindfulness training for teachers changes the behavior of their preschool students. *Research in Human Development, 10*(3), 211–233.

Singh, N. N., Lancioni, G. E., Winton, A. S. W., Singh, J., Curtis, W. J., Wahler, R. G., et al. (2007). Mindful parenting decreases aggression and increases social behavior in children with developmental disabilities. *Behavior Modification, 31*, 749–771.

Singh, N. N., Lancioni, G. E., Winton, A. S. W., Singh, J., Singh, A. N. A., & Singh, D. A. (2014). Mindful caregiving and support. In J. K. Luiselli (Ed.), *Children and Youth with Autism-Spectrum Disorders (ASD): Recent advances and innovations in assessment, education and intervention* (pp. 208–221). New York: Oxford University Press.

Sukhodolsky, D. G., & Scahill, L. (2012). *Cognitive-behavioral therapy for anger and aggression in children*. New York: Guilford Press.

Vitiello, B., & Stoff, D. M. (1997). Subtypes of aggression and their relevance to child psychiatry. *Journal of the American Academy of Child and Adolescent Psychiatry, 36*, 307–315.

Yorke, I., White, P., Weston, A., Rafla, M., Charman, T., & Simonoff, E. (2018). The association between emotional and behavioral problems in children with autism spectrum disorder and psychological distress in their parents: A systematic review and meta-analysis. *Journal of Autism and Developmental Disorders, 48*, 3393–3415.

Index

A
ABA assessment, 133
Academic-demand condition, 48
Accuracy, 8
Actual physical aggression, 76
Actuarial assessments, 145
Adapted-CBT, 134, 137
Aggression, 57
    DAs, 157
    in FAs, 155, 157
    in inpatient and residential
        settings, 160
    performance management, 175, 178,
        182, 183
    precursors, 158
    staff stress and burnout, 154
    traditional FA methodology, 157
    treatment components, 160
    treatment costs, 154
    and violence, 173, 183
Aggressive behavior, 4, 195
    BST, 161, 162
    clinical significance, 4
    data, 161
    direct assessment, 4
    effects of treatment, 20
    efficacy of treatment, 20
    environmental modifications, 155
    extended FA, 159
    FBA and FA procedures, 155
    function-based treatment
        evaluations, 163
    intervention, 160
    latency FAs, 157
    medications, 154
    natural environment DAs, 156
    neurodevelopmental disabilities, 154
    on staff, 154
    physical management procedures, 155
    problem behaviors, 154
    protective equipment, 156
    rating scale, 11
    risk factors, 4
    social negative reinforcement, 157
    staff injuries, 155
    statistical measures, 21
Antecedent-behavior-consequence (ABC)
    methods, 35, 134
Antecedent strategies, 176
Applied behavior analysis (ABA), 6, 47, 86,
    130, 170, 190
Arousal suppression technique, 133
Assessment of Risk Manageability for
    Individuals with Developmental
    and Intellectual Limitations who
    Offend-Sexually
    (ARMIDILO-S), 145
Assessment or How Behavior Analysis, 87
Attention-deficit hyperactivity disorder
    (ADHD), 134
Autism, 173, 177, 180
Autism spectrum disorder (ASD), 5, 46, 131,
    171, 190
    deviant sexual behavior, 139
    diagnostic features, 139
    sex offenders, 139
    symptomology, 139
Automated training, 172

B

Behavioral acquisition programming, 174
Behavioral risk assessment
  aggression and violence, 72, 73
  aggressive risk, 73
  aggressive topographies, 77
  challenging behavior, 72, 74, 79
  clinical interview, 75
  clinician, 80, 82
  dynamic variables, 79
  functional assessment, 75
  harmful effects, 72
  high-intensity aggression, 79
  individual targets, 78
  intellectual disability, 74, 75
  interviewed caregivers, 80
  MOs, 79
  physical aggression, 78
  positive findings, 77
  principles, 80
  rating scale, 76
  Screening Tool, 77
  self-directed aggression, 78
  significant problem, 73
  topography, 76, 80
Behavioral skills training (BST), 121, 161, 162
  BIPs, 170, 171
  care providers, 170
  in inpatient and residential settings, 162
    self-instructional packages, 162, 163
    trainer availability, 162
  pyramidal training, 171, 172
  role-play, 170
  staff training, 170
  substantial research, 170
Behavioral treatment, 160
Behavior analysts, 130
Behavior-analytic framework, 5
Behavior intervention plans (BIPs), 170, 171
Behavior management training, 155
Behavior Problems Inventory (BPI), 76
Board Certified Behavior Analysts (BCBAs), 144
Brief FAs, 158

C

Caregivers, 195
Child psychopathology, 194
Classroom Ecology Checklist (CEC), 180
Clinical-behavioral assessments, 74, 75
Closed-ended assessments, 33

Closed-ended questions, 31
Close-ended indirect assessments, 32
Cognitive-behavioral therapy (CBT), 130, 190
Communication-focused treatment
  aggression, 108
  antecedent-based strategies, 111
  behavioral interventions, 111
  communication skills, 117
  consequence-based strategies, 112
  DRA, 108
  FCR, 110
  FCR, teaching strategies
    FCT, 118
    increasing complexity, 120
    naturalistic-training approach, 118
    NDD, 119
    time-delay, 119
  FCT, 109, 110
  increasing practicality, 113, 115
  limitations, future research, 122, 123
  multiple-schedule reinforcement thinning, 114
  NDD, 108, 123
  promoting generalization, 120, 121
  reinforcers, 108
  response topography
    FCR, 115, 116
    NDD, 115
    preference, 117
    proficiency, 116
    social validity, 117
  violence, 108–110
Community participation skills, 147
Community-based cognitive therapy, 131
Computer-based training, 173, 174
Concurrent operants assessment (COA), 159
Contingency management, 138
Continuous measures, 10
Continuous response measures, 14
Core Sex Offender Treatment Program (Core-SOTP), 130

D

Data collection system, 6
Data measurements, 19
  graphs, 20
Data transformation, 21
  distant, 22
  intimate, 22
  rules, 22
Decision-making models, 14
Descriptive analysis (DA), 156, 157

Index

Descriptive assessment, 34
   ABC, 35, 36
   conditional, 35
   narrative, 34
   observations, 34
   probability, 35
   scatterplot, 34
   strength, 34
   three-way comparison, 36
   validity, 35, 36
Differential reinforcement of alternative behavior (DRA), 97
Differential reinforcement of other behavior (DRO), 97, 134
Direct measures, 10, 11
Direct observation, 135, 137
Discontinuous measures, 11, 12
   benefit, 12
   target response, 13
   time sampling, 13
   types, 12
Discontinuous response measures, 14
Discrete trial training (DTT), 173
Duration per occurrence, 11
Duration recording, 11
Dynamic risk assessments, 145

E

Effective practices, 181
Environmental variables, 145
Establishing operation (EO), 51, 52, 159
Evidenced-based supervisory practices, 178
Exact agreement, 18
Experimental analysis, 30
Exposure therapy, 133
Extended FAs, 159

F

Fourth generation approach, 147
Frequency measures, 10
Frequency within interval agreement, 17, 18
Functional analysis (FA), 29, 30, 46
   academic-demand condition, 49
   aggression, 63
   aggressive behavior, 155
   automatic reinforcement, 157
   brief FAs, 158
   changes to approach, 51, 52
   changes to format, 51
   components, 46
   contingency analyses, 52, 53
   extended FAs, 159
   flexibility/versatility, 54
   injury risk behavior, 62
   latency-based, 51
   latency FAs, 157, 158
   medical screening, 56
   modifications, 159
   multielement design, 49
   OVI, 61
   patient PPE, 59, 61
   PICA, 63
   PPE, 57
   practice recommendations, 55
   precursor FAs, 158
   problem, 47
   problem behavior, 156
   property destruction, 64
   protective equipment, 156
   purpose, 46, 47
   purpose of conducting, 47
   research, 61, 62
   safety precautions, 55
   setting modifications, 56, 57
   standard FA methodology, 157
   test/control conditions, 50
   therapist PPE, 58, 60
   traditional, 48, 49
   variations, 48
Functional analysis methods, 108
Functional Analysis Screening Tool (FAST), 31
Functional Assessment for Multiple Casualty (FACT), 32
Functional Assessment Interview (FAI), 31
Functional behavior assessment (FBA), 27, 134, 155, 156
   analysis of information, 38
   analyze, 29
   caregivers/experts, 33
   categories, 29
   describe/verify, problem, 28
   evidence based practice, 37
   experimental, 29
   FA, 29, 30
   hypothesis statement, 29, 39
   indirect assessment, 30, 31
   intervention, 28
   intervention plan, 29, 39
   methods/data, 29
   practitioners, 36, 37
   professions, 37
   reliability, 31
   research, 39–41

Functional behavior assessment (FBA) (cont.)
  respondents, 32
  select/collect data, 38
  strengths/limitations, 31
  target, 38
  targets, 29
  test hypothesis, 29, 39
  validity, 32
  verify the problem, 38
Functional communication responses, 117
Functional communication training (FCT), 109
Functionally equivalent, communication response (FCR), 110
Function-based intervention, 28
Function-based treatment, 138

G
General Aggression Model, 191
Good Lives Model (GLM), 146
Graphs, 20
Group supervision, 180

I
Inadvertent probes, 138
Independent living skills, 146
Indirect measures, 9
Individuals with Disabilities Education Improvement Act (IDEIA), 28
Intellectual and developmental disabilities (IDD), 153, 154, 191, 194, 195, 197, 198
Intellectual disabilities and other neurodevelopmental disorders (IDND), 129
  CBT-based program, 131
  core-SOTP, 132
  domains, 146
  environmental factors, 146
  ethical code, 144, 145
  level of treatment, 147
  outcome measures, 130, 131
  risk assessment, 145, 146
  sexual offenders, 133
  sexual offending behavior, 130
  SOTSEC-ID, 131
Intellectual disability (ID), 130, 180, 181
Intensity recording, 11
Internet, 141
Interobserver agreement (IOA), 15
  frequency within interval, 17
  interval, 16, 17
  issue, 19
  standards/interpretation, 19
  total, 15
Interpretive aid, 21
Interresponse time, 11
Interval agreement, 16
  calculations, 16
  primary/secondary observers, 16
  variations, 16
Interview-Informed Synthesized Contingency Analysis (IISCA), 52
  ecological validity, 53
  primary purpose, 52
  reinforcer, 53
  reliability, 53
  traditional FA, 53, 54
  treatments, 53

L
Latency, 11
Latency FAs, 157, 158
Learning theory, 193
Legal issues, 142
Level system, 135

M
Mand-topography assessment, 116
Mean duration, 11
Mean latency, 11
Measurement procedure, selection, 13, 14
Medications, 154
Mindfulness-Based Positive Behavior Support (MBPBS), 194
Mindfulness-based programs and practices
  adult antisocial behavior, 190
  aggression, 191
  anger, 191
  attention-maintained aggressive behavior, 190
  caregivers, 195
  cognitive and speech limitations, 190
  cognitive behavior therapy, 190
  definition, 191
  diversity, 190
  emotion regulation practices, 190, 191
  implementation, 198, 199
  interventions, 190
  maladaptive emotional regulation, 191
  mechanisms, 192, 193
  parent training programs, 190
  parents, 194, 195
  qualities, 192

Index

social dimensions, 191
teachers, 197, 198
trained clinical caregivers, 196, 197
treatment, 190
verbal and physical aggression, 190
Mindfulness strategies, 132
Motivating operations (MOs), 79
Multi-Agency Public Protection Arrangements (MAPPA), 142
Multicomponent behavioral treatment (MCBT), 130, 134
Multielement design, 49, 143

N
Narrative descriptive assessments, 34
Naturalistic-training approach, 118
Neurodevelopmental disabilities, 86, 89, 90, 92–94, 97, 100, 101, 108, 154
Noncontact Internet-related sexual offense, 139
Non-contact sexual offenses, 130
Non-contingent reinforcement (NCR), 97
Nondeviant stimuli, 133
Nonoccurrence agreement, 17, 18

O
Occurrence agreement, 16, 17
One-to-one therapy, 137
One-way observation window, 57
Ongoing visual inspection (OVI), 61
Online safety, 141
Open-ended assessments, 33
Open-ended questions, 31
Operational definitions
 biting, 6
 clinical characteristics, 6
 construction/measurement, 8
 core characteristics, 6
Organizational behavior management (OBM), 170

P
Parental stress, 194
Parents, 194, 195
Partial-interval recording, 12
PDC-Safety, 178
Penile plethysmography, 133
Percentage duration, 11
Performance Diagnostic Checklist – Human Services (PDC-HS), 177, 181
Performance Diagnostic Checklist (PDC), 177

Performance management, 169, 175–177
 antecedent strategies, 176
 CEC, 180
 consequence strategies, 176
 curriculum options, 178
 ecological factors, 180
 empirically supported practices, 183
 interpersonal and professional skills, 180
 job responsibilities, 169
 practice recommendations, 181
 praise and feedback, 176
 procedural fidelity, 175
 quality client services, 181
 quality implementation, 175
 staff performance, 175
 and staff training (*see* Staff training)
 systematic contingencies, 175
 tools, curricula and guidelines for best practices, 182
Permanent-product data, 9
Permanent-product recording, 9, 11
Personal protective equipment (PPE), 57
Person-centered planning, 147
Positive behavior support (PBS), 194
Potential environmental considerations, 14
PowerPoint training, 173
Practical Functional Assessment, 52, 158
Problem behavior, 49
Procedural fidelity, 175
Program community-based activities, 137
Psychological treatments, 132
Putative reinforcers, 53
Pyramidal training, 171, 172, 174, 175, 178

Q
Questionnaire on Attitudes Consistent with Sexual Offending (QACSO), 131
Questions About Behavior Function (QABF), 31

R
Randomized controlled trial (RCT), 194
Registered behavior technician (RBT), 175
Regulatory agencies, 146
Relapse-prevention behaviors, 144
Relapse-prevention skills, 143
Relationship and sex education, 140, 141
Reliability, 8, 15
Response latency, 11
Response rate, 10

Review status, 135
Risk assessment and management plan (RAMP), 137
Rumination, 193

S

Safety precautions, 55, 62
Sample operational definitions, 7–8
Scatterplot, 34
Self-injurious behavior (SIB), 64
Self-injury trauma (SIT) Scale, 9
Self-instructional packages, 163
Several behavior management curricula, 155
Severe intellectual disability, 154
Severe problem behaviors, 154
Sexual Offences Prevention Orders (SOPO), 142
Sexual offending behavior
　direct observation, 133
　renewal relapse, 142, 143
　research findings, 142
Single-case experimental designs, 20
Slat system, 58
SOBER breathing space, 197
Social media, 141
Social validity assessment
　ABA, 87–90, 92, 93
　accuracy, 88
　consumer populations, 88
　definition, 85
　effective procedures, 86
　intellectual and developmental disabilities, 92
　intellectual disability and challenging behavior, 91
　intervention, 88
　measures, 89
　methodologies, 93–95, 97
　methods, 85
　physical restraint, 90, 92
　ratings, 91
　results, 85
　strategies, 93
　supervisory intervention, 93
　target behaviors, 87
　targets and objectives, 99
　treatment acceptability, 89, 90
　violence and aggression, 86
Soles of the feet (SoF), 196
Special educators, 161
Speech and language pathologists (SLPs), 161

Staff performance, 176
Staff training
　ABA and OBM, 170
　antecedent strategies, 174
　behavioral interventions, 161
　BIPs, 170, 171
　BST, 161, 162 (*see also* Behavioral skills training (BST))
　BST components, 174
　and caregivers, 161
　computer-based training, 173
　DTT, 173
　evidence-based procedures, 163
　mastery, 183
　performance management, 169, 175, 176 (*see also* Performance management)
　procedures, 169
　pyramidal training, 171, 172
　video/automated training, 172, 173
Standard functional analysis, 158
Static risks assessments, 145
Static-99R, 145
Supervisor-supervisee relationship, 179
Supervisory practices, 179, 180, 183
Surrogate destructive response, 54
Sustained bite marks, 10
Synthesized contingency analysis, 52, 54

T

Target response, 13, 15
Teachers, 197, 198
Technology, 174
Topography-based approach, 72, 80
Topography-based model, 79
Topography-based responses, 116
Topography-based risk assessment, 76
Total agreement, 15
Total agreement equation, 16
Trained clinical caregivers, 196, 197
Training as usual (TAU), 195
Training videos, 174
Translational researchers, 143
Treatment data point, 21
Treatment Evaluation Inventory (TEI), 91
Trial-based functional analysis, 48, 51
Trumpet Behavioral Health, 178

V

Video modeling, 176
Video trainings, 172–174, 176

Violence, 173, 183
Violence aggression, 3, 12, 47, 62
  inpatient and residential treatment, 153, 154
Visual inspection, 20

W
Whole-interval recording, 13
Within-subject experimental designs, 48

Lightning Source UK Ltd.
Milton Keynes UK
UKHW020628140122
397133UK00001B/10